The Campus History Series

BOB JONES UNIVERSITY

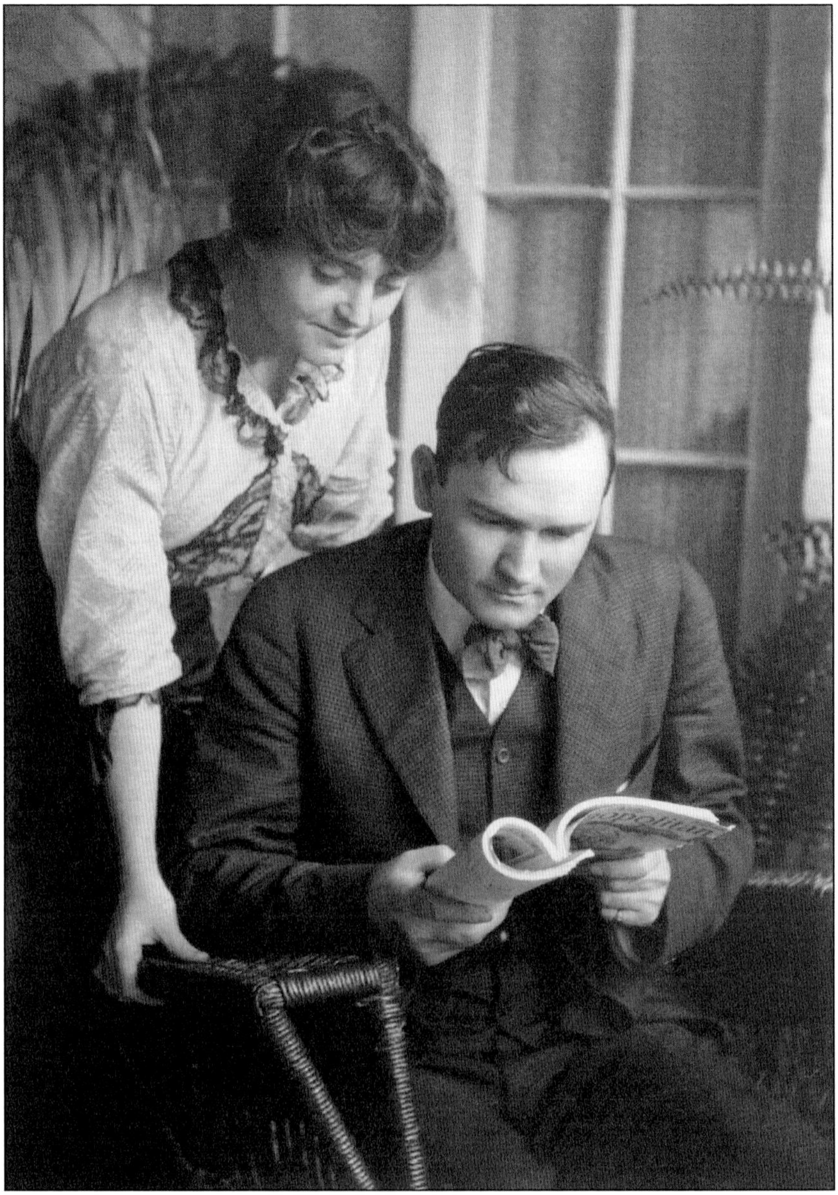

Evangelist Bob Jones Sr., shown here with his wife Mary Gaston Jones, founded Bob Jones College in College Point, Florida, in 1927. Dr. Bob Jones Sr. was 44 years old and, by this time, was a well-known evangelist across the United States. Although he was primarily a minister of the Gospel, Dr. Bob was used by God to establish a school that is known all around the world for its vigorous Christian testimony and high academic standards. (Courtesy of Bob Jones University.)

On the Cover: Affectionately called "Old Main," the primary building on Bob Jones College's Cleveland, Tennessee, campus accommodated the entire college operation in the 1933–1934 school year, the first year after the school moved from its College Point, Florida, location. Classrooms, an auditorium, administrative offices, the library, the dining room, and a swimming pool occupied the first floor. Dormitory suites, accommodating two students each, were located on the second floor. (Courtesy of Bob Jones University.)

The Campus History Series

BOB JONES UNIVERSITY

BOB A. NESTOR

ARCADIA
PUBLISHING

ISBN 978-0-7385-5389-4

Published by Arcadia Publishing
Charleston, South Carolina

Printed in the United States of America

Library of Congress Catalog Card Number: 2007942673

For all general information contact Arcadia Publishing at:
Telephone 843-853-2070
Fax 843-853-0044
E-mail sales@arcadiapublishing.com
For customer service and orders:
Toll-Free 1-888-313-2665

Visit us on the Internet at www.arcadiapublishing.com

Contents

ACKNOWLEDGMENTS

The author is sincerely grateful for the numerous individuals at Bob Jones University who helped in so many ways to make this book possible. Because of their reluctance to have the author list them all personally, however, he is expressing his special gratitude to them collectively in the Communications Division, the University Archives Research Center, and the Photo Studio. The 196 photographs appearing in this book are all courtesy of Bob Jones University, who not only allowed their use, but who actually prepared them for publication.

Having been a freshman at Bob Jones University (BJU) more than a half century ago, the author counts it a privilege to have a part in the production of this book that focuses upon a school for which he is eternally grateful. It was at BJU where he met his wife, Peggy, whose patience and encouraging words were helpful throughout this project.

One other person deserves special mention, and that is Maggie Bullwinkel, the author's editor at Arcadia, with whom it has been a privilege to work.

INTRODUCTION

Bob Jones University (BJU), an accredited Christian liberal arts university founded by evangelist Bob Jones Sr., opened its doors as Bob Jones College on September 14, 1927, at College Point, Florida, nine miles north of Panama City. After relocating to Cleveland, Tennessee, from 1933 to 1947, Bob Jones College made a third move to Greenville, South Carolina, in the fall of 1947 and became a university. With an enrollment of 4,200 students from every state and more than 50 foreign countries, BJU today offers more than 100 undergraduate and 70 graduate majors.

As an evangelist who had addressed audiences estimated at 15 million in 80 U.S. cities, Dr. Bob Jones Sr. became burdened for Christian young people whose faith was being undermined in both public and Christian institutions. While with Dr. Bob Jones Sr. at the Winona Lake Bible Conference in Indiana in 1924, William Jennings Bryan said to him, "If schools and colleges do not stop teaching evolution as a fact, we are going to become a nation of atheists."

Dr. Jones concurred, and he was determined that the school he founded would be a place where young people could be educated in an environment that recognized the absolute authority of the Bible while maintaining high academic and cultural standards.

On opening day at College Point, the then two-year college had a faculty of nine and a student body of 88. The first semester began with a revival service, and 40 students made decisions relating to their spiritual lives. Since then, every semester at BJU has begun with a revival service.

In 1932, with the country in the throes of the Great Depression, the school found itself in great difficulty, as $352,000 in mortgages owed to the college from surrounding property owners could not be collected. In April 1933, the board of trustees decided to move the school to Cleveland, Tennessee, selling the Florida property and assets for $3,100. After holding its last Florida commencement on May 31, 1933, the college moved its operation to the then vacant campus of Centenary College in Cleveland. It opened at this location on September 6, 1933, with an enrollment 50 percent higher than in the highest Florida year.

In 1934, Bob Jones Jr., to allow his father to remain actively engaged as an evangelist, became the acting president at the age of 23. For more than 13 years, the new four-year college flourished in the Tennessee city, reaching an enrollment of over 1,580 students in 1946.

University officials consider the Cleveland years to be the institution's "maturing years." Academically, the college was greatly strengthened under the leadership of Dr. Eunice Hutto, who served as dean of the college from 1932 until 1941. Recognized as the first female dean of a coeducational college in America, Dr. Hutto is credited with making invaluable contributions toward curriculum standardization, class scheduling, and faculty direction.

But the school faced problems in the mid-1940s: additional space was needed to accommodate the influx of students, and the land near the college was not affordable.

When an announcement was made to the student body that the college was looking for a new campus location, Martha Stone, a sophomore music major, mentioned the announcement as a postscript in a letter to her father, E. Roy Stone, a Greenville, South Carolina, realtor. Thanks to his efforts, a 220-acre plot of red clay, located on the outskirts of the city on U.S. 29, proved to be just the place Dr. Bob Jones Sr. was looking for to construct the new campus. The Cleveland campus was sold to the Church of God for close to $1.5 million and is now the home of Lee College. At the close of the 1946–1947 school year, Bob Jones College became Bob Jones University, with Dr. Bob Jones Jr. installed as its second president.

The Greenville campus opened on October 1, 1947, with nearly 2,500 students, already surpassing the planned accommodations for 2,000 students, and the school began almost immediately to expand its ministries. Recognizing the power of the media in spreading the Gospel, in 1949, the university started its own radio station, WMUU, where Dr. Bob Jones Sr. conducted daily live broadcasts. Unusual Films, a Christian film department, began in 1950, and in 1951, Dr. Bob Jones Jr. founded the Museum and Gallery to acquaint students and the public with art of the masters.

On January 16, 1968, the beloved founder, Dr. Bob Jones Sr., died at age 84. Three years later, Dr. Bob Jones Jr. assumed the role of chancellor, and Dr. Bob Jones III, who had become vice president in 1964, became president and continued the growth and expansion.

To meet the needs in Christian education, for example, BJU Press was started in the 1970s. It produces educational material with an integrated Christian philosophy for use in classrooms and homeschools.

In the 1980s, Dr. Bob Jones III encouraged local and worldwide outreach through church planting and missions, and started the Timothy and World Funds, which help international students attend BJU and then return to their home countries to serve the Lord. During the summers since the 1980s, the university has sent out nearly 15 student mission teams each summer led by faculty and staff members to assist pastors and missionaries abroad.

Satellite educational programs—BJ LINC (Bob Jones Live Interactive Network Classroom) and BJ HomeSat—have extended the BJU outreach to more than 45,000 homeschooled students, as well as to Christian schools and individual off-campus students.

The Bob Jones Jr. Memorial Seminary and Evangelism Center, which honors the memory of the school's second president, was dedicated on March 23, 2000. And in the 1990s, an annual tradition was begun near Easter week—Living Gallery, a unique presentation of the Gospel through music, drama, and live characters who actually form living reproductions of works of art.

In the new century, a variety of campus improvements have taken place, including a face-lift on Founder's Memorial Amphitorium and the front campus fountain; the Davis Field House, which replaced the gymnasium; a new Welcome Center on Wade Hampton Boulevard; and a 400-car parking garage behind Rodeheaver Auditorium that facilitates on-campus parking.

In 2005, Dr. Stephen Jones, great-grandson of the founder, became the fourth president of Bob Jones University, at which time his father, Dr. Bob Jones III, moved into the chancellor's position.

During the six decades the university has been in Greenville, in addition to many new buildings and extensive landscaping, multiple offerings on both the undergraduate and graduate levels have been added to the curriculum, and many programs have been initiated to help students develop Christlike character and leadership skills. Most importantly, the founder's emphasis on "the old-time religion and the absolute authority of the Bible" remains paramount.

One

The Florida Years 1927–1933

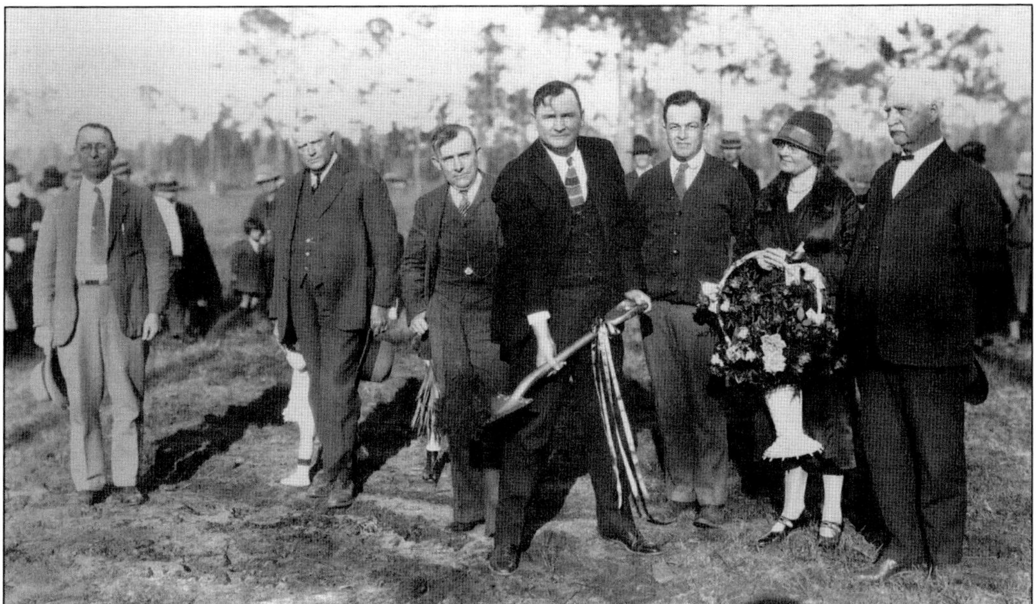

More than 700 people gathered for the ground-breaking of Bob Jones College (BJC) in College Point, Florida, on December 1, 1926. Turning the first shovel of dirt was the school's founder, Dr. Bob Jones Sr. The local newspaper called that day "the finest day that nature could offer at this season of the year." Others in the photograph are, from left to right, J. M. Sapp, R. I. McKenzie, Alabama governor-elect David "Bibb" Graves, Willis Haymaker, Mary Gaston Jones, and M. F. Boone.

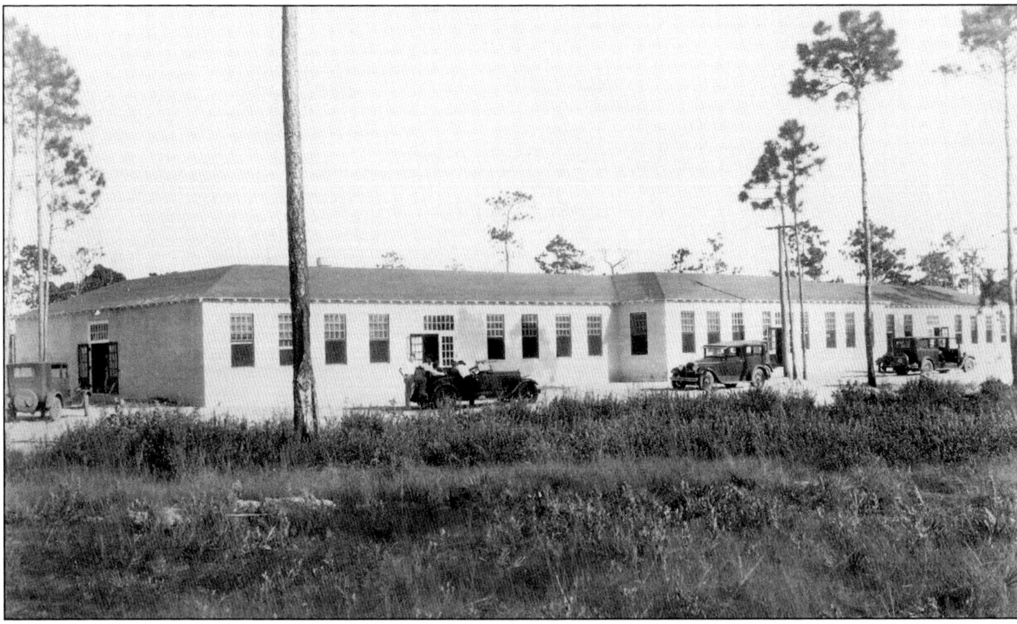

From 1917 until 1933, this building on the College Point, Florida, campus housed both administrative offices and classrooms. It was one of the six original Spanish-style stucco buildings constructed on the 470-acre BJC campus that bordered St. Andrews Bay.

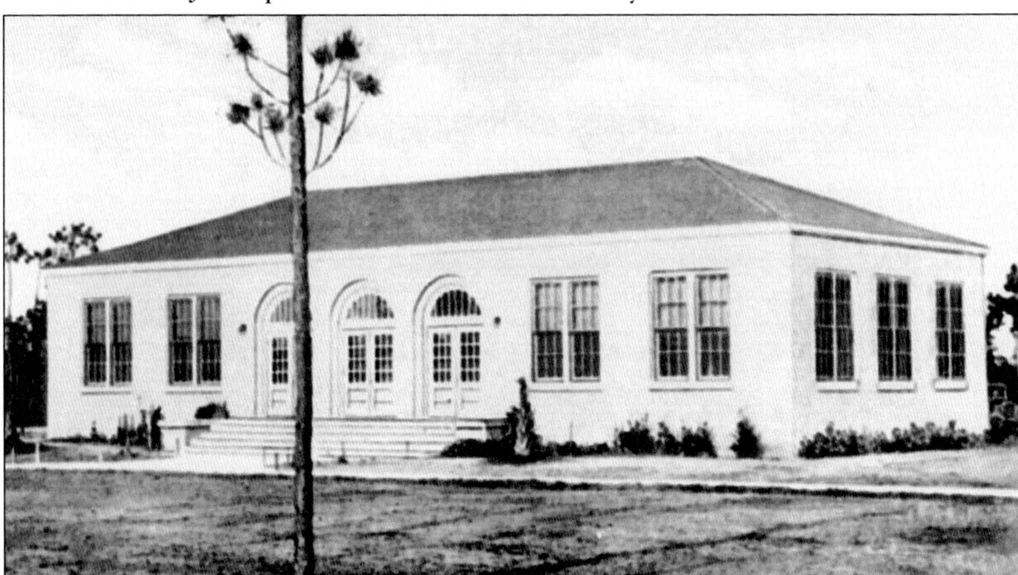

Family-style seating in the dining hall at College Point afforded opportunities for students to fellowship with each other and the faculty. One of the first meals served was a banquet for guests who attended the September 14, 1927, opening ceremony, including Gov. Bibb Graves of Alabama, along with his wife, Dixie Graves; Congressman William Upshaw of Georgia; representatives of the Florida and Alabama departments of education; presidents of other colleges; and pastors of churches in several states. The dining hall director proved to be inexperienced in planning large meals, and Mary Gaston Jones ended up planning and overseeing the preparation of the banquet and doing some of the baking herself.

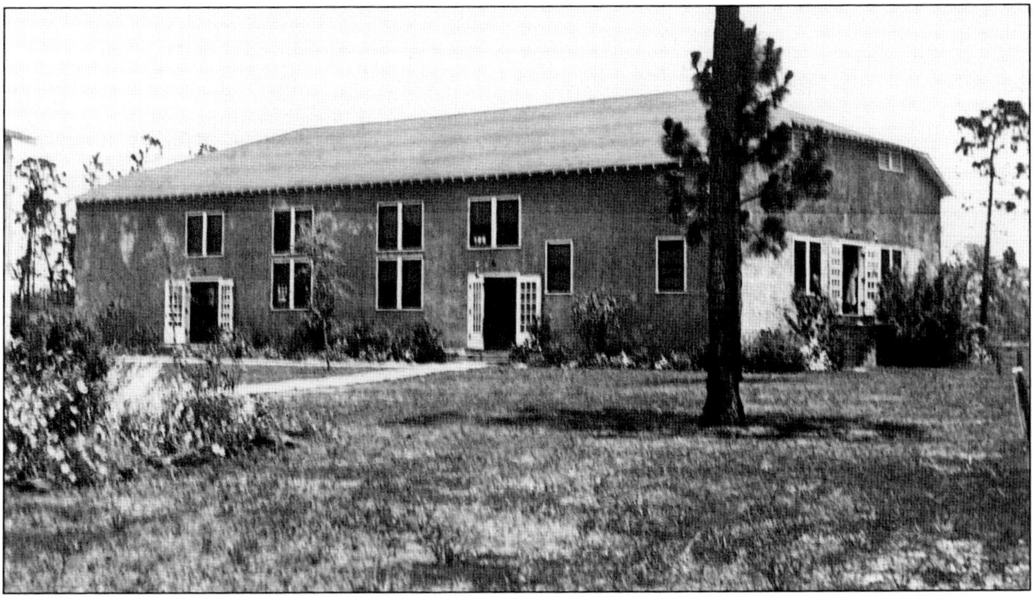

The student body and faculty came together every day for chapel in the Dixon-McKenzie Auditorium on the College Point campus. Every chapel session, students and faculty recite the university creed, which reaffirms their belief in essential doctrines such as the inerrancy of Scripture and the virgin birth of Jesus Christ.

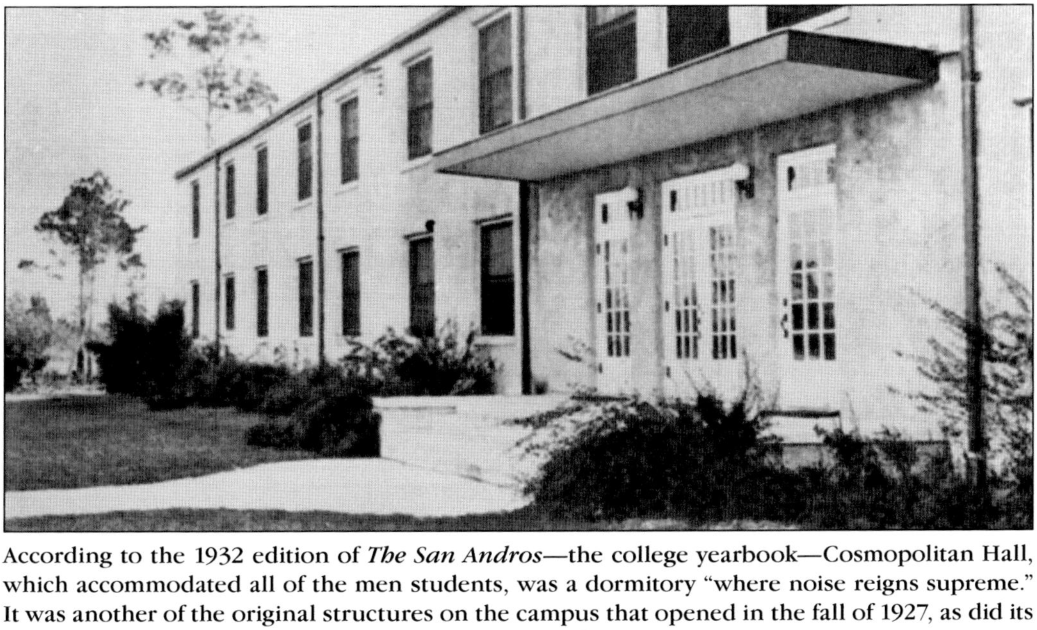

According to the 1932 edition of *The San Andros*—the college yearbook—Cosmopolitan Hall, which accommodated all of the men students, was a dormitory "where noise reigns supreme." It was another of the original structures on the campus that opened in the fall of 1927, as did its counterpart, Jennie Brandenberg Hall, the women's dormitory.

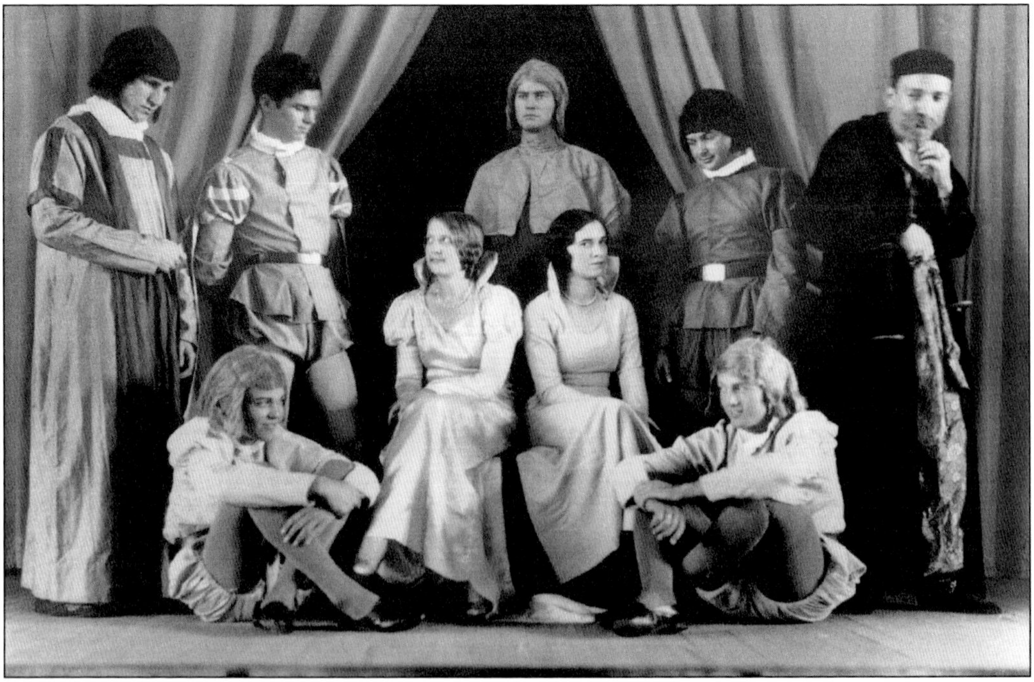

Bob Jones Jr. (far right) portrayed Shylock in the Classic Players' 1930 presentation of *The Merchant of Venice*. Since that inaugural year, Shakespearean productions have been an annual event performed before capacity crowds of the university family and people from the surrounding communities. In 1931, the Classic Players performed *Othello*, their second production.

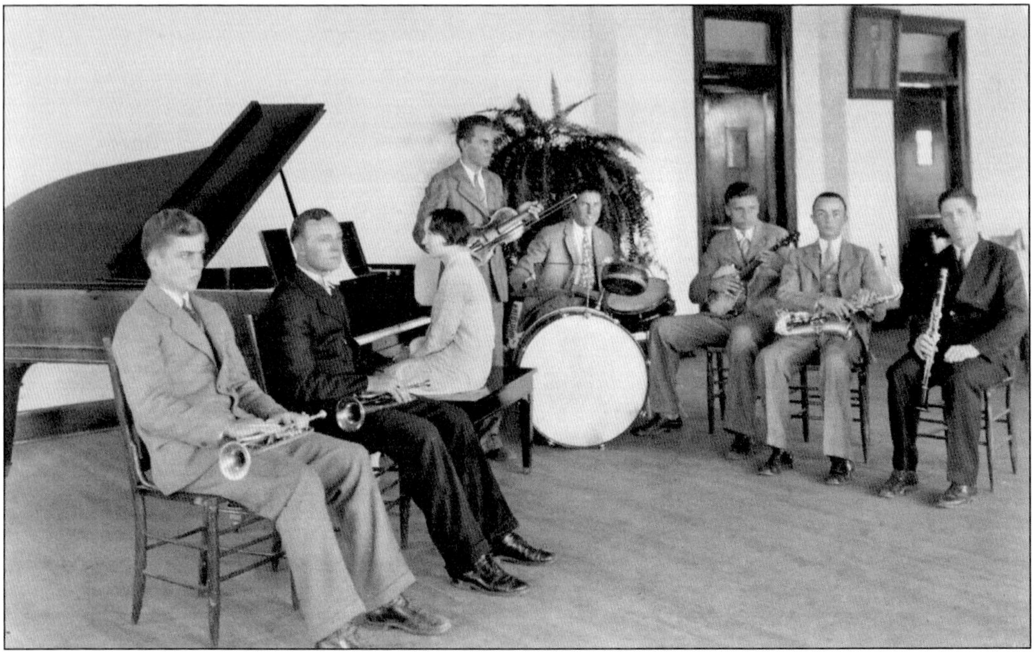

During the initial school year, 1927–1928, this seven-man contingent of instrumentalists joined pianist Minnie Monk to form Bob Jones College's first orchestra. Instruments played by the musical group included trumpets, a violin, drums, a banjo, a saxophone, and a clarinet.

In the 1930 gridiron season, two men were key players for the Bob Jones College Swamp Angels—John Parks Tyson (below) and Monroe "Monk" Parker (right). As the team's quarterback and captain, Tyson won the respect of every man on the team with his uncanny ability to make the necessary yards for a first down. Parker, alternate captain and fullback, was the strong man on the team, the one depended upon for his ability to plunge through the defensive line to keep the team moving. In four years of interscholastic competition, the football team lost only one game. In 1931, the Swampers overwhelmed all opposition in 10 games by scoring 322 points to a total of 138. Most of the team's games were played at the Collins Stadium in College Point.

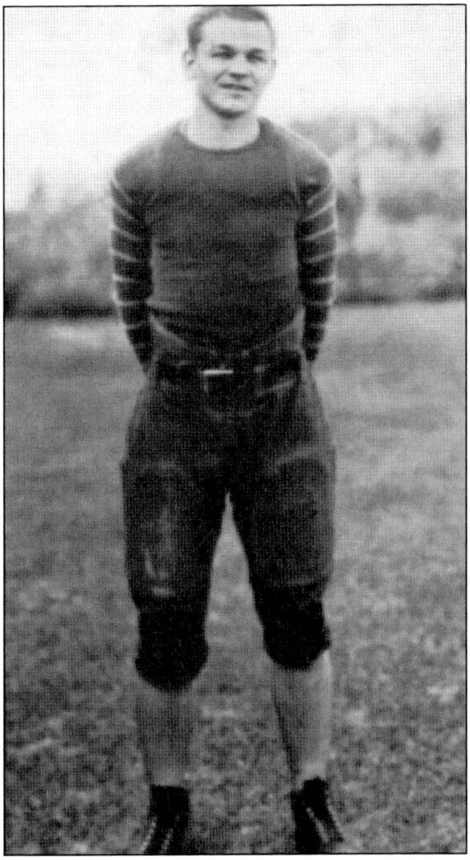

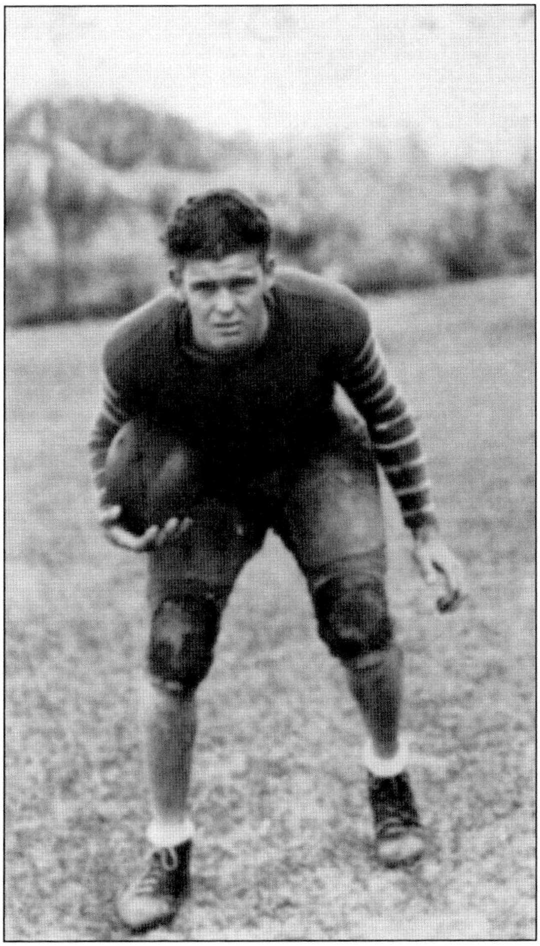

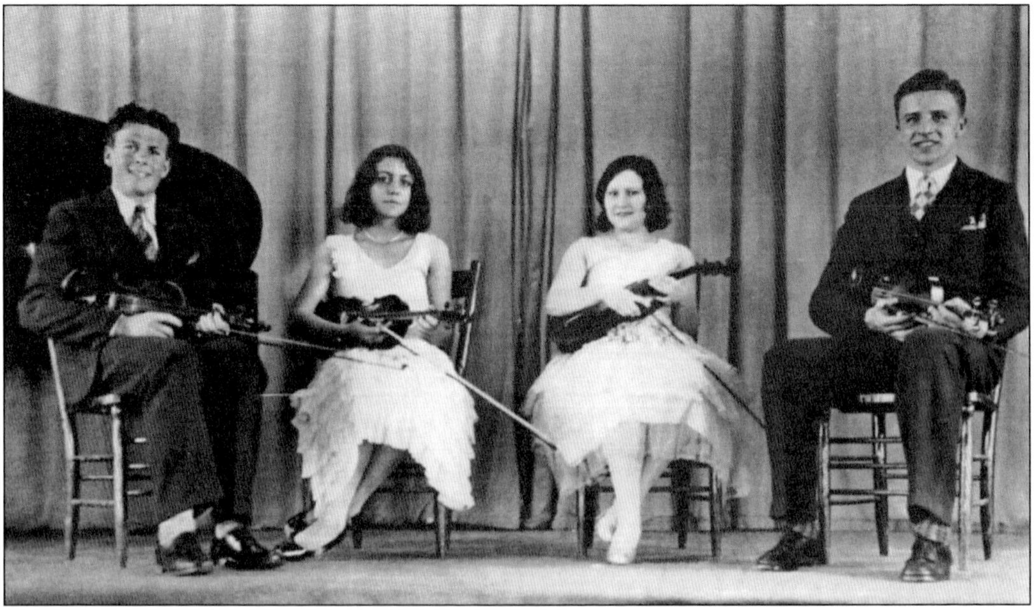

This Bob Jones College String Quartette performed during the 1929–1930 school year. The musicians—(from left to right) Philip Unsworth, Charlotte Perpetuo, Ione Gryder, and Henry Bloker—provided music for Vespers and concerts.

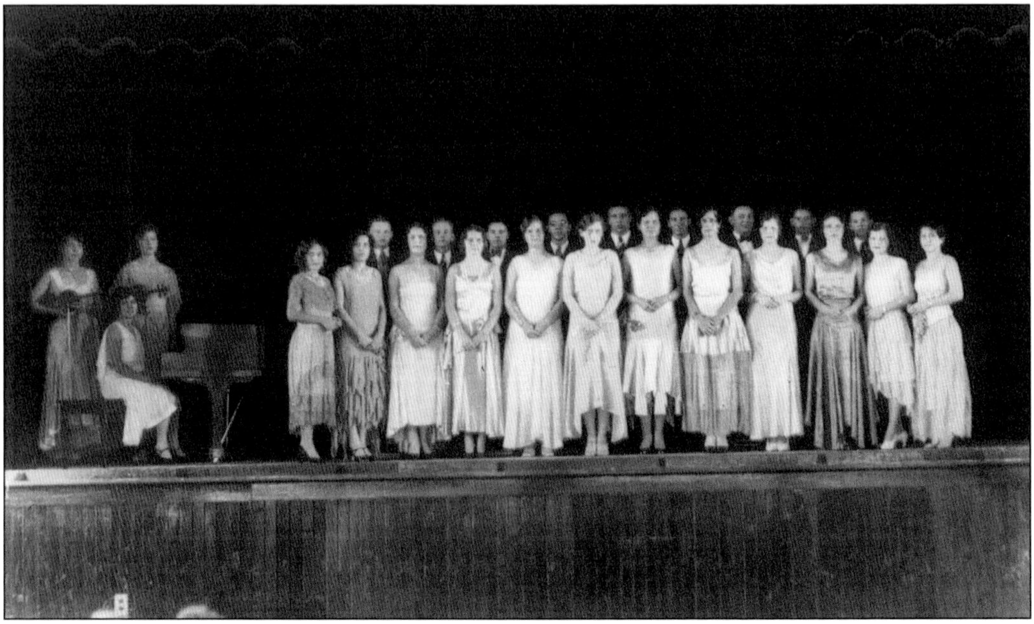

In the first year of BJC, each student sang, recited poetry, or made a dramatic presentation to the student body. These presentations were put together into *Twilight Musicales*, which in 1928 became Vespers.

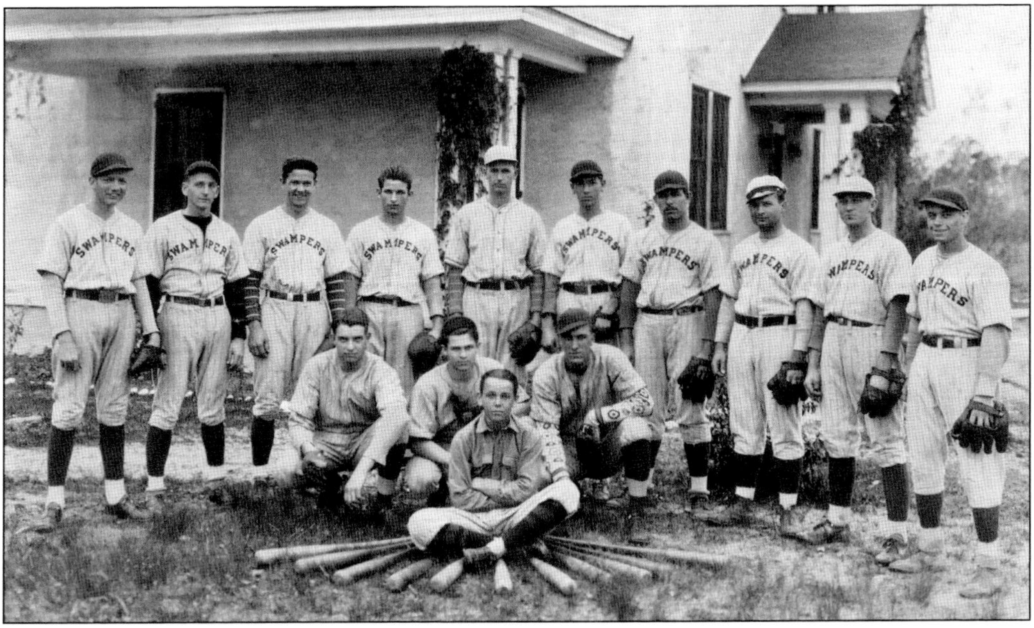

The Bob Jones College Swamp Angels baseball team was very competitive during its six years in Florida. Because the team did not travel the first two years, the Swamp Angels hosted all of their opponents on their home field. Their schedule was made up of games against both college and high school teams. The college engaged in several scholastic sports during its years in College Point: baseball, basketball, football, track, and tennis.

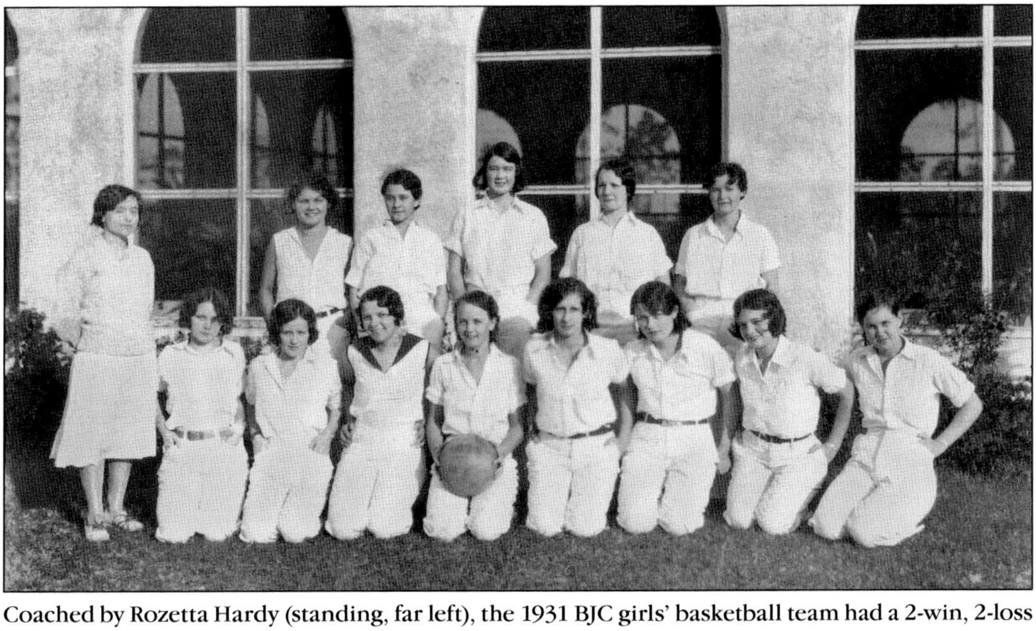

Coached by Rozetta Hardy (standing, far left), the 1931 BJC girls' basketball team had a 2-win, 2-loss season, scoring a total of 59 points against their opponents' 59 points. They defeated Apalachicola, Florida, 24-18 and Port St. Joe, Florida, 16-7 but lost to Headland, Alabama, 10-9 and Cottondale, Florida, 24-10. Team members were (kneeling) Martha Lee Patterson, Mildred Edwards, Ruth Newberry, Aileen Williams, Peggy Folks, Evelyn Roton, Lois Russ, and Monta Moore; (standing) Margaret Hoskins, Mary Stapleton, Lola Wilson, Rebecca Smartt, and Maitle Derby.

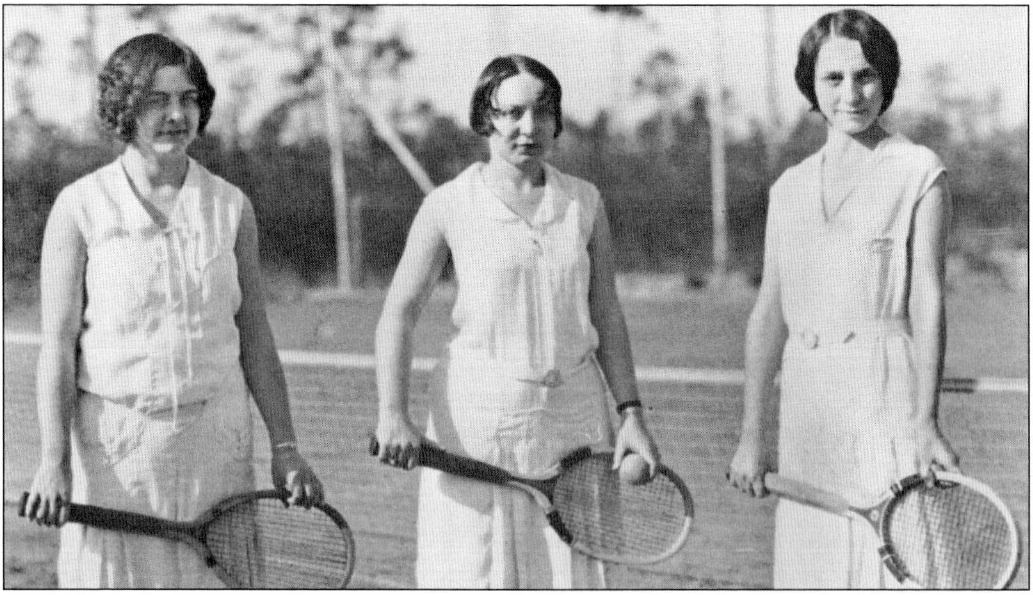

From left to right, Ruth Meriwether, Minnie Monk, and Fannie Mae Holmes were the Bob Jones College girls' tennis champions in 1930. After Holmes's graduation in 1931, she earned a master's degree in home economics from Colorado State Teachers College and returned to BJC as a dietitian and home economics instructor. She later married Bob Jones Jr. in a ceremony held in the Margaret Mack Auditorium on the Cleveland campus on June 1, 1938.

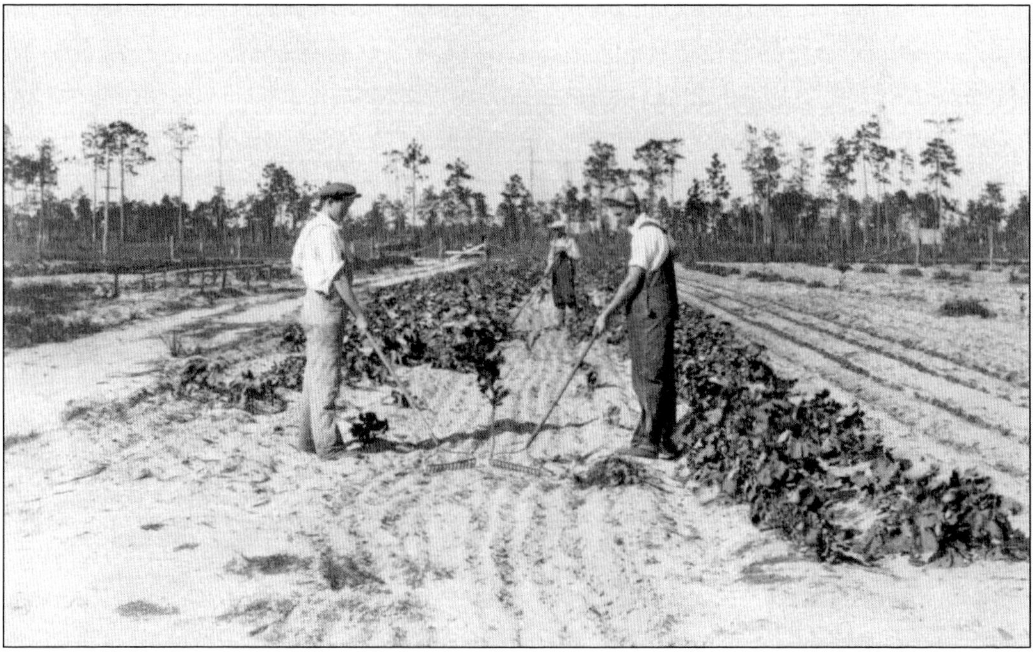

Since 1927, Bob Jones University has endeavored to keep tuition and room and board costs as low as possible so no student would be prohibited from enrolling because of finances. Twenty acres of the College Point campus were set aside as a vegetable farm, and the college also had a canning plant, a dairy consisting of 12 head of milk cows, and a sawmill to meet student employment needs while generating some profit for the school.

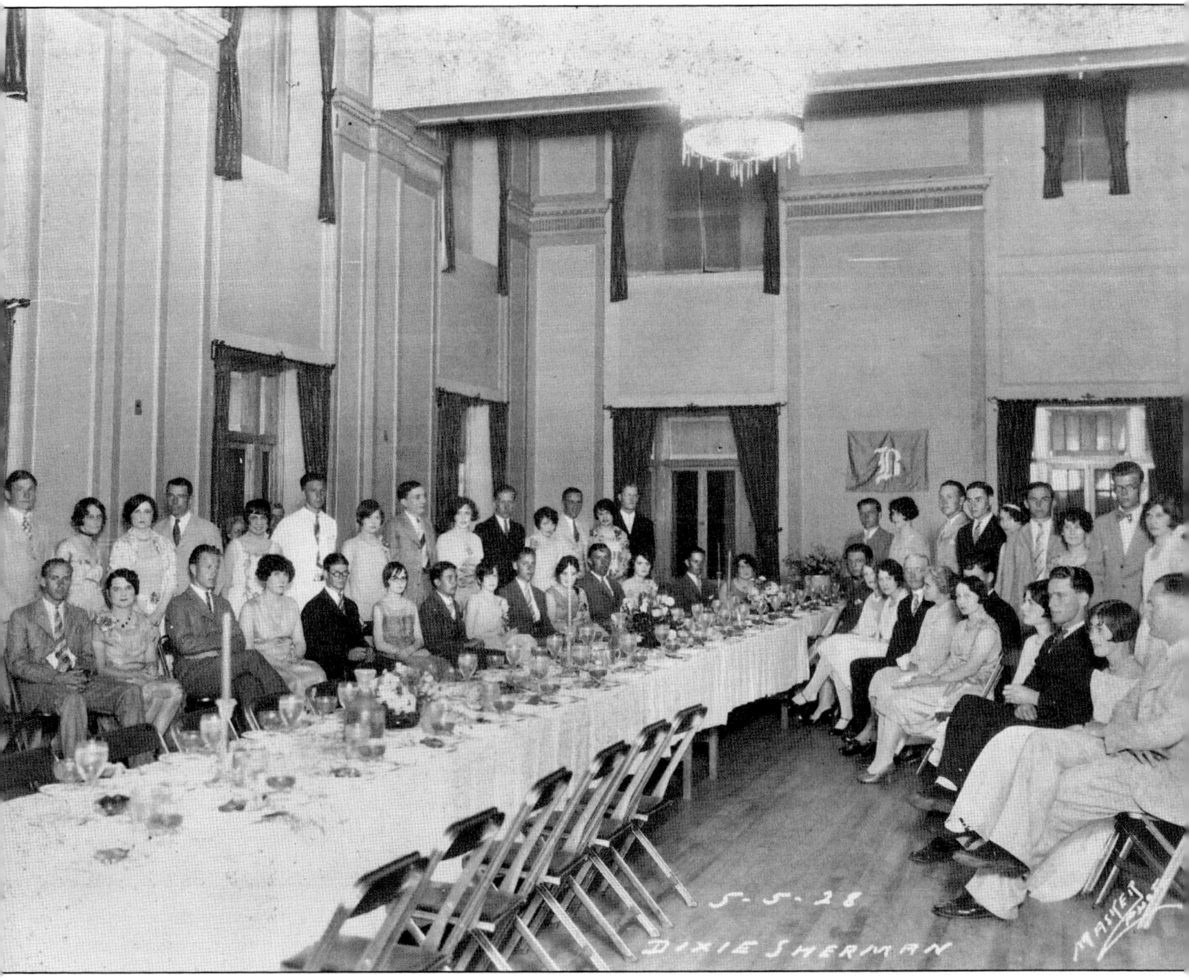

The William Jennings Bryan literary society's 1928 outing was a formal banquet at the Dixie Sherman Hotel in Panama City. The students reportedly enjoyed riding the hotel's elevator, which for some was a new experience. Every student at Bob Jones University today—just as at Bob Jones College in 1928—is a member of a literary society, which provides opportunities for spiritual growth and leadership training, along with fellowship and service. The university does not have fraternities or sororities.

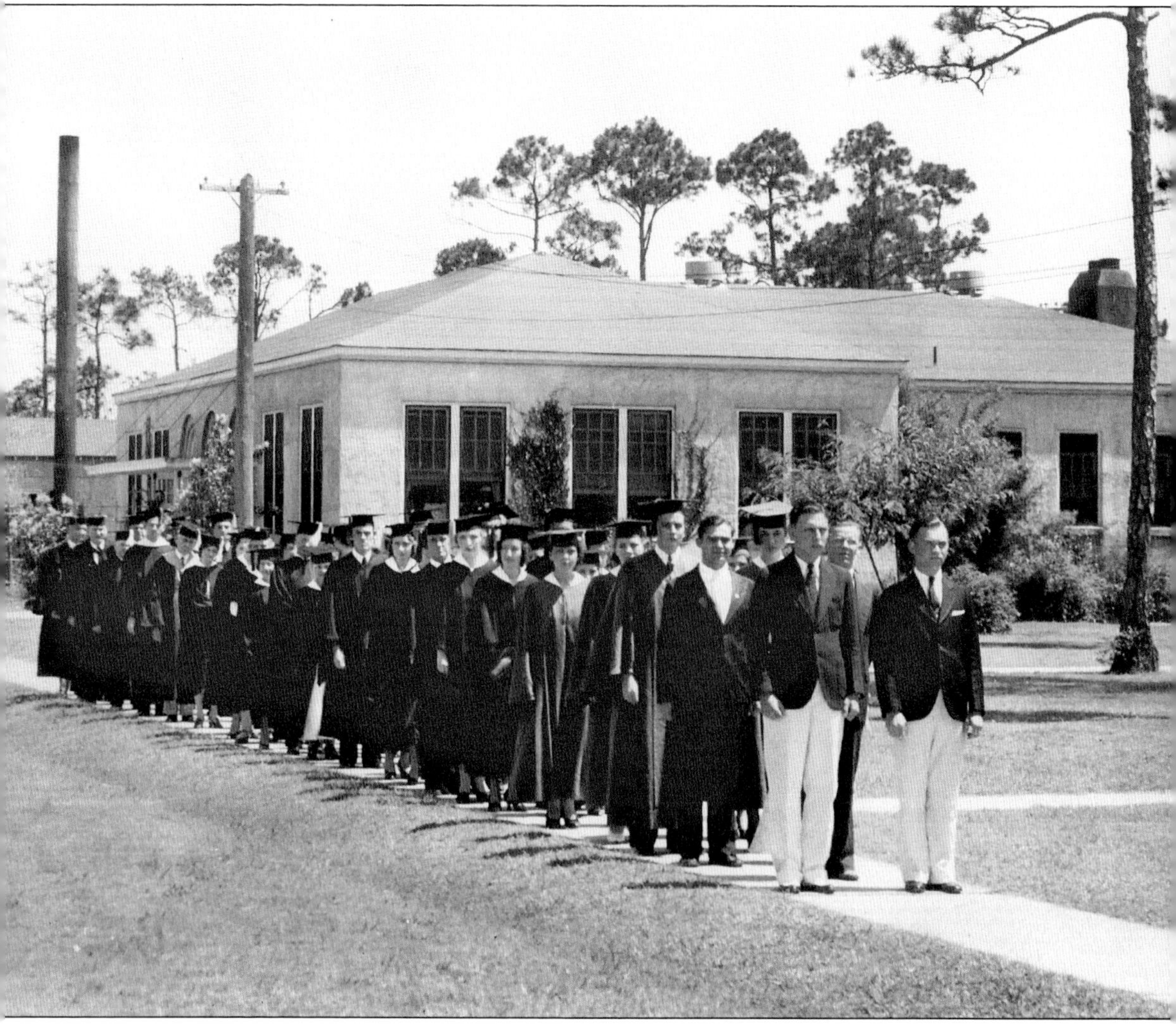

BJC graduates and faculty members take part in the final commencement procession on the College Point campus on May 31, 1933. In the fall, the college would be relocated to the campus of Centenary College in Cleveland, Tennessee. Many memories of their six years in Florida were fresh as school officials and students said good-bye to their school's first home. All believed that God's hand was in control in spite of the nation's financial woes, a factor making the move necessary.

Two

The Tennessee Years 1933–1947

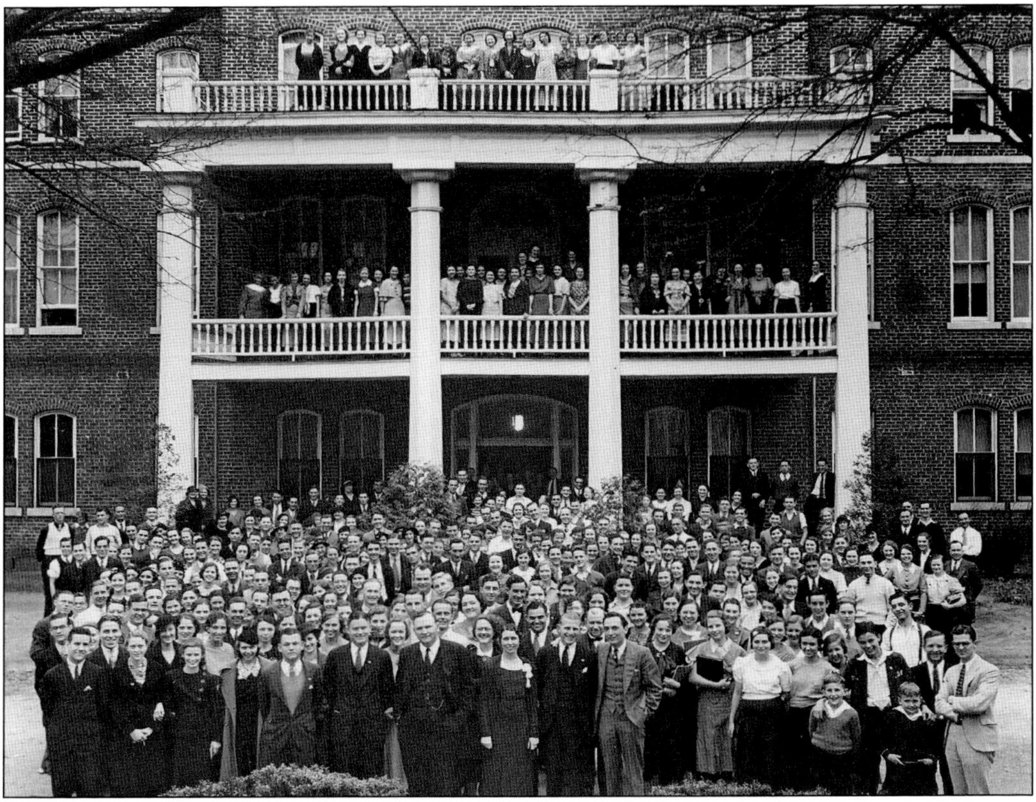

Following extensive renovation of the primary building, Old Main, Bob Jones College opened its doors to students in Cleveland, Tennessee, in September 1933. Two years later, the Young People's Fellowship Club and faculty members assembled for this photograph in front of Old Main and on the two porches of the venerable old building. Dr. Bob Jones Sr. is in the center foreground, and Dr. Bob Jones Jr. is standing on the far right of the group in the center. The school grew to a 24-building campus valued at $2.4 million by 1945.

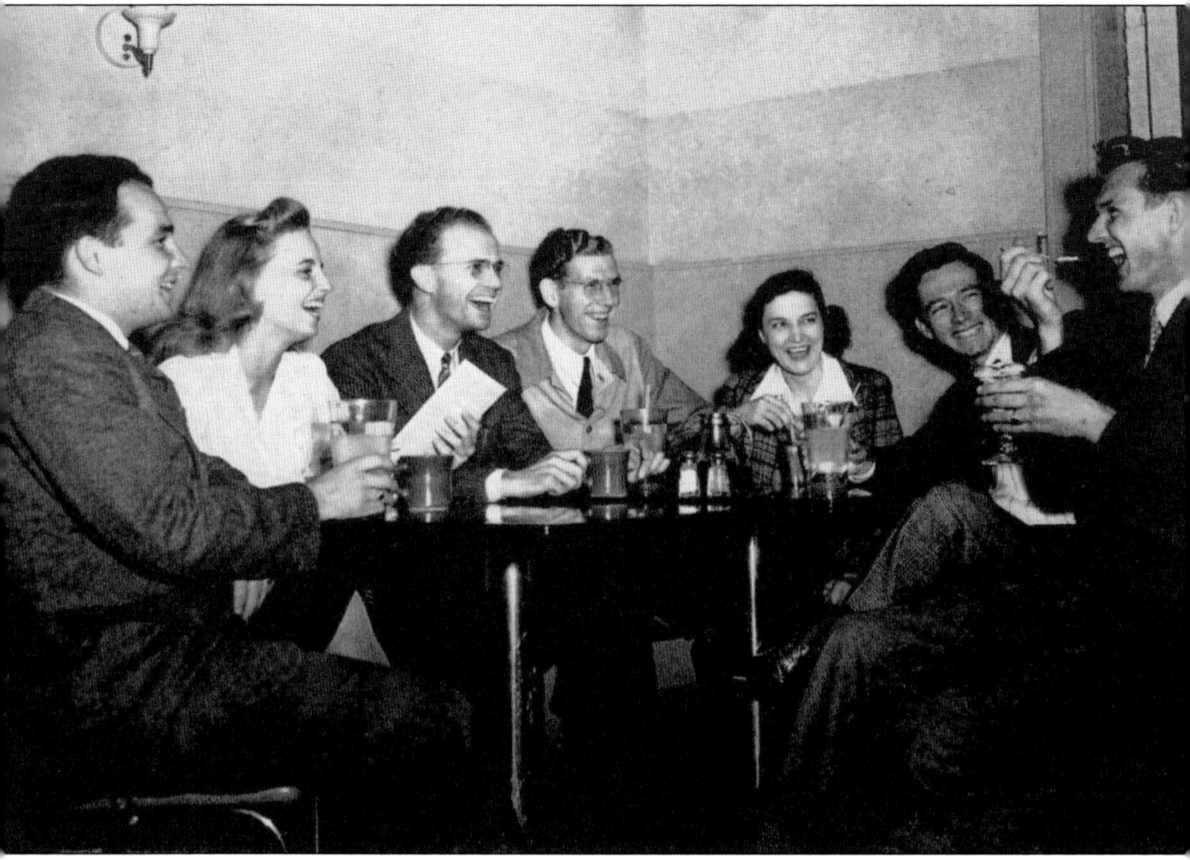

During the second semester of the 1943–1944 school year, these student body officers met in the chapel every weekday morning to conduct business. One of the most important duties of these officers was to represent the students at the weekly meeting of the Discipline Committee. On some occasions, the officers gathered in the Snack Shop over chocolate malts, caramel sundaes, and coffee. Officers were J. R. Faulkner, president; Vern Taylor, vice president; Horace Sams, chaplain; Anna Lloyd Pace, secretary; Fred Afman, sergeant-at-arms; Victor Werner, chorister; and Erna Lee Wall, pianist.

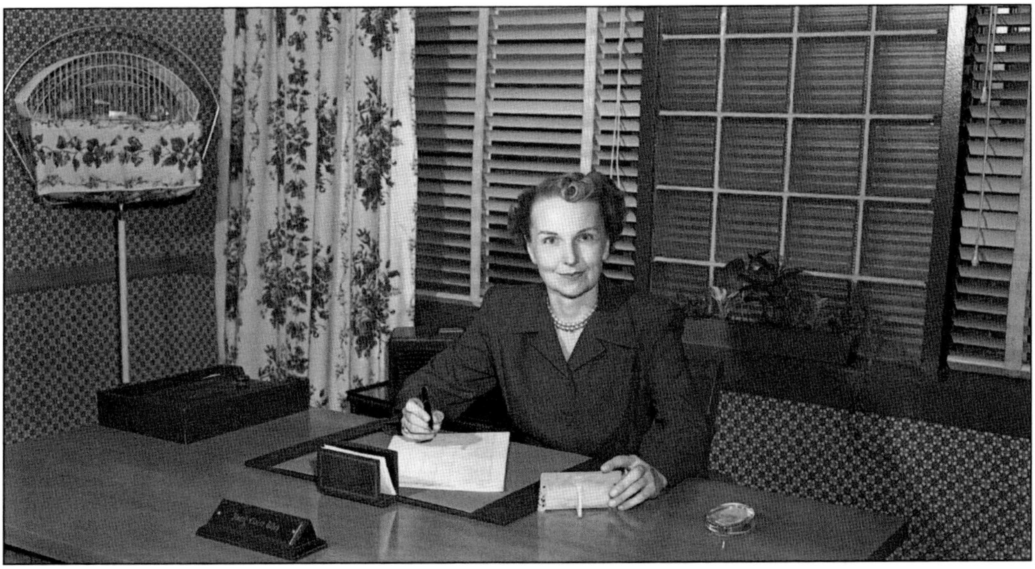

Hazel Clair Riley became the assistant dean of women in 1935 and served as the dean of women in both Cleveland, Tennessee, and Greenville, South Carolina, from 1941 until her retirement in 1977, when Luena Barker succeeded her. With a gentle Christian spirit, she guided thousands of young women for 36 years. She died in April 1982. Her legacy includes the residence hall prayer captain and assistant prayer captain structure.

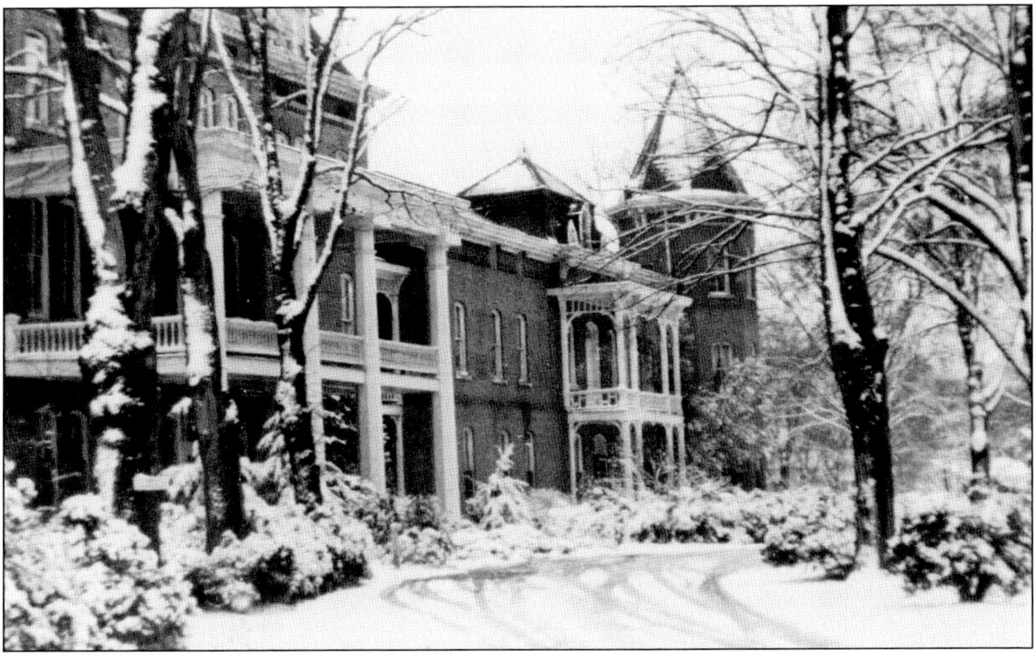

Cleveland, Tennessee, is not particularly known for its snowy winters, but occasionally, the Creator turned the Bob Jones College campus into a winter wonderland. During the first year in Tennessee, a classroom building was constructed to supplement Old Main, pictured here. By 1935, a gymnasium, auditorium, and men's residence hall were under construction. During the 13 years the school was in Cleveland, a new building was constructed each year, and several nearby homes were purchased and renovated for college use.

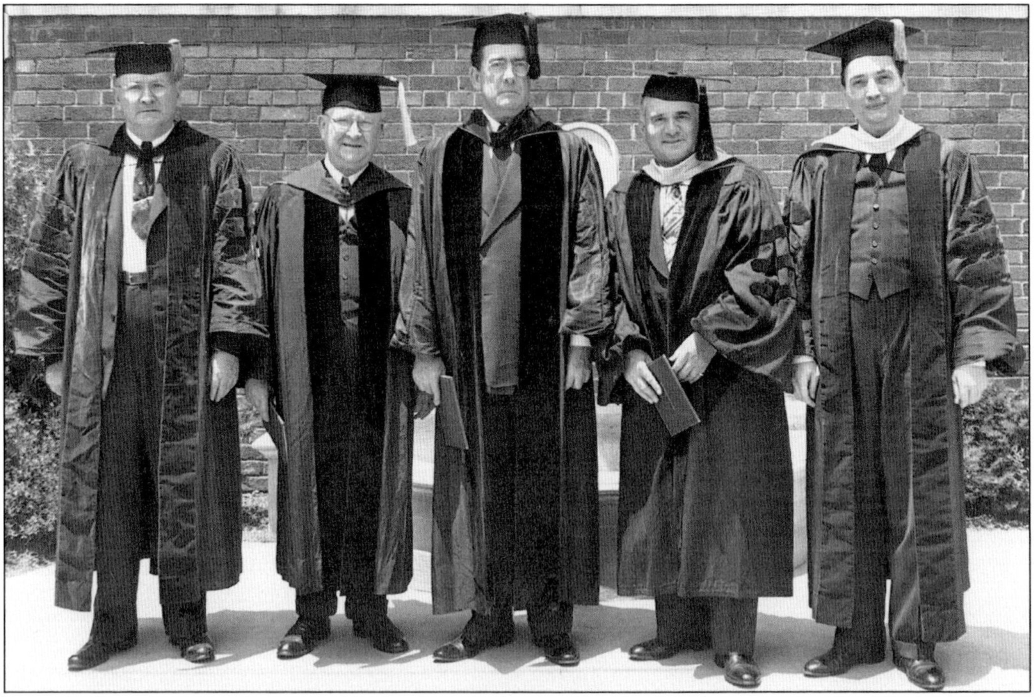

In the 1942 commencement, Bob Jones College presented honorary doctorates to, from left to right, (between Dr. Bob Jones Sr. on the left and Dr. Bob Jones Jr. on the right) Harry Ironside, pastor of Moody Memorial Church in Chicago; Will Houghton, president of Moody Bible Institute; and Homer Rodeheaver, longtime song leader for evangelist Billy Sunday.

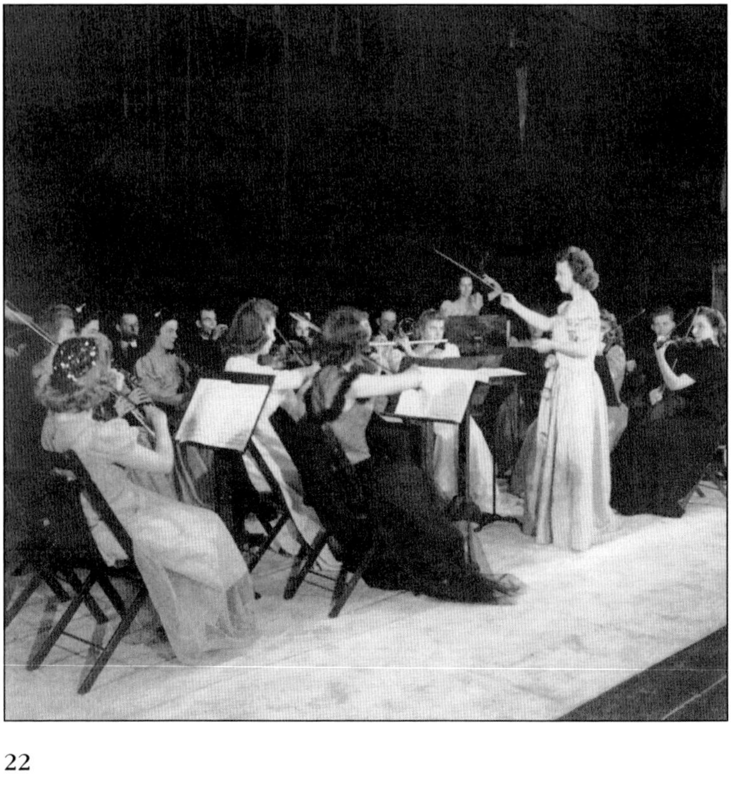

For its first public appearance in the 1942–1943 academic year, the BJC Orchestra, under the direction of Julia Rosser, played the accompaniment for the chorus and guest soloists of the opera *Il Trovatore*. The orchestra also played several times during the year in Sunday afternoon Vespers.

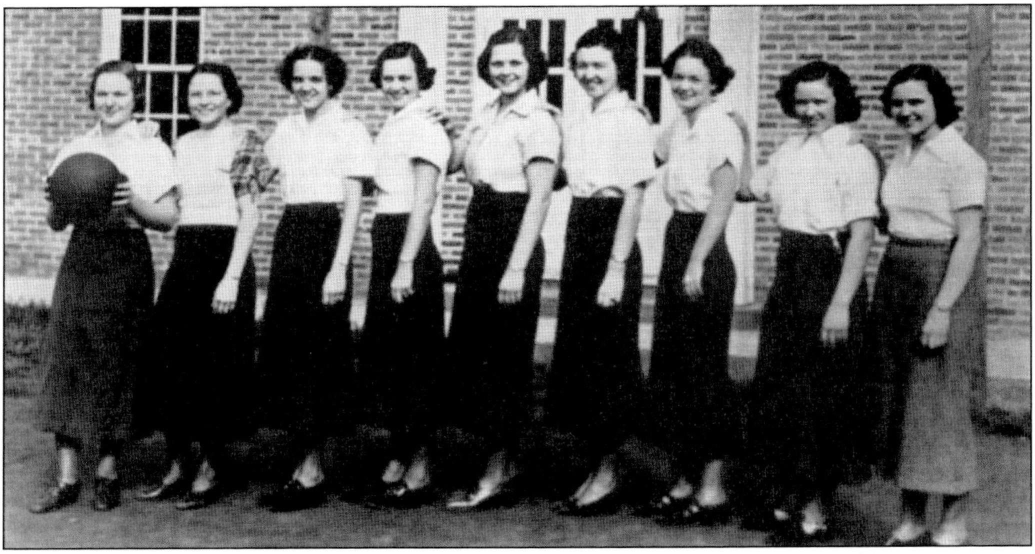

These young women comprised the 1937 upper-class girls' basketball squad. Women students on the Cleveland campus also competed in tennis, volleyball, and softball. In addition, all students were required to physically exercise for an hour each day. The BJC catalog noted, "The physical health of the students is cared for by supervised calisthenics, baseball, volleyball, basketball, tennis, playground ball, and hiking."

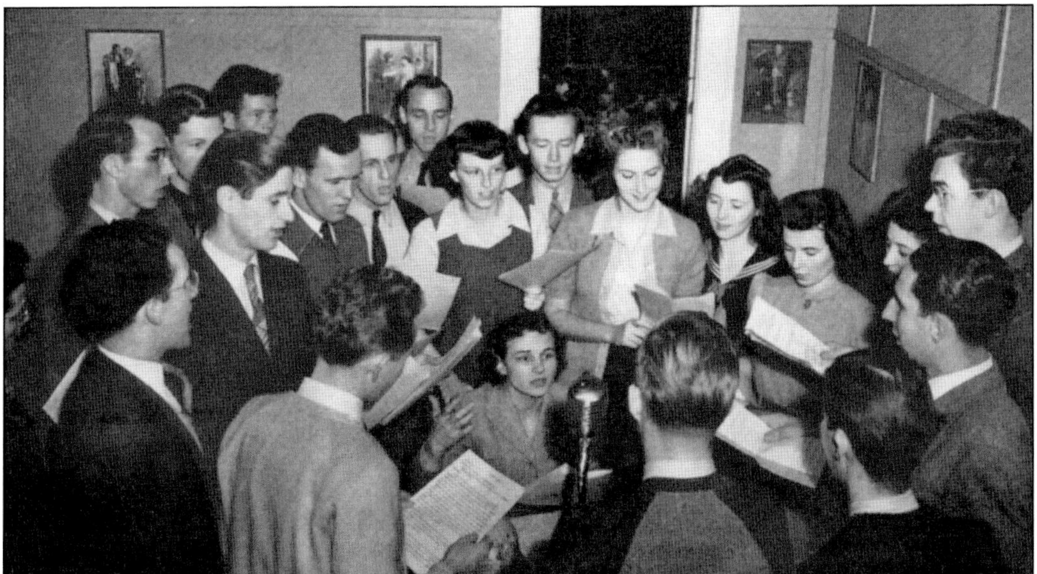

Students in Katherine Stenholm's 1943 Radio Technique class gather around her to learn how to master the "mic." These students wrote and directed programs for once-a-week broadcasts over WDOD-Chattanooga. Stenholm later became the first director of Unusual Films and has been highly recognized for her work in cinema.

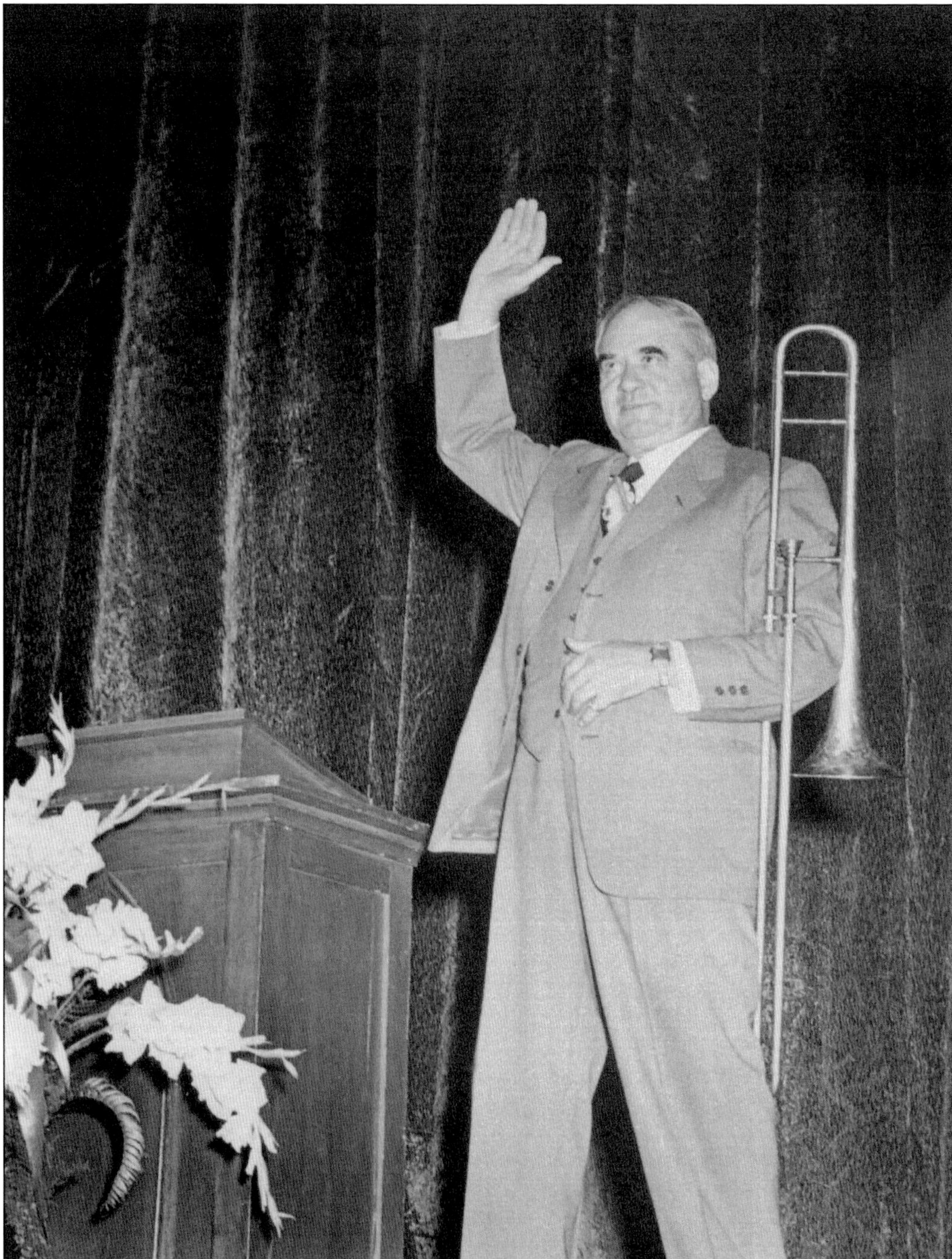

Dr. Homer Rodeheaver, with a trombone on his arm, leads the student body, faculty, and staff in singing. Having served as evangelist Billy Sunday's song leader from 1909 to 1931, Rodeheaver was a frequent campus guest and the major donor to the construction of the 3,000-seat Rodeheaver Auditorium on the Greenville, South Carolina, campus.

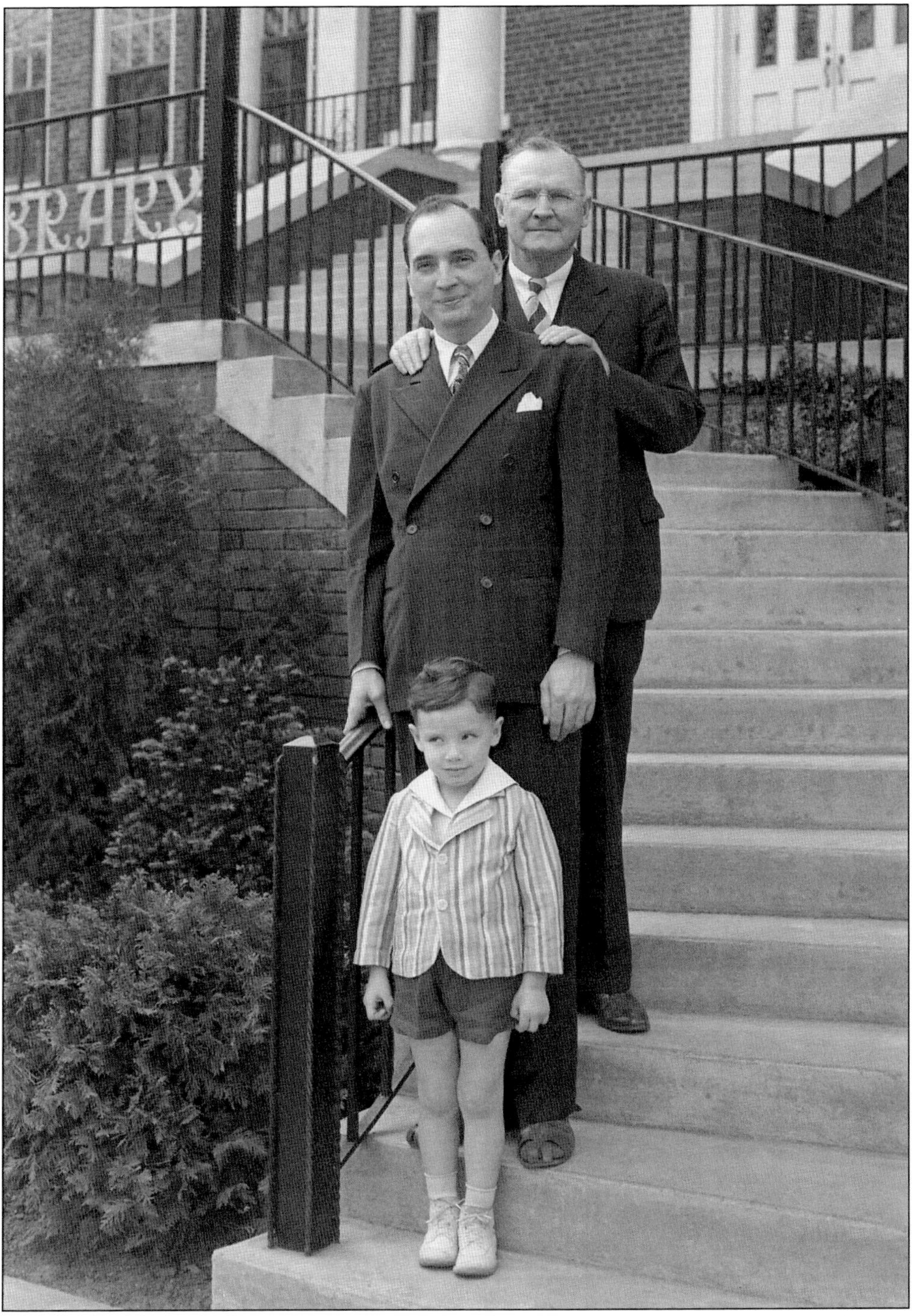

Standing on the steps of the Mack Library on the Cleveland, Tennessee, campus in 1944 are three Bob Joneses—young Bob III, Bob Jr., and Bob Sr. Succeeding his father as president of the school in 1947, when Bob Jones College moved to Greenville, South Carolina, and became a university, Dr. Bob Jones Jr. served in the chief administrative position until he was succeeded in 1971 by Dr. Bob Jones III.

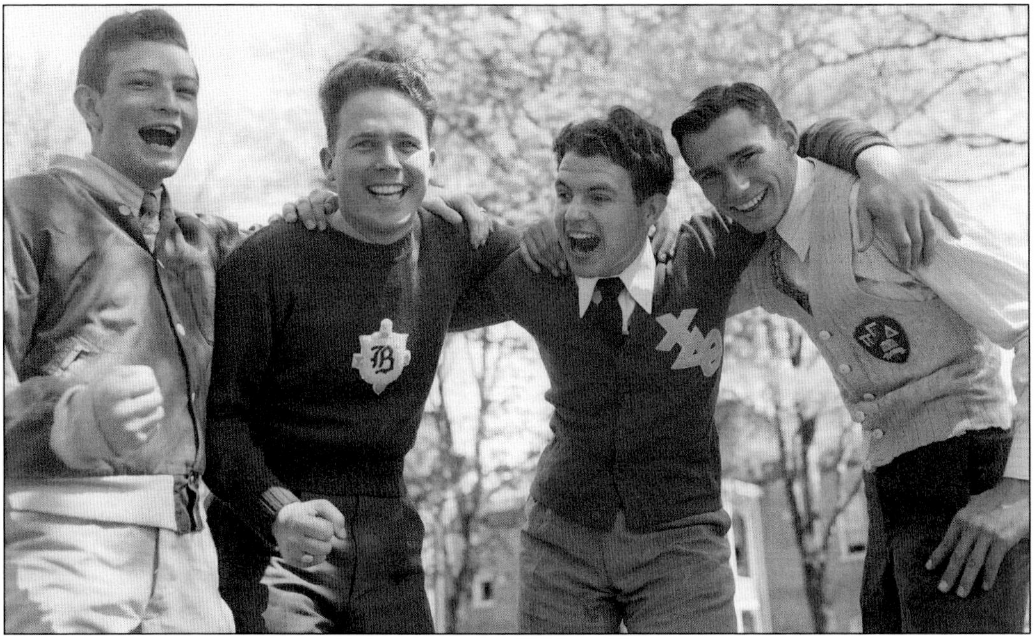

These young men on the Cleveland campus sport their respective literary societies' colors and emblems. Every student at Bob Jones College in the past and at Bob Jones University today chooses a society that he or she will belong to throughout college. Societies were started to encourage productive, cooperative, godly relationships.

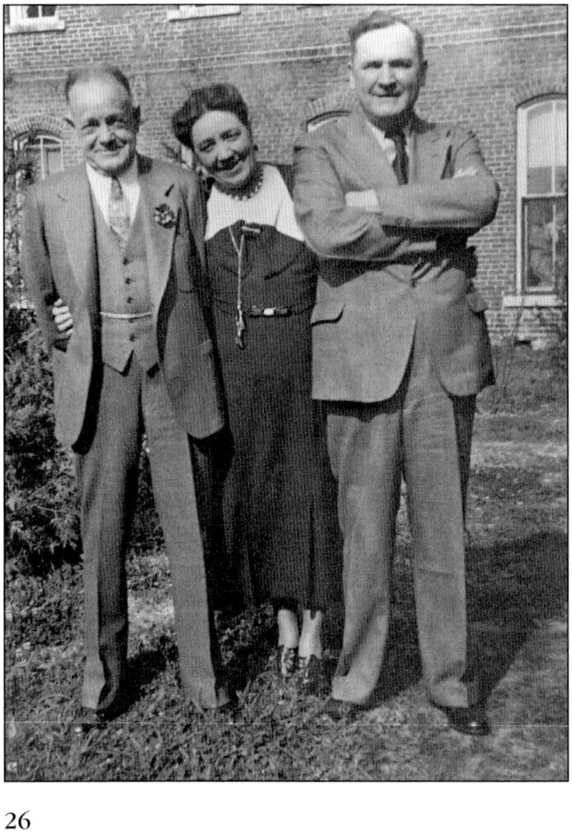

Shown here on the Cleveland campus, from left to right, are evangelist Billy Sunday, Ma Sunday, and Dr. Bob Jones Sr., who all had a common goal: winning people to the Lord Jesus. Billy Sunday was an early supporter of the idea of building Bob Jones College, and the school later recognized him with the honorary degree of doctor of laws. Billy Sunday preached at BJC every year from the school's founding until his death in 1935. Ma Sunday, for whom the Nell Sunday residence hall is named, served on the BJC and BJU Boards of Trustees from 1936 to 1957.

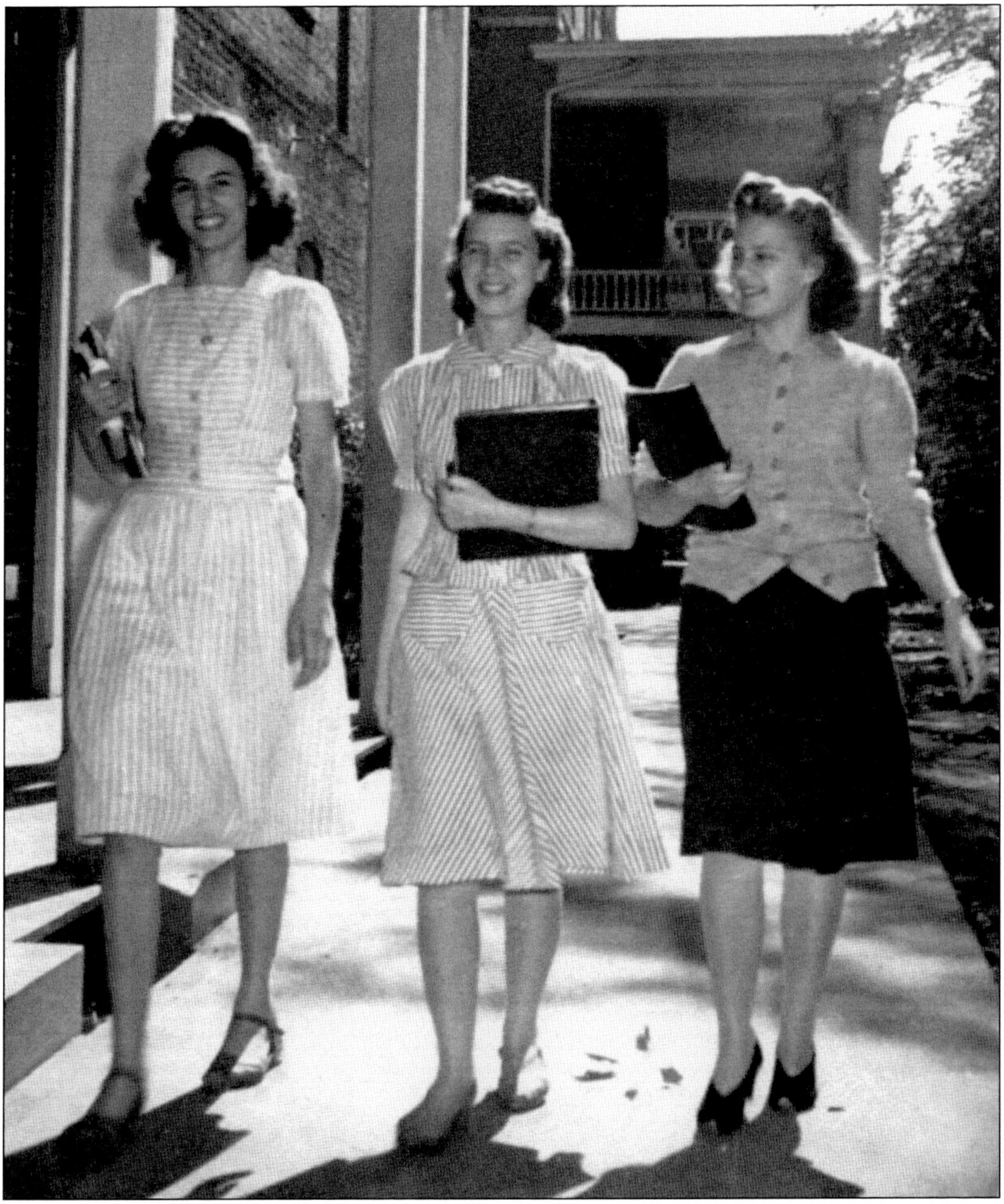

These young women were students on the Cleveland campus in 1942. From the beginning, the founder said he wanted the school he started to produce "show-window material for Jesus Christ." One aspect of training young people to be show-window material was inculcating standards of appropriate dress.

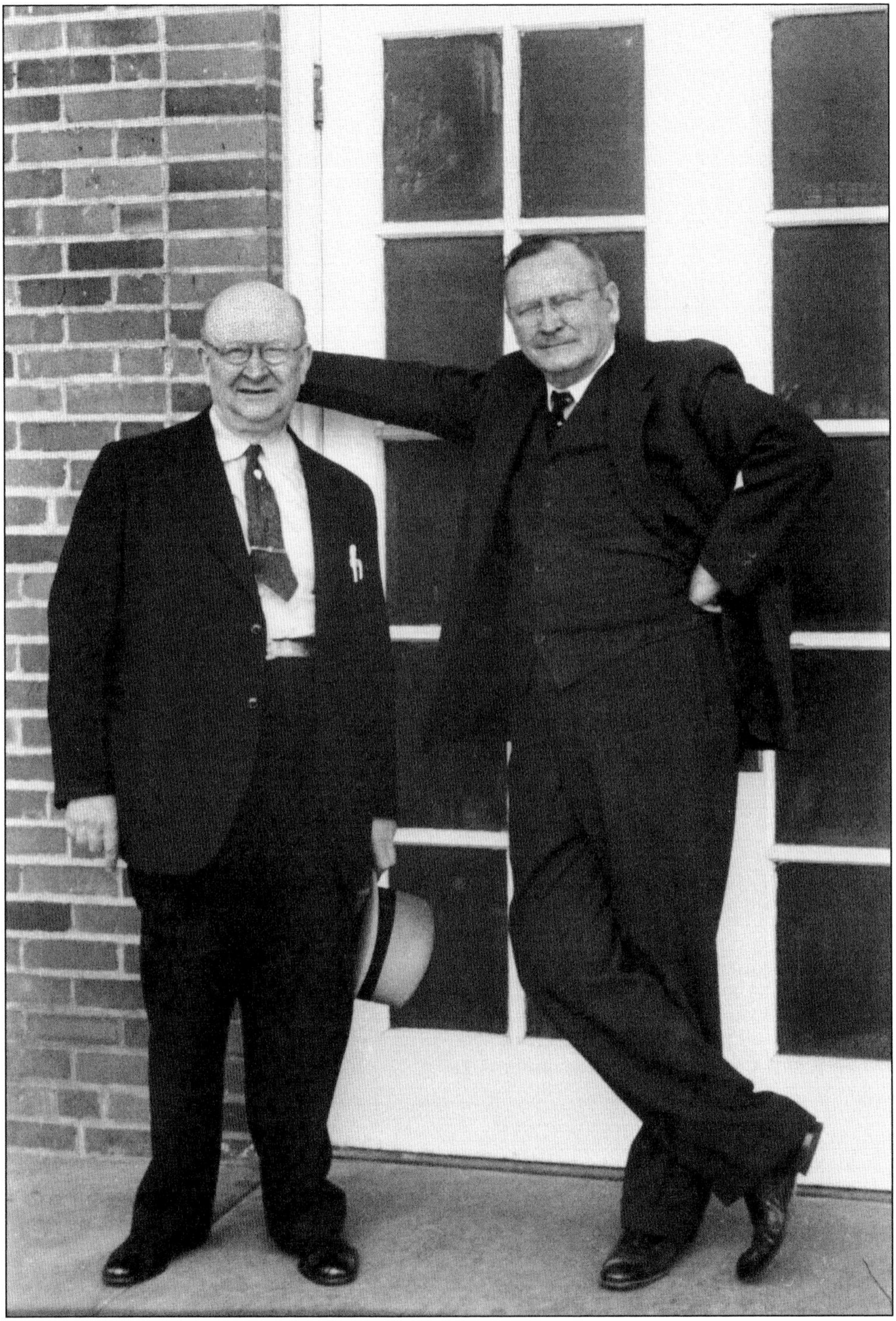

Two friends and warriors for the faith—Dr. Harry Ironside (left) and Dr. Bob Jones Sr.—pause during one of Dr. Ironside's visits to the Cleveland campus of Bob Jones College. Pastor of Moody Memorial Church in Chicago and the author of numerous books, Dr. Ironside has been called "the archbishop of Fundamentalism."

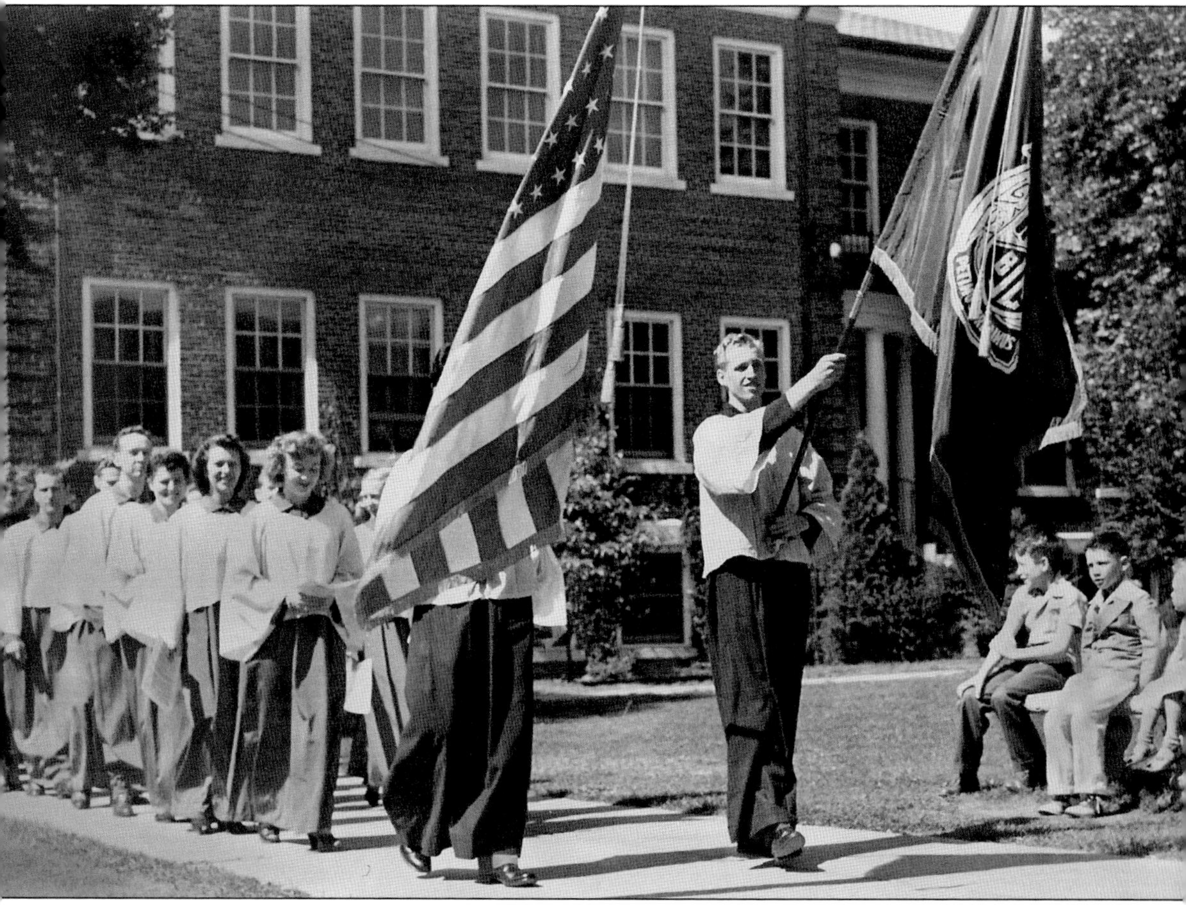

Commencement on the Cleveland campus of Bob Jones College began with this procession of flag bearers, choir members, faculty, and graduates making their way across the campus to the Mack Auditorium, where the ceremony was held. During the years in Cleveland, Bob Jones College experienced remarkable growth, both in undergraduate students and graduate students. The total yearly enrollment increased as follows: 1935—214; 1937—335; 1939—416; and in postwar 1946—1,581. The college began offering a master of arts in religion in 1942 and a doctor of philosophy in religion in 1943. The faculty more than doubled from 30 in 1936 to 66 in 1946.

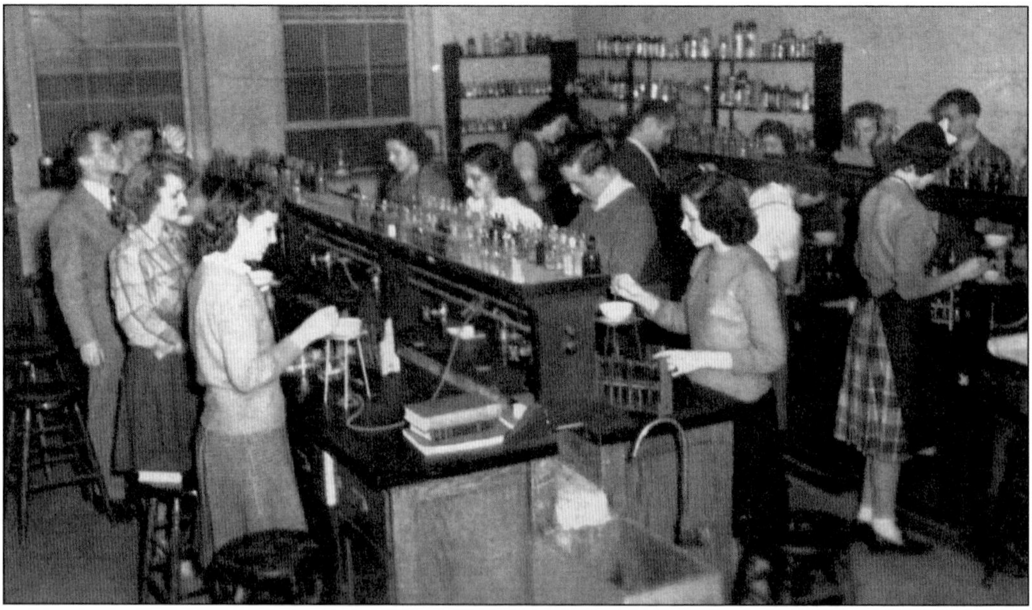

Pictured here is the 1945 chemistry lab at Bob Jones College. Two years later, after the college moved to Greenville, South Carolina, the 1947 academic catalog listed a full range of biology, botany, chemistry, and physics courses—an example of the expansion of the academic offerings when the college became a university.

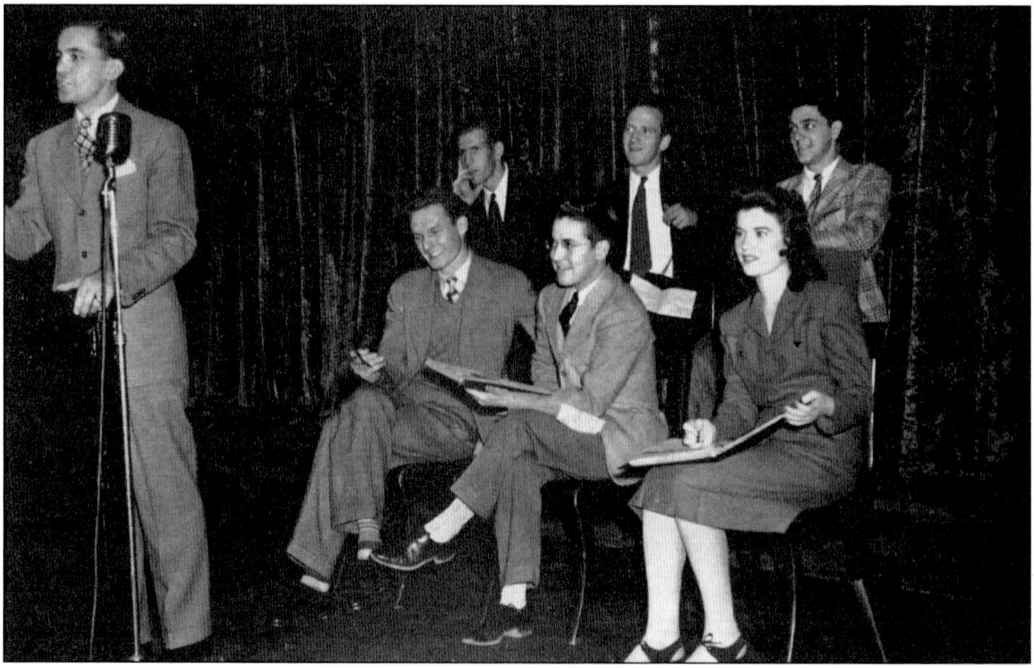

Student body officers for the first semester of the 1944–1945 school year had charge of chapel on Monday mornings, conducting student body business, and providing an inspirational program. Serving with Pres. Charles Bishop are Verne Taylor, vice president; Elizabeth Browning, secretary; Herbert Noe, chaplain; Ferris Hough, chorister; Dick Grenell, pianist; and Fred Afman, master-at-arms.

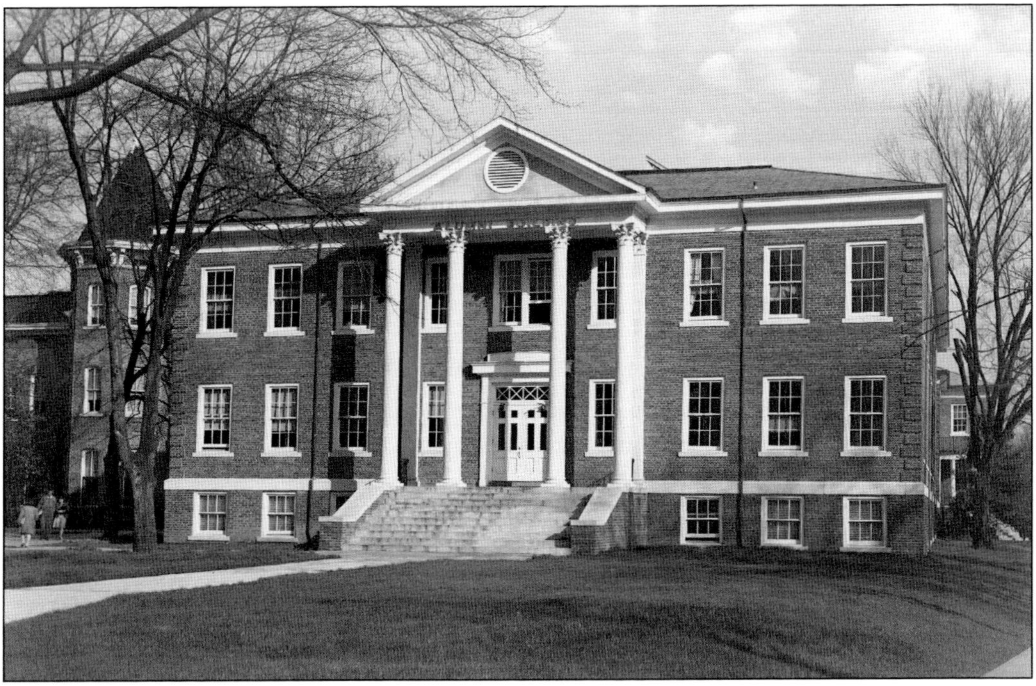

The Alumni Building (above) was one of the last two construction projects on the Cleveland campus of Bob Jones College. Primarily a classroom structure, it was built in 1945. A men's dormitory, Victory Hall, was built in 1946. This bird's-eye view (below) of the Cleveland campus shows some of the 13 new buildings that were constructed during the 14 years the college was located in Cleveland. The need for more land necessitated the move to South Carolina in 1947.

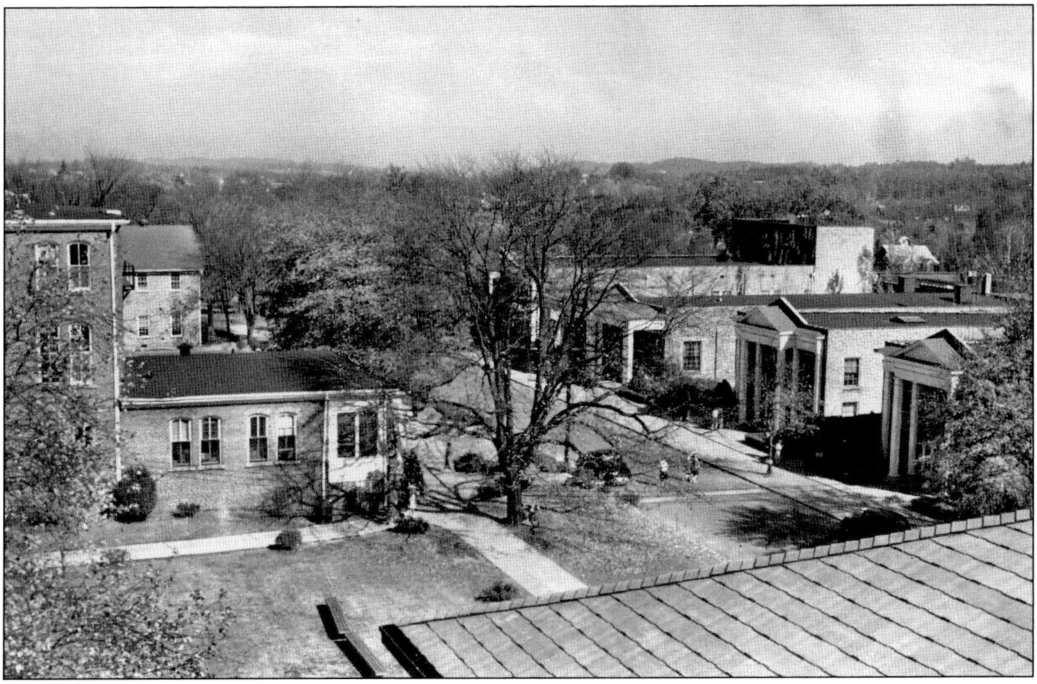

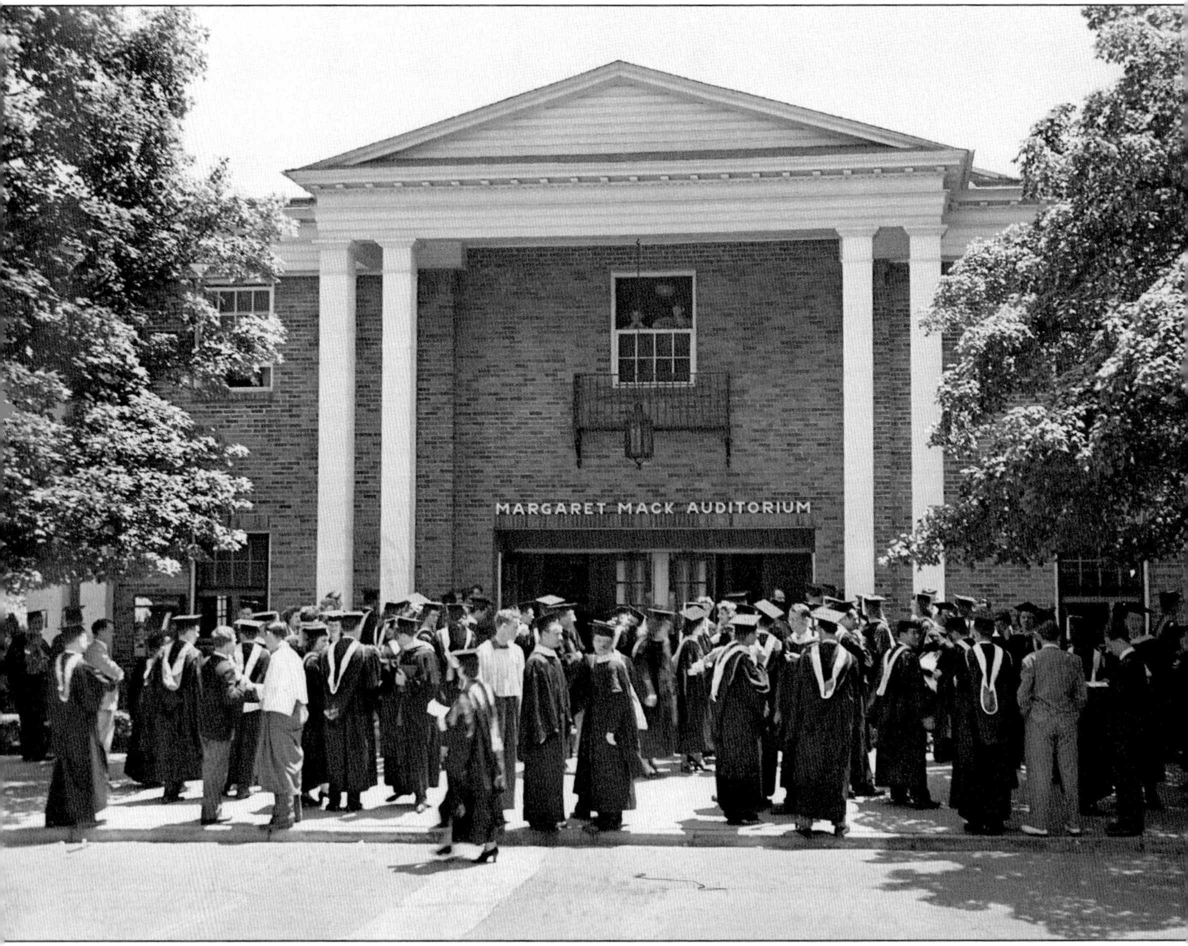

Margaret Mack Auditorium, dedicated on the Cleveland campus in 1936, was made possible by the generosity of John Sephus Mack, a Pennsylvania businessman who first met Dr. Bob Jones Sr. during a 1927 evangelistic campaign in McKeesport, Pennsylvania. When he later visited the campus, Mack was so impressed with the work God was doing at Bob Jones College that he said to Dr. Bob, "Construct your buildings and send me the bill." The above photograph shows graduates outside the Margaret Mack Auditorium following the 1945 commencement. John and Margaret Mack are still honored today by two buildings on the Greenville, South Carolina, campus that bear their names: the J. S. Mack Library and the Margaret Mack Residence Hall.

Three

The South Carolina Years 1947–1976

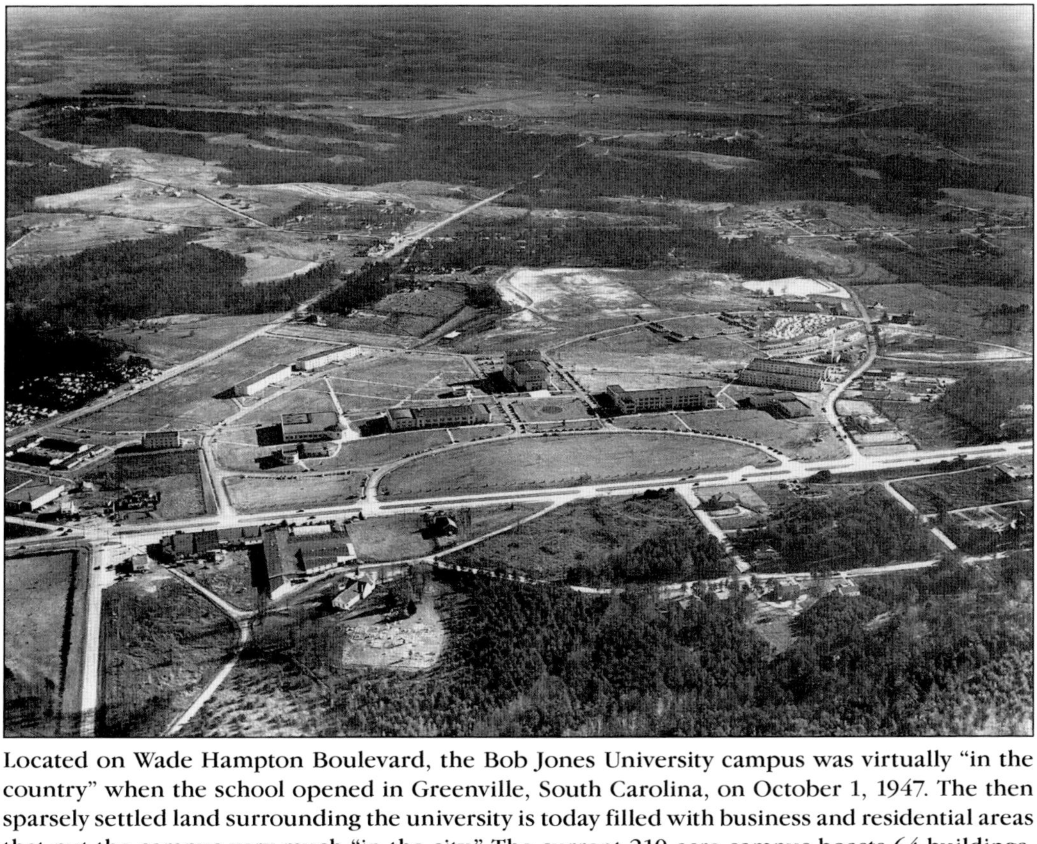

Located on Wade Hampton Boulevard, the Bob Jones University campus was virtually "in the country" when the school opened in Greenville, South Carolina, on October 1, 1947. The then sparsely settled land surrounding the university is today filled with business and residential areas that put the campus very much "in the city." The current 210-acre campus boasts 64 buildings, mature shrubs and trees, and a student body that exceeds 4,200.

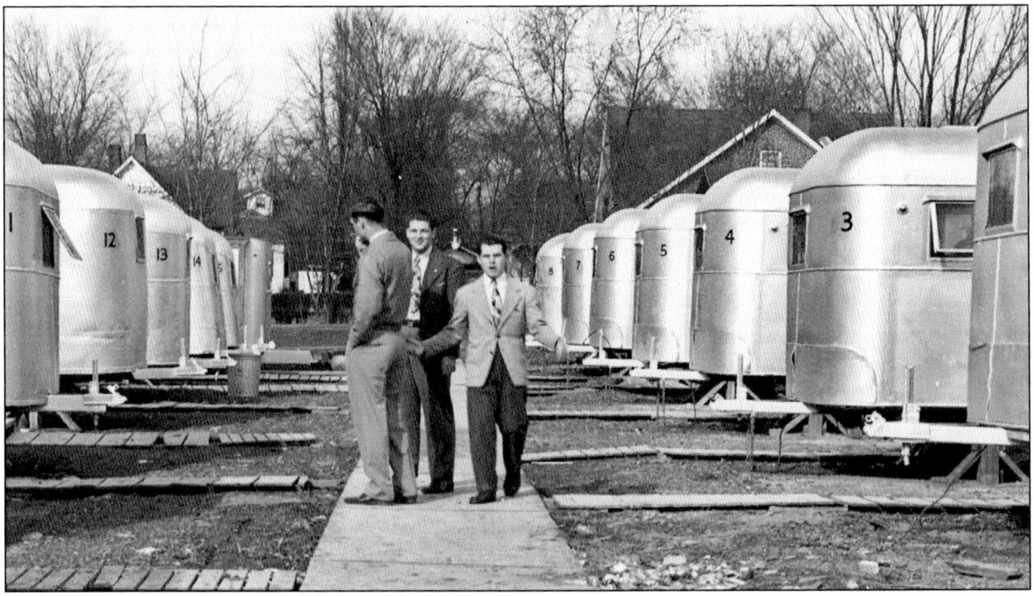

Silver City—a back-campus community of 50 house trailers purchased from the federal government in Oak Ridge, Tennessee—was assembled in 1947 to accommodate the many World War II veterans who were entering BJU to study under the GI Bill. Many of these men responded to the Lord's call to prepare for the ministry either as pastors or as missionaries. Bibb Graves Hall and J. Y. Smith Hall, the two men's residence halls, were filled, making Silver City a necessity to provide on-campus housing for veterans and married students.

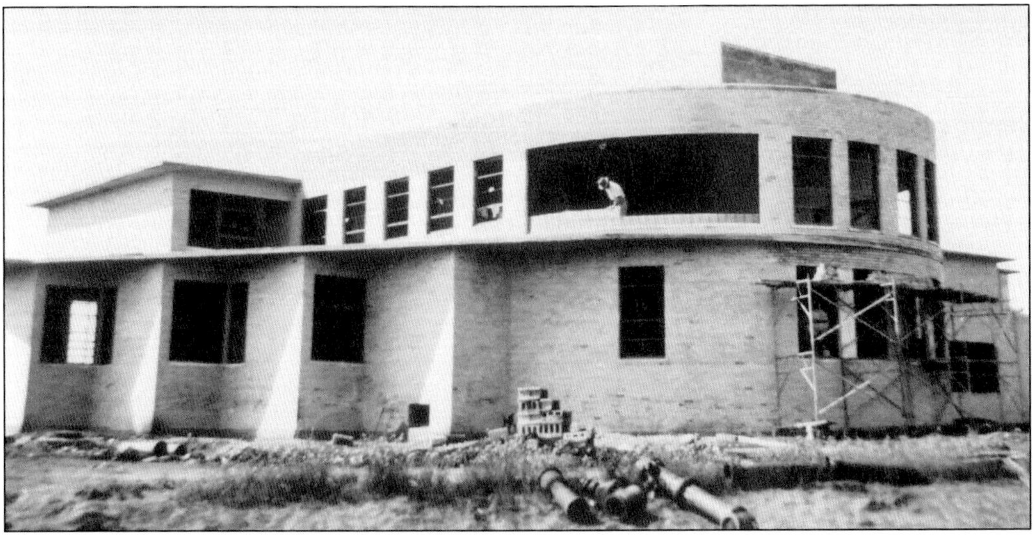

The Administration Building, on the east end of the front campus, is beginning to take shape in the summer of 1947, during the construction of the original Greenville campus. As construction progressed that year, shortages of construction materials following the war put the fall completion date in jeopardy. According to R. K. Johnson, business manager, who moved to Greenville to oversee construction, God miraculously supplied critical materials at just the right times, including 6,000 doors built especially for the school by Christian businessmen in Seattle, Washington, nails gathered up in the Cleveland, Tennessee, area and driven to Greenville, and electrical transformers made available when another Westinghouse customer cancelled its order.

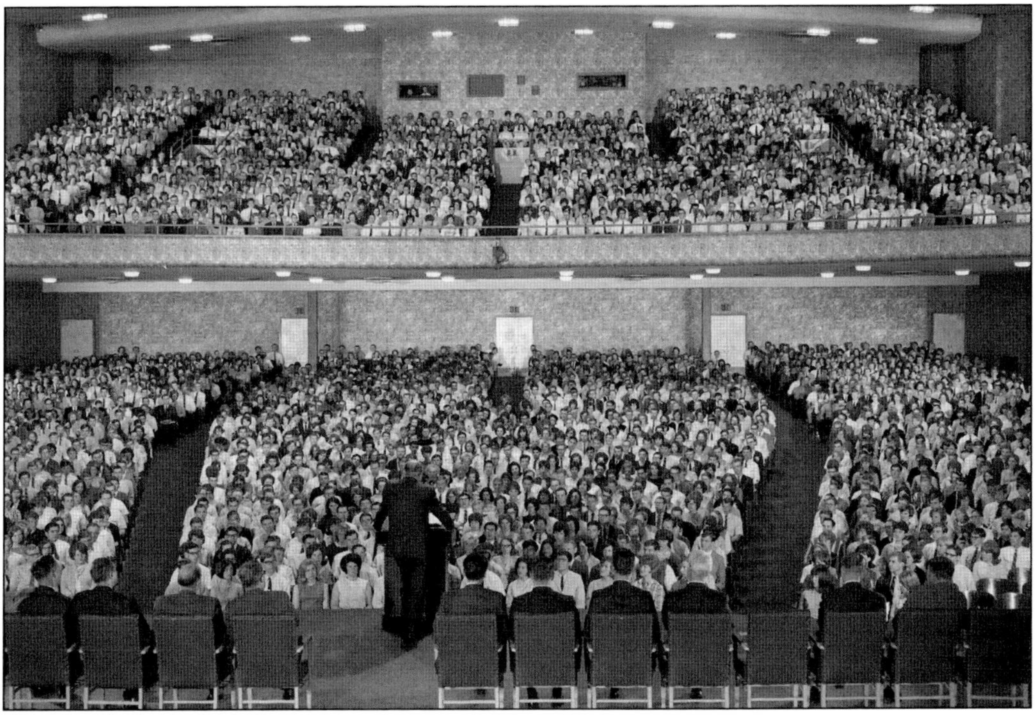

Dr. Bob Jones Jr. speaks to the over 3,000 BJU students in the late 1940s during daily chapel in a full Rodeheaver Auditorium. He, Dr. Bob Jones Sr., and guest speakers always endeavored to "keep the chapel platform hot" with practical messages true to the Bible.

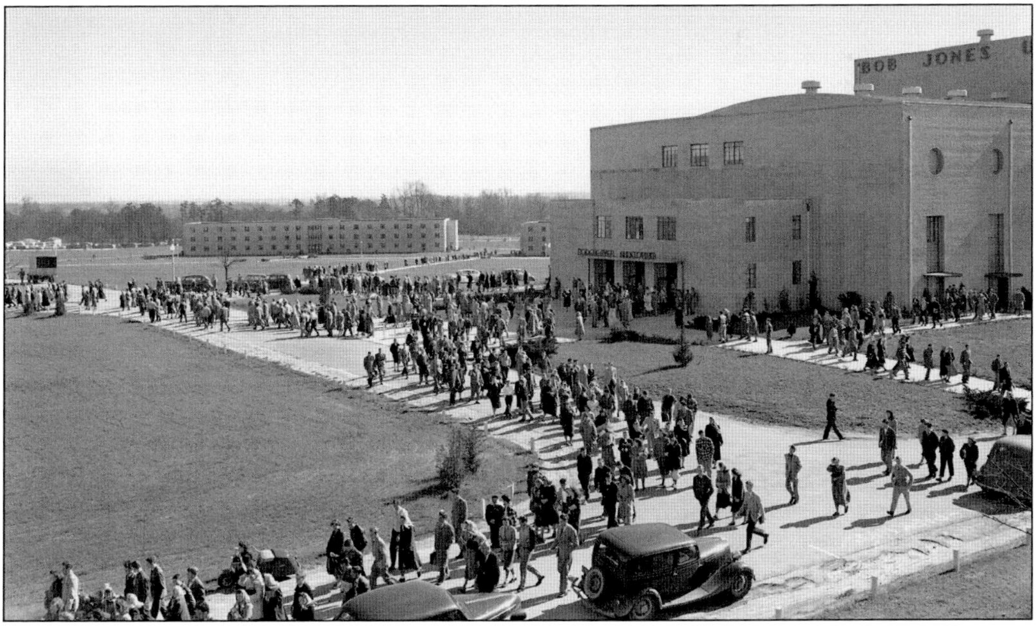

Students exit Rodeheaver Auditorium during the 1949 school year. Until the Founder's Memorial Amphitorium was constructed in 1972, Rodeheaver Auditorium was a multi-purpose building used for chapel, Sunday church services, Artist Series programs, Vespers, commencement, and all dramatic performances.

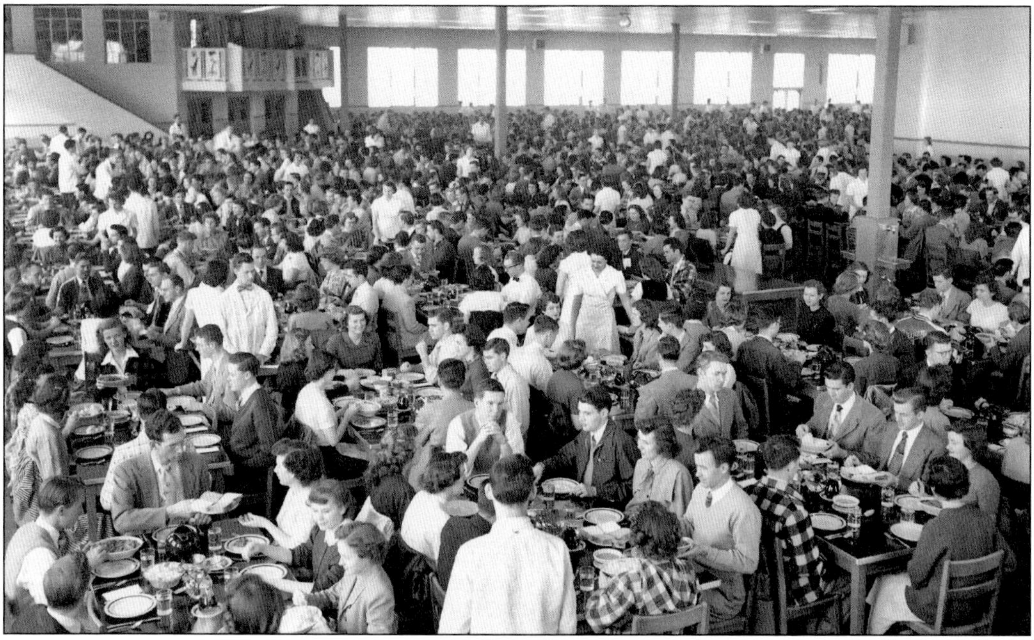

Through 1987, when it became nearly impossible to fit fixed meal times into the students' schedules, meals were served family-style, with students, faculty, and staff rotating tables every few weeks where they were served by waiters and waitresses. Before sitting down, students sang a hymn and someone led in prayer. This photograph pictures the original Greenville Dixon-McKenzie Dining Common, which today is the Museum and Gallery at Bob Jones University.

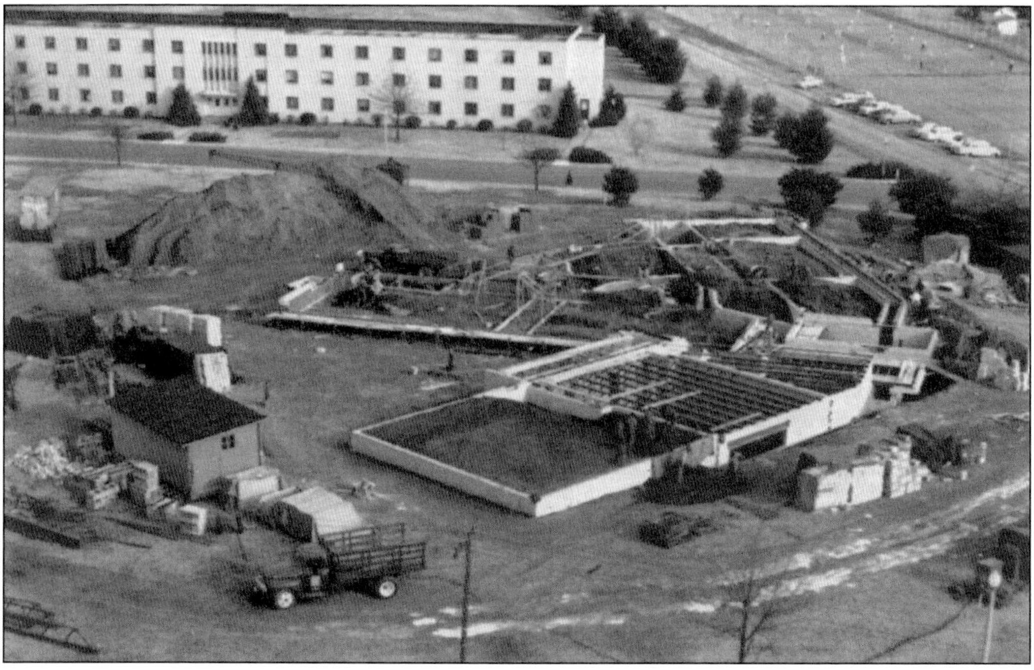

Construction was under way for the Howell Memorial Science Building in the 1959–1960 school year. The building houses classrooms, lecture amphitheaters, laboratories, a planetarium, and offices for the departments of natural science and family and consumer science.

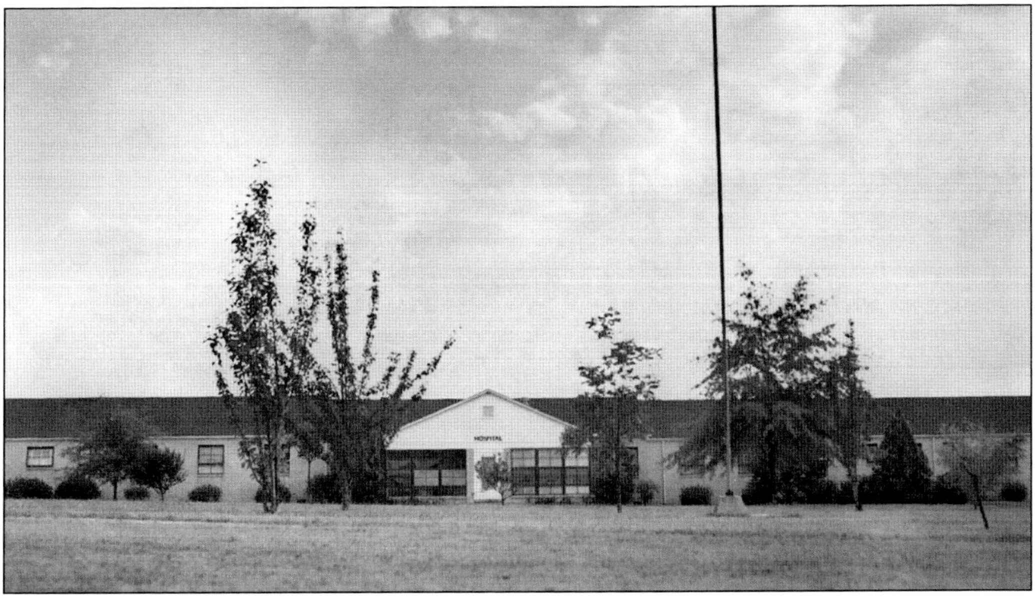

Constructed in 1948, the original University Hospital served the campus family until the W. J. Barge Memorial Hospital was built in 1969. In 1951, a surgery wing was added to the original hospital building. Today the building is a Bob Jones Academy classroom building known as the Brown Building.

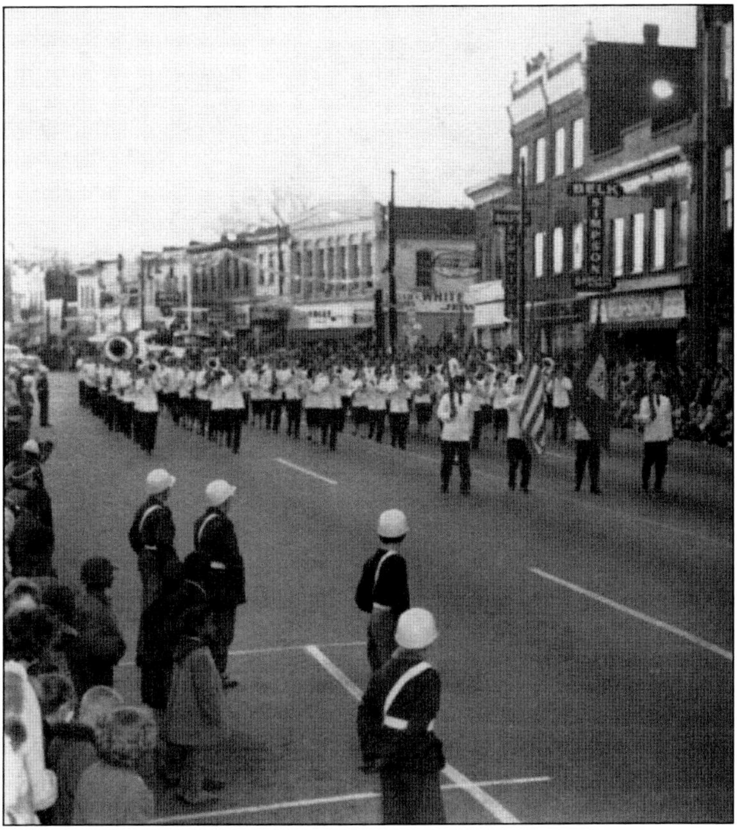

The 1949 university band under the direction of James Conley marches down Main Street in the annual Greenville Christmas parade. BJU students continue to participate frequently in community events, including the annual Christmas parade.

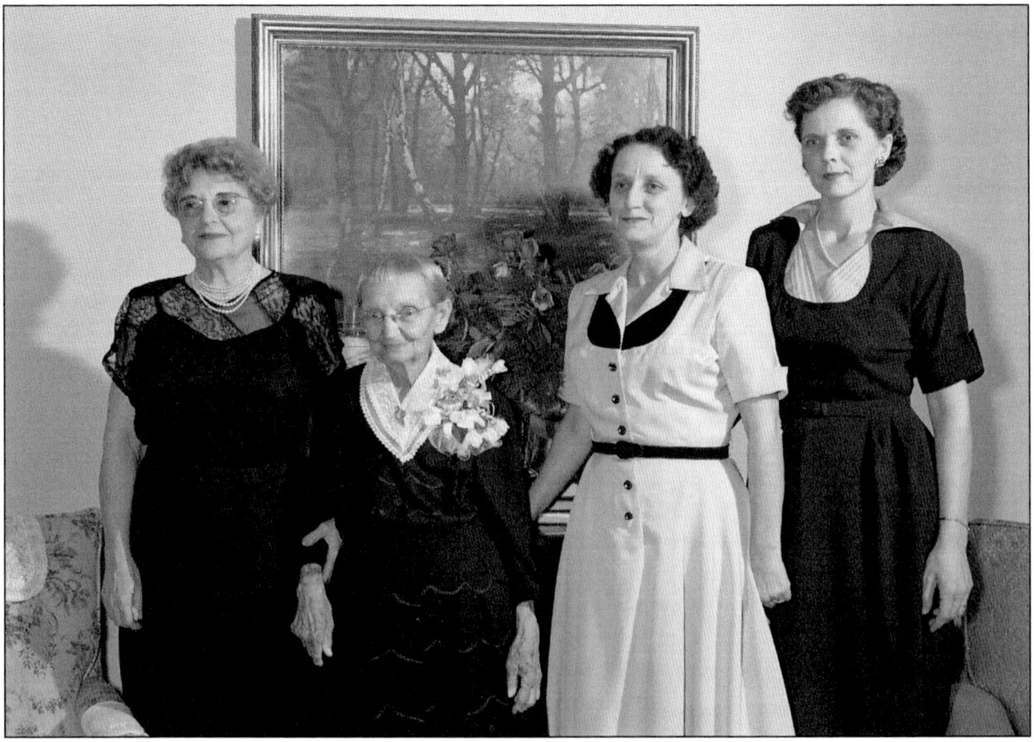

Four familiar faces on the Greenville campus during the 1940s were, from left to right, Mary Gaston Jones, the founder's wife; Dr. Grace Haight, who edited the *Fellowship News* and taught missions and hymnology; Fannie Mae Jones, the president's wife; and Elizabeth Edwards, speech instructor and wife of the dean of students. The building currently housing the university's nursing program is named for Dr. Haight, who served as a missionary in both Egypt and China before coming to Bob Jones College.

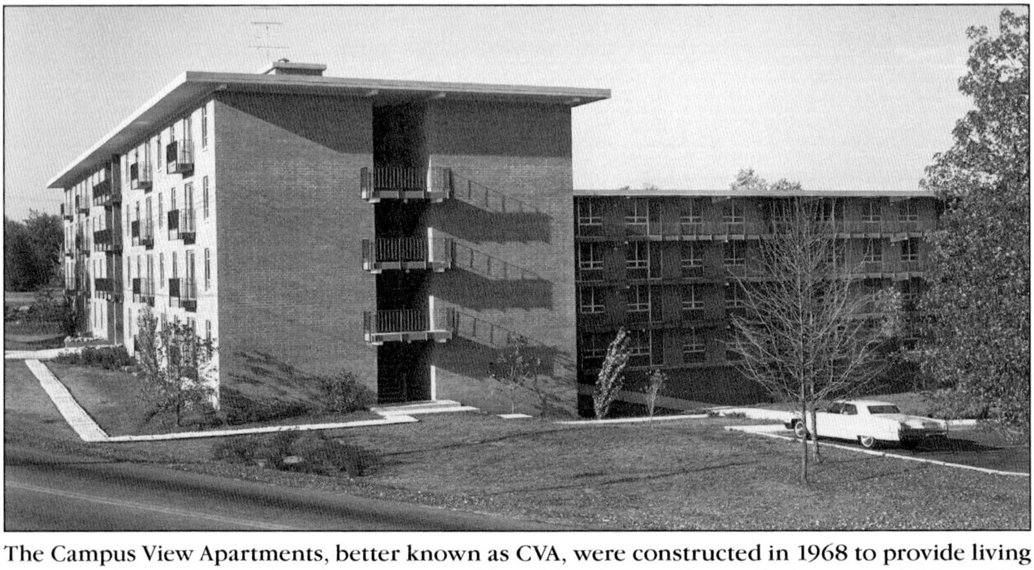

The Campus View Apartments, better known as CVA, were constructed in 1968 to provide living accommodations for graduate assistants, staff, and faculty members who have no children. The building is located directly across Wade Hampton Boulevard from BJU's main entrance.

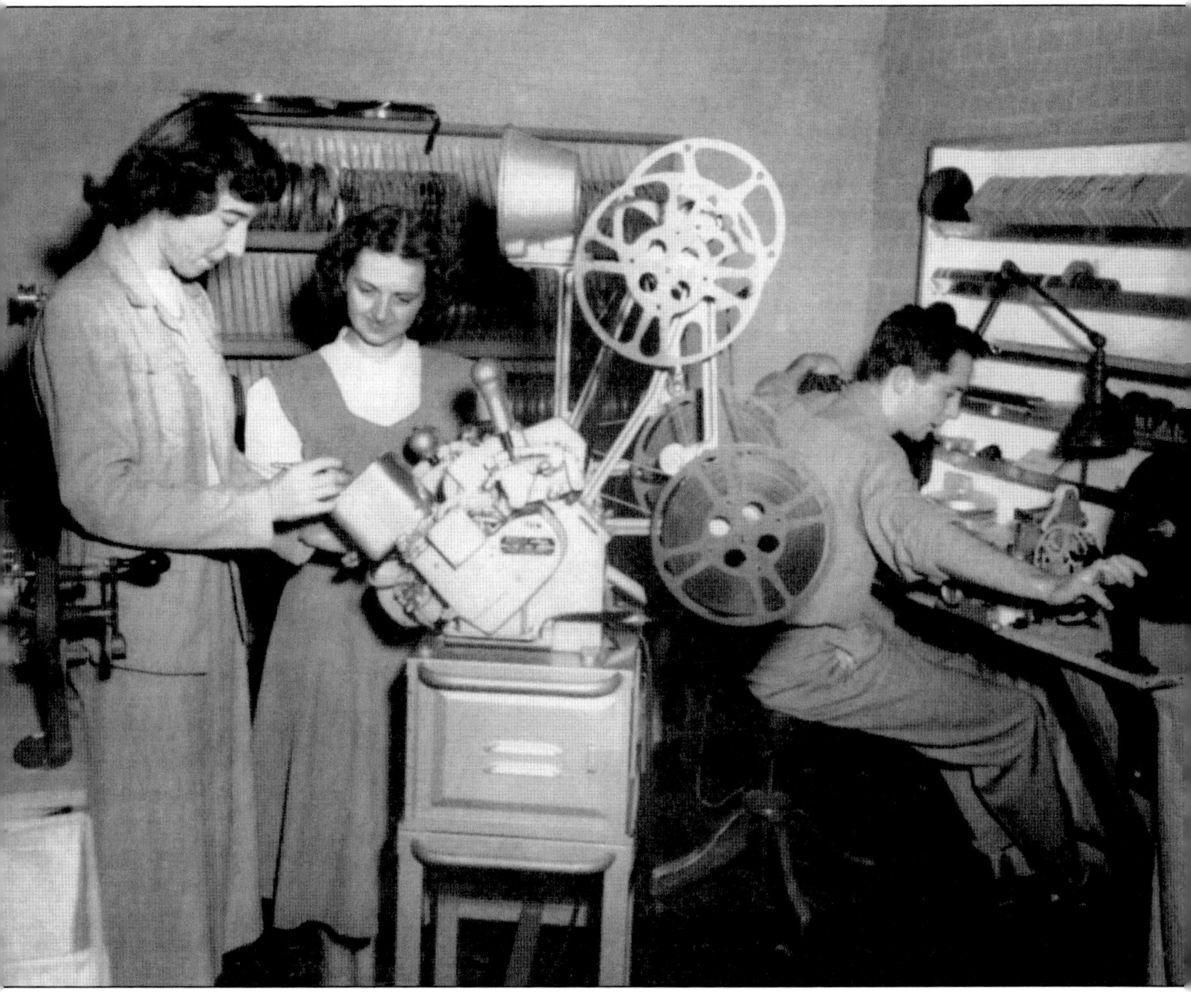

From left to right, Alice Cromley, Betty Rae Campbell, and George Jensen worked as the 1952 editing staff in the Unusual Films Studio, which produces Christian films to spread the Gospel. Today's studio is a large soundstage with a camera crane and boom microphone, catwalks, and multiple lights. The film editing and cutting offices, the makeup and hair styling department, and numerous dressing rooms have all contributed to make Unusual Films a leader in university cinema. Alice Cromley has served on the Unusual Films and Photo Studio staff for more than a half century.

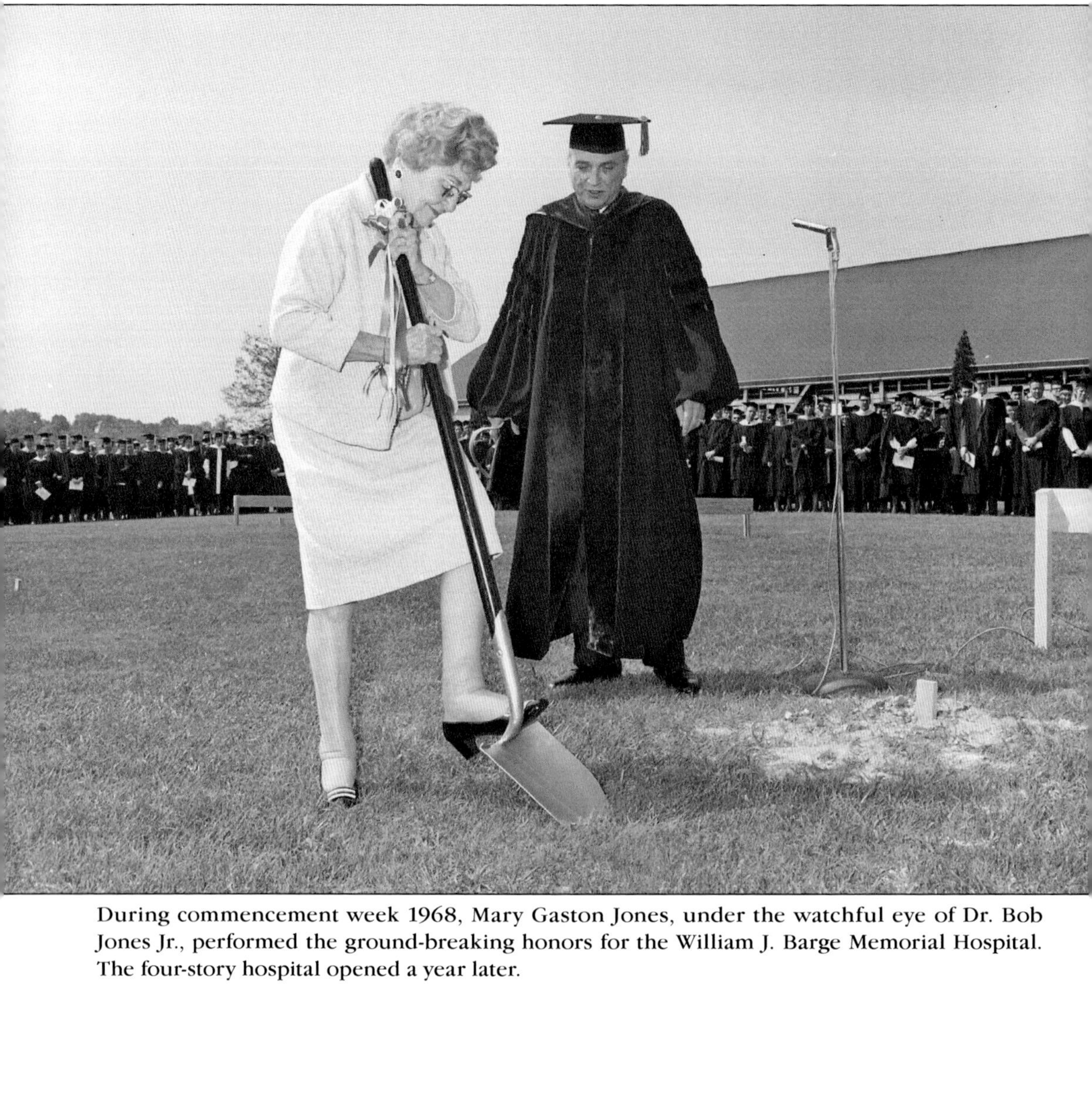

During commencement week 1968, Mary Gaston Jones, under the watchful eye of Dr. Bob Jones Jr., performed the ground-breaking honors for the William J. Barge Memorial Hospital. The four-story hospital opened a year later.

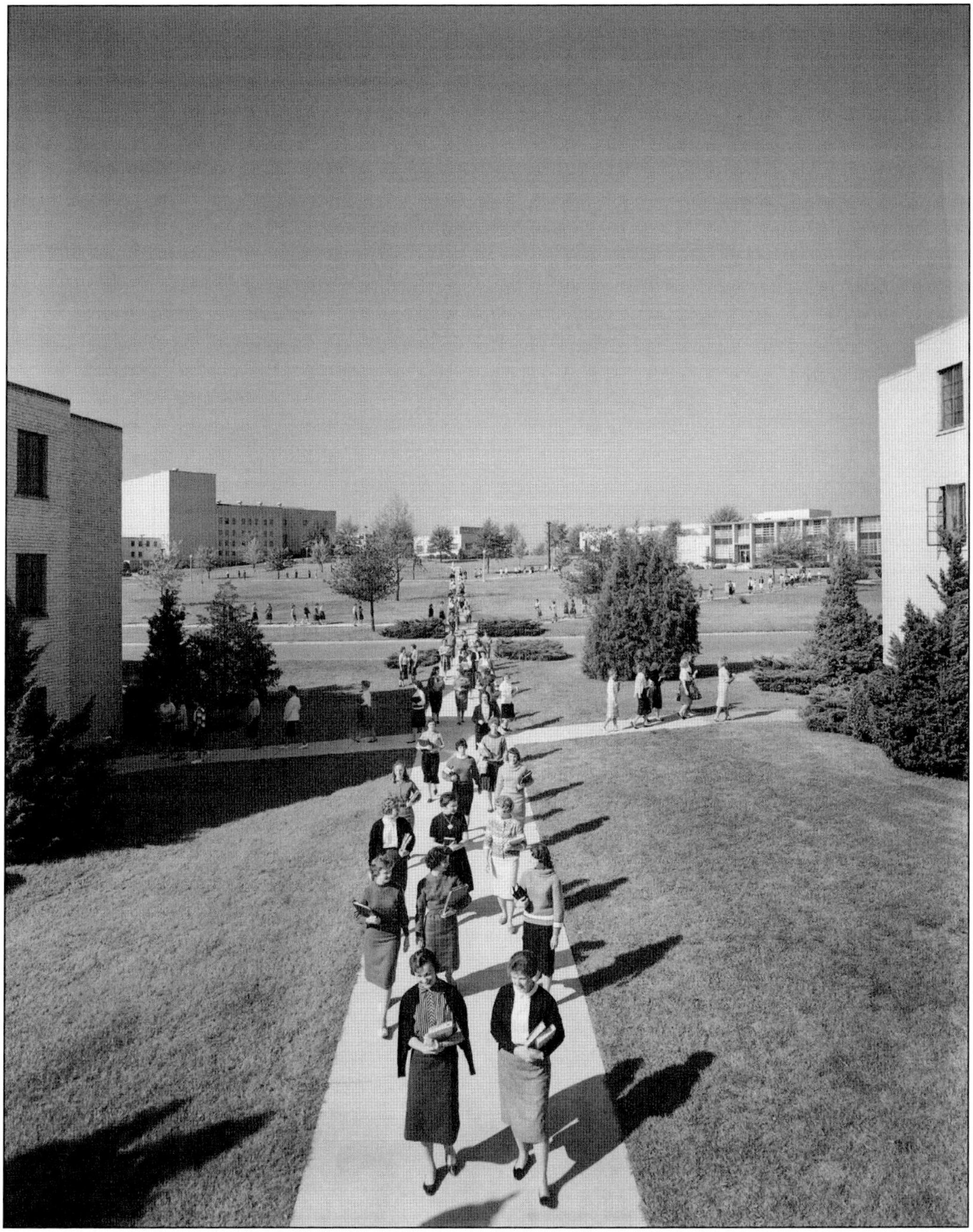

In the late 1950s, no Founder's Memorial Amphitorium or other buildings blocked the view of Rodeheaver Auditorium from the women's residence halls, and covered sidewalks were nowhere to be found. The building to the right of Rodeheaver Auditorium in this photograph was the original WMUU studio. The original three women's residence halls were Margaret Mack, Nell Sunday, and Grace Haight.

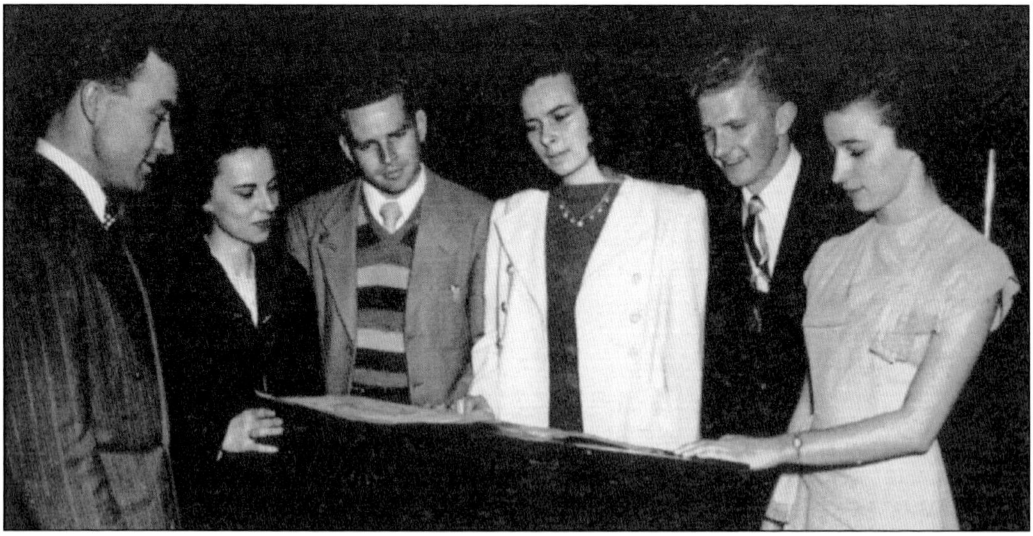

In 1948, students met daily in Mission Prayer Band to pray for missionaries, and as a result, many answered the Lord's call to serve on mission fields around the world. The 1948 Mission Prayer Band officers were Willard Wyatt, president; Earl Carlberg, vice president; Wanda Grider, vice president; June Cook, secretary; Grant Yeatman, chorister; and Frances Ackley, pianist. In addition to Mission Prayer Band, which continues to meet, the university now designates one week each year as Missions Emphasis Week to keep the need for missionaries continually before the student body.

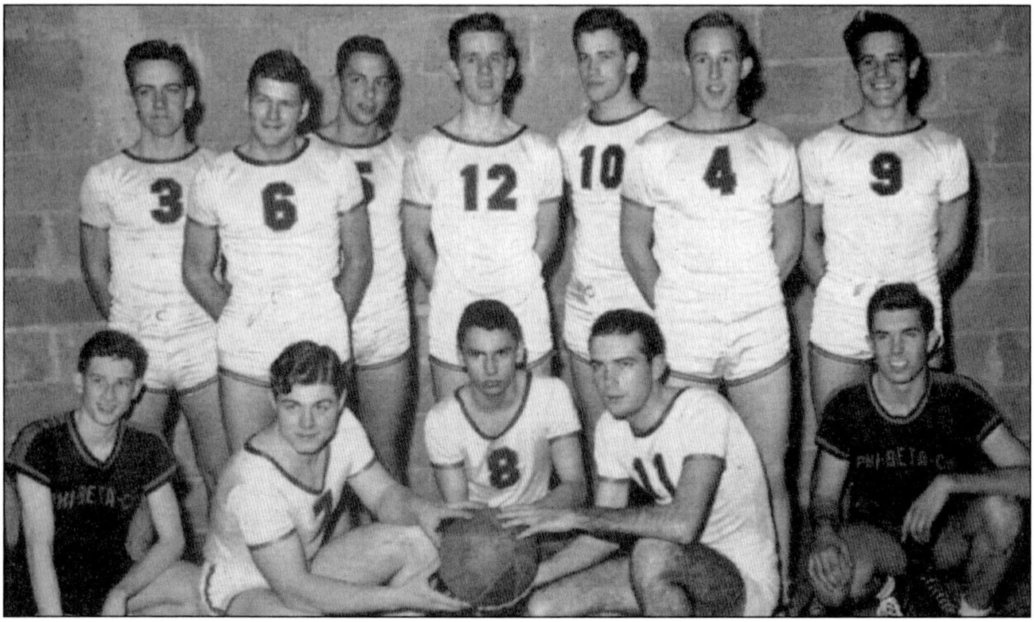

These 12 young men were the 1948 Phi Beta Chi basketball team. BJU's intramural sports program creates a lot of competition and rivalry among the various societies, especially in basketball and soccer. The games in 1948 were played in the gymnasium at the north end of the Student Center. When the second gymnasium was built in 1959, the original gymnasium became the Concert Hall and is now completely refurbished and known as Stratton Hall, as a memorial to Mel Stratton, the longtime BJU stage manager.

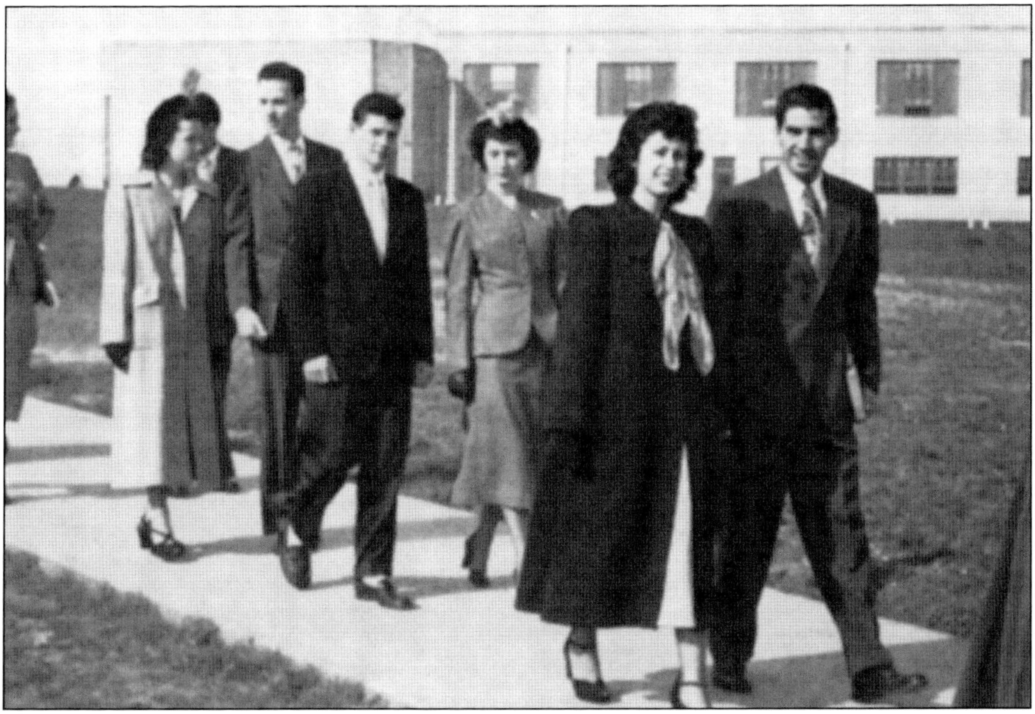

These three couples walk the "snail trail"—sometimes called the "date line"—leading to the women's residence halls. Each evening following dinner, men students escort their dates home. After Sunday services and special performances, the snail trail originates at Founder's Memorial Amphitorium or Rodeheaver Auditorium.

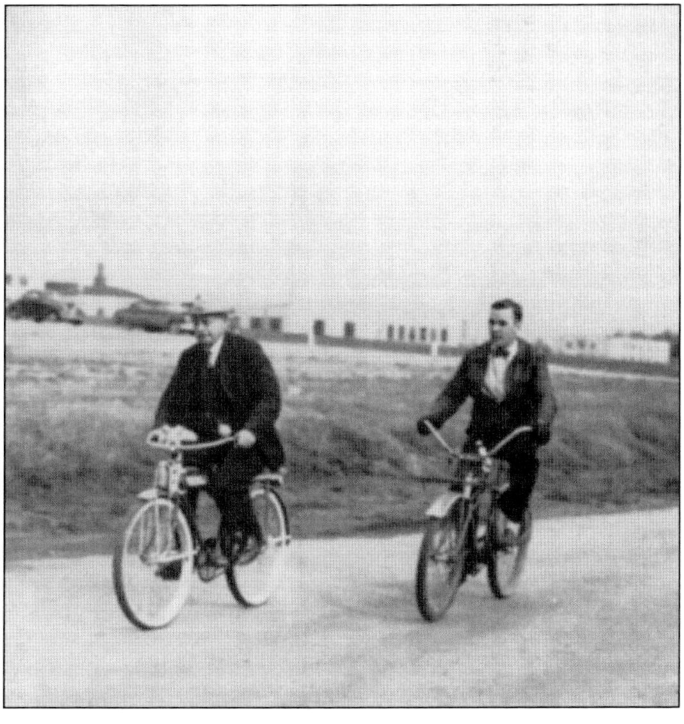

In the late 1940s, Dr. Charles Brokenshire (left), who had the reputation of being the most gifted linguist Bob Jones University ever had, made his way around campus on his bicycle. A Princeton and University of Chicago scholar who spoke and read more than 35 languages, Dr. Brokenshire joined the BJC faculty in 1943 and stayed through his death on May 28, 1954. He died shortly after he submitted his second-semester grades.

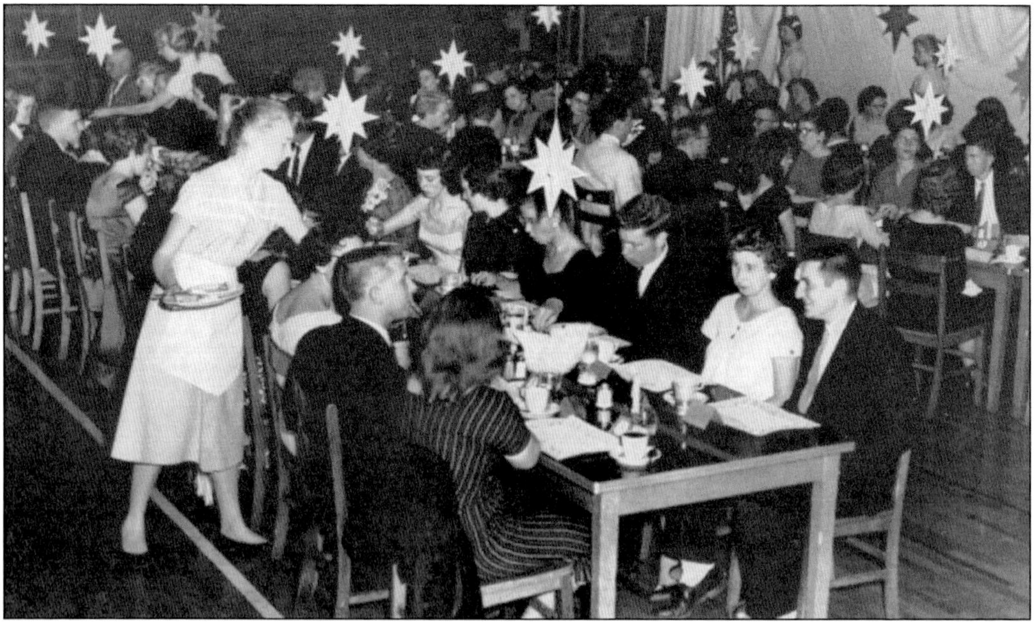

Begun during the 1957–1958 school year, the Association of Christian Teachers boasted 400 members by its second year. Speakers from Christian day schools, mission schools, and public schools frequently addressed the group. "Disneyland" provided the theme of the 1959 annual party climaxing the year's events.

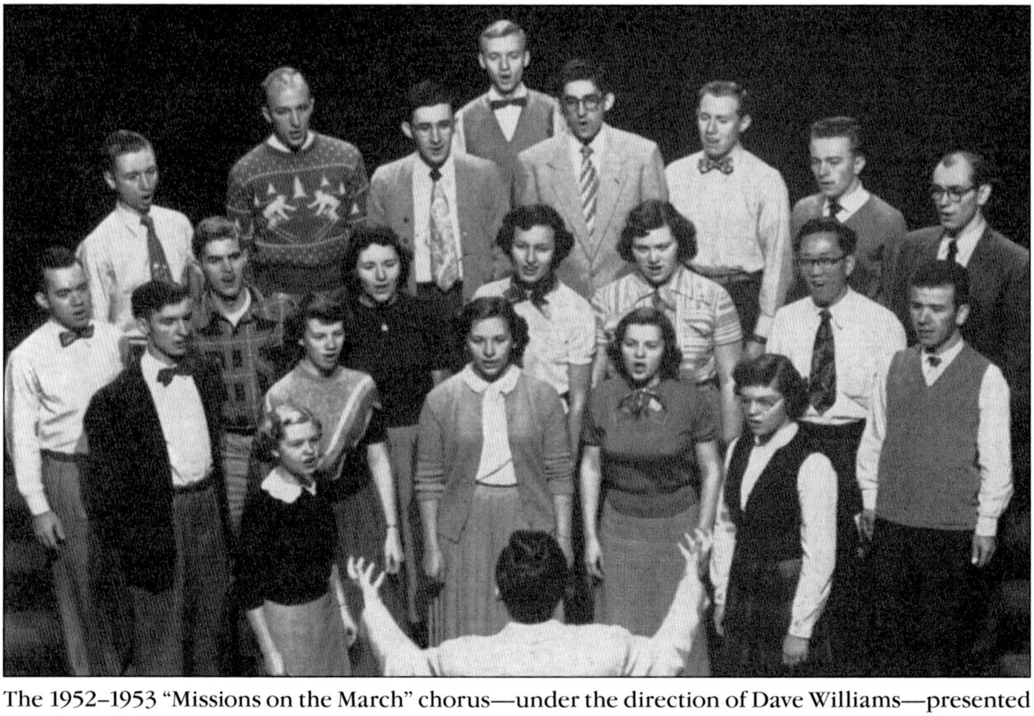

The 1952–1953 "Missions on the March" chorus—under the direction of Dave Williams—presented a live program every Saturday morning over radio station WMUU. A project of Mission Prayer Band, the 15-minute program focused on the challenges of various mission fields through hymns and anthems. Hundreds of BJU graduates have become missionaries in countries around the world.

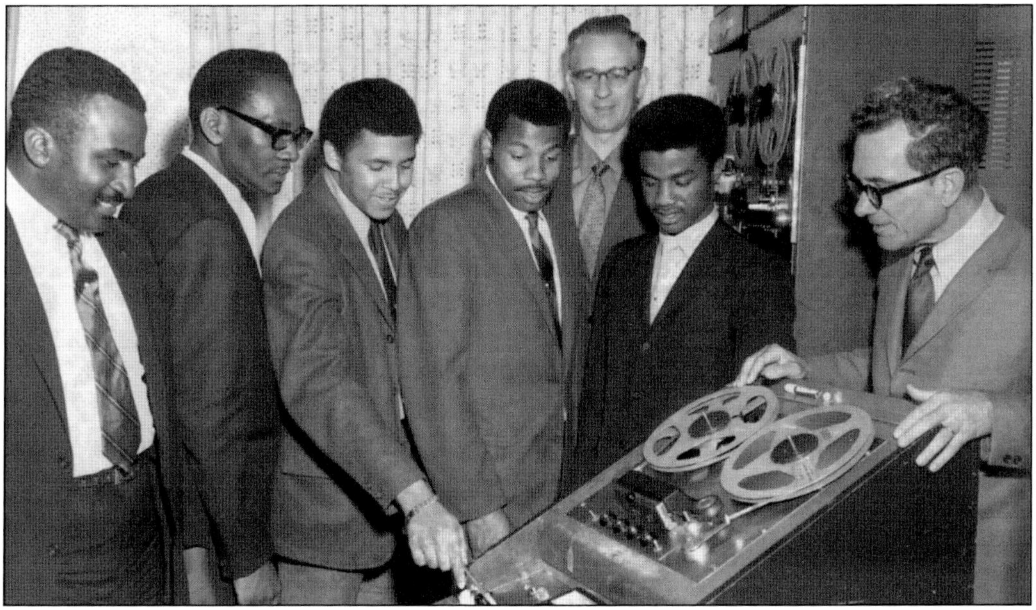

Five students from Carver College in Atlanta, Georgia, visit the BJU campus in 1972 to see the broadcast facilities of radio station WMUU and to attend a workshop conducted by WMUU staff members. The visitors were enrolled in a three-hour course taught by Elmer Rumminger (fifth from left), which met at BJU's other station, WAVO-FM and AM in Decatur, Georgia, where Rumminger was manager from 1963 to 1971. Jim Ryerson (far right), the station manager, is explaining the features of the WMUU recording equipment.

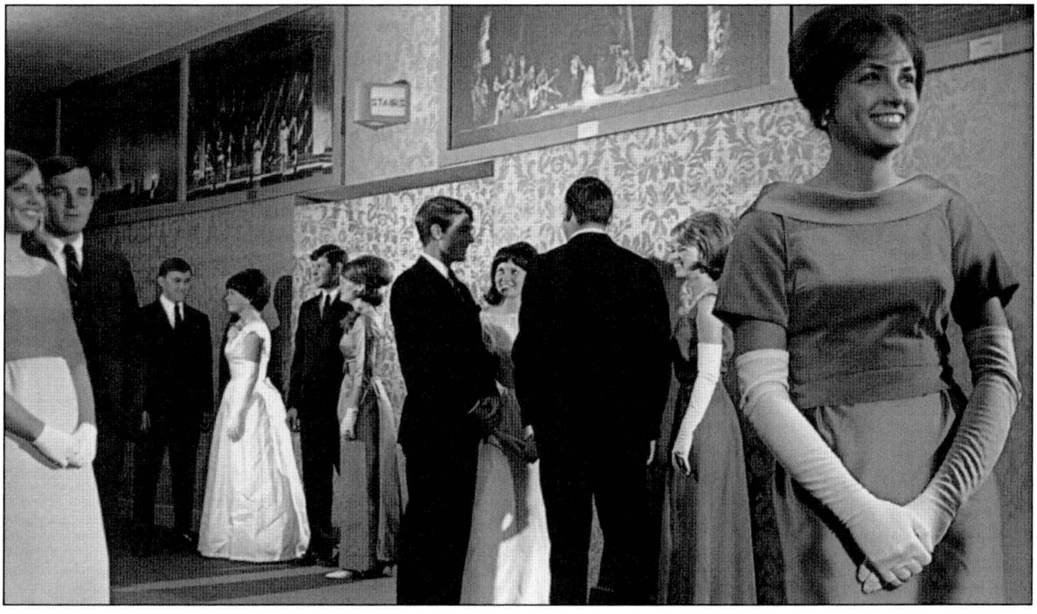

Students chat with their dates in the Rodeheaver Auditorium lobby at a 1967 Artist Series program. Artist Series are a perfect setting for developing students' appreciation for the fine arts. Artist Series programs include the productions of the Classic Players and the annual opera, as well as guest artists such as soloists, ensembles, and full orchestras. At BJU, Artist Series programs are considered part of the educational process, and all students attend.

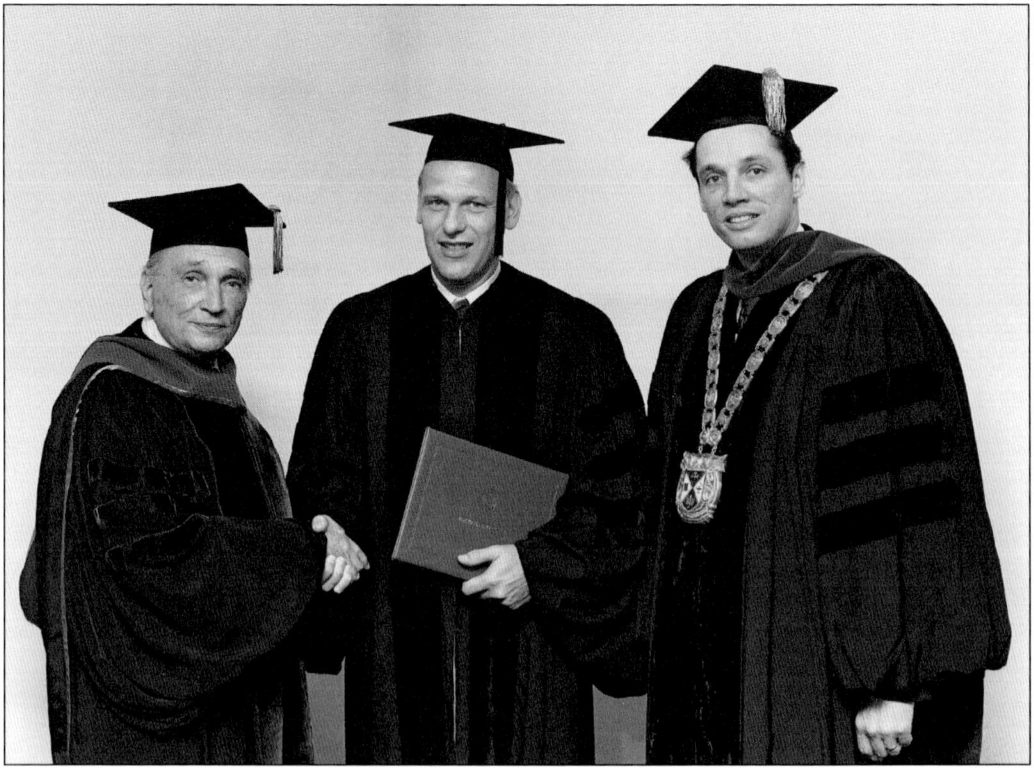

Dr. Bob Jones Jr., chancellor, (left) and Dr. Bob Jones III, president, (right) congratulate Ken Hay following the 1975 commencement where he was awarded an honorary doctorate. Dr. Hay is the founder of the Wilds Christian Camp and Conference Center in North Carolina, which over the years has ministered to thousands of young people and adults. Dr. Hay previously served on the university faculty as the first director of the Institute of Christian Service.

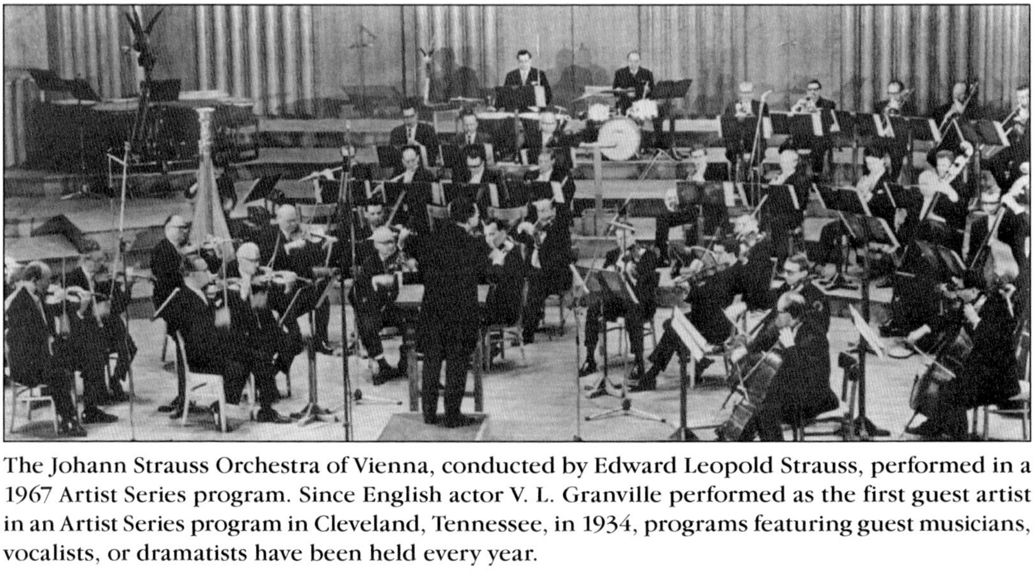

The Johann Strauss Orchestra of Vienna, conducted by Edward Leopold Strauss, performed in a 1967 Artist Series program. Since English actor V. L. Granville performed as the first guest artist in an Artist Series program in Cleveland, Tennessee, in 1934, programs featuring guest musicians, vocalists, or dramatists have been held every year.

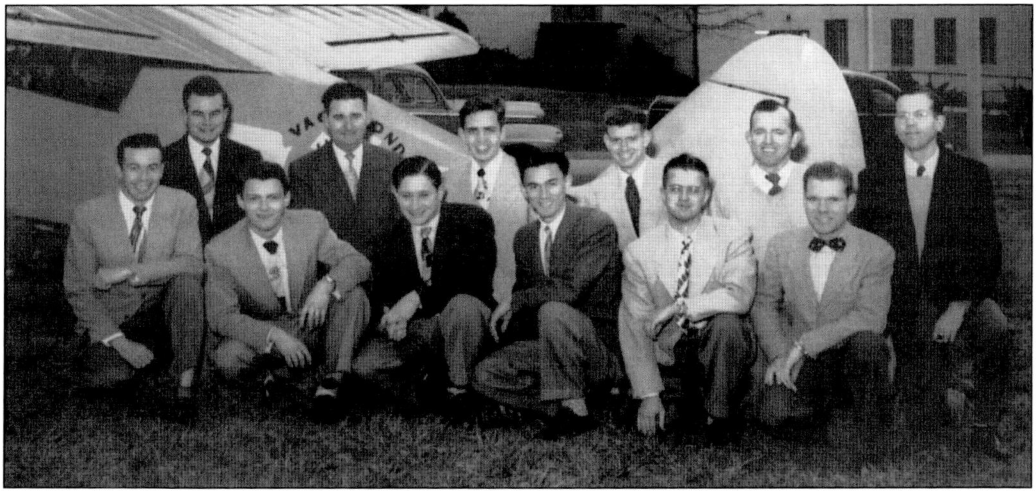

Members of the 1952 Vagabond Flight Club kneel by their plane, a Piper NC4 12111, which was co-owned by the club members. All of the men in the club that year were ministerial students who wanted to use their flying skills in missionary aviation. Officers are Bill Bathman, president; Grover Ausburn, secretary; Eli Ardelean, treasurer; and Jim Benefiel, maintenance.

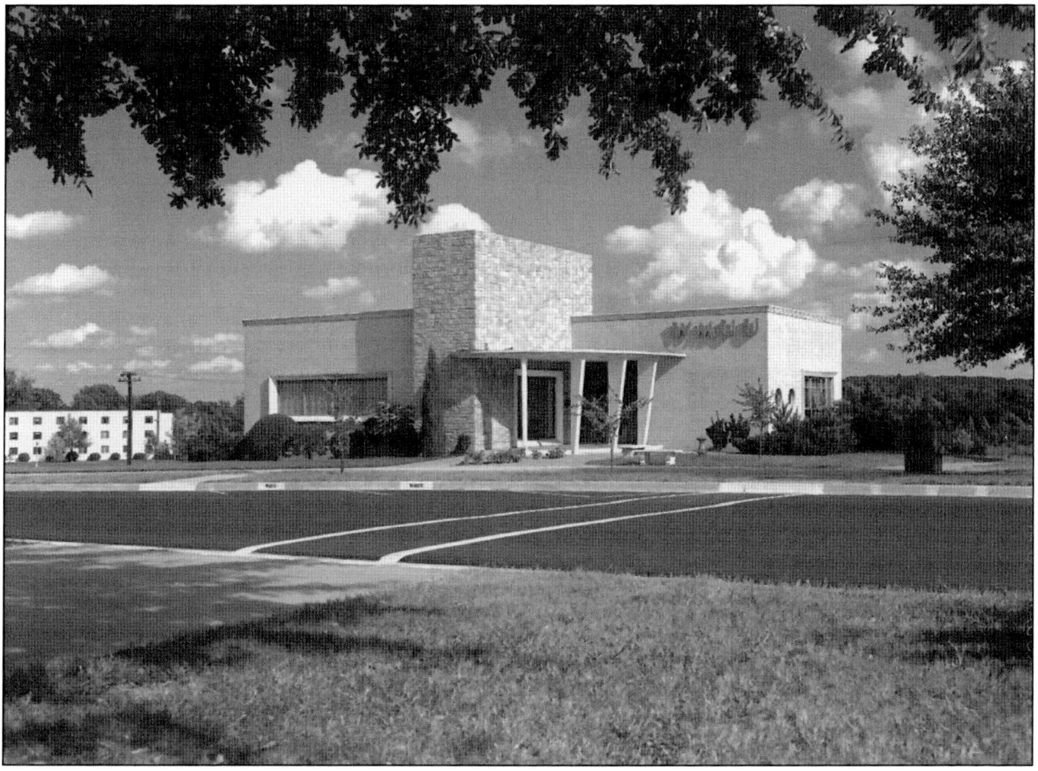

Originally, radio station WMUU was located where the entrance to Founder's Memorial Amphitorium now stands. The 3,000-square-foot building, as it appeared in the 1950–1951 school year, was the home base for the Upstate's "Beautiful Music Station." Jim Ryerson served as the station's general manager for more than 30 years.

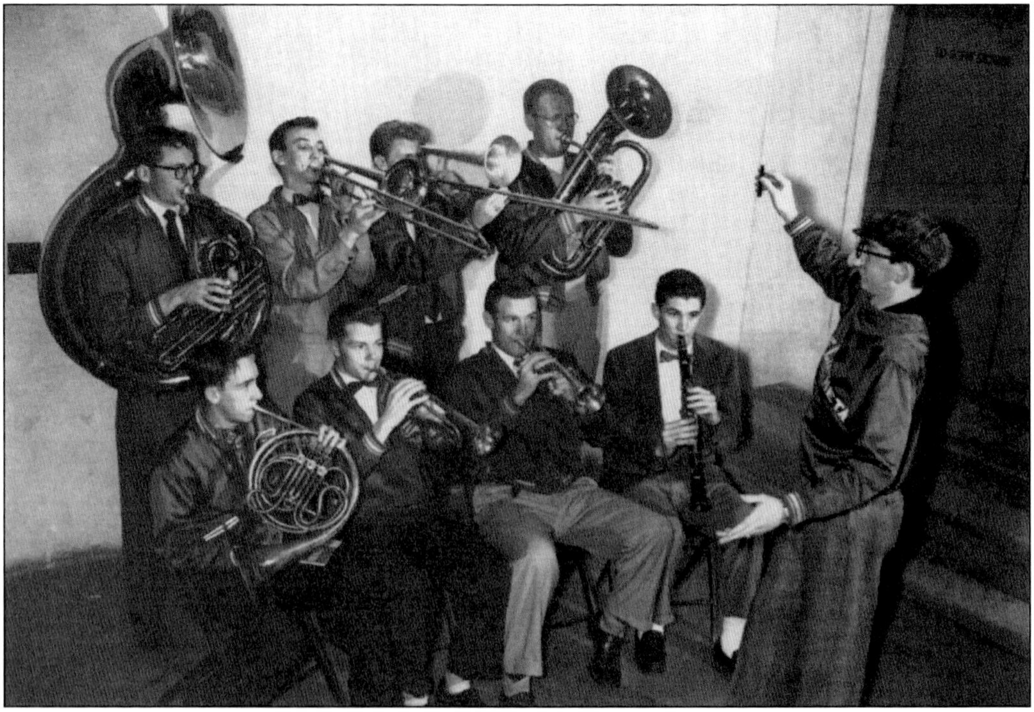

In the 1952–1953 school year, Chi Delt's unique and sometimes "infamous" combo—whether participating in society Rush Week on campus or generating spirit on the soccer field or basketball court—always caused foot tapping and hand clapping by anyone within hearing distance of their high-decibel output.

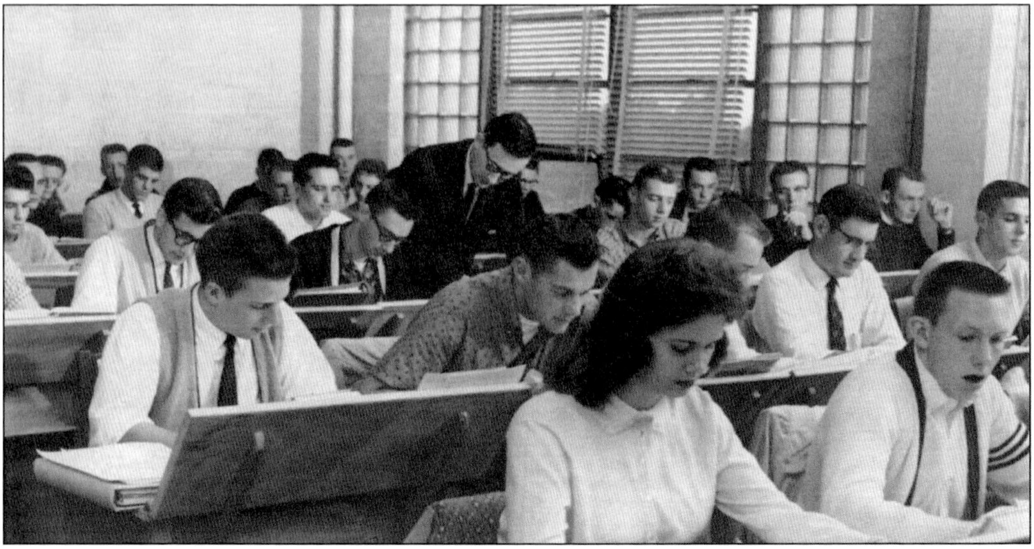

Jim Martin, seen here with his 1960 accounting class, served at Bob Jones University for 45 years. Like many BJU faculty and staff, he also served faithfully in a local church—in his case, as organist at Hampton Park Baptist Church. Martin was also a partner in a private accounting business. His son, Kris, currently serves on the accounting faculty.

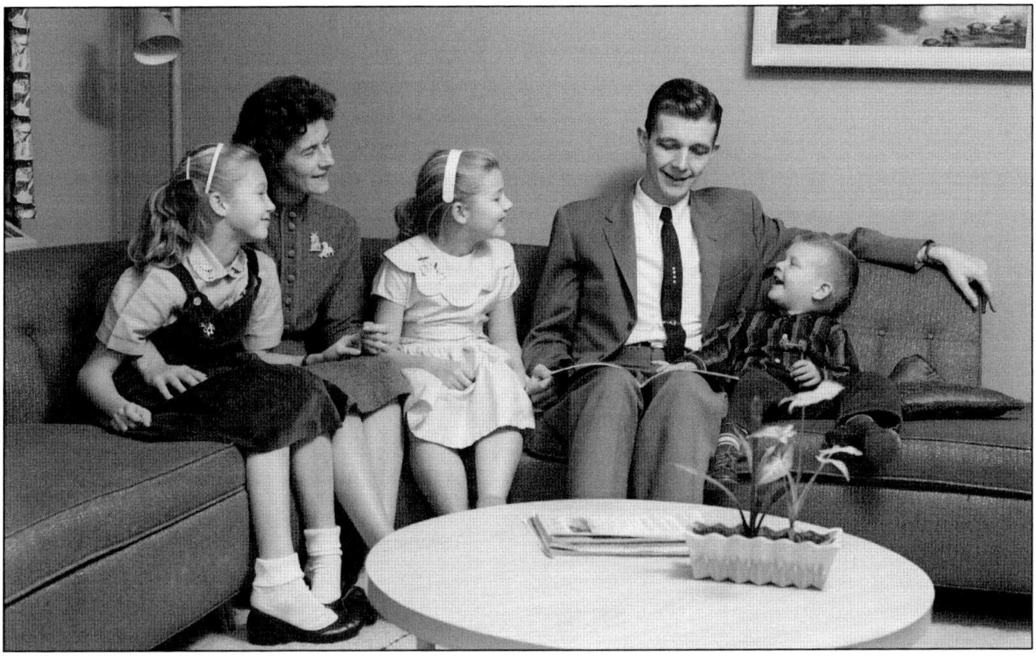

Dr. Walter Fremont, dean of the School of Education from 1951 to 1990, and his wife, Trudy, served on the BJU faculty for more than four decades. They are pictured here in 1960 with their children (from left to right) Gayle, Elaine, and Gilbert. Gilbert today teaches history at Bob Jones Junior High.

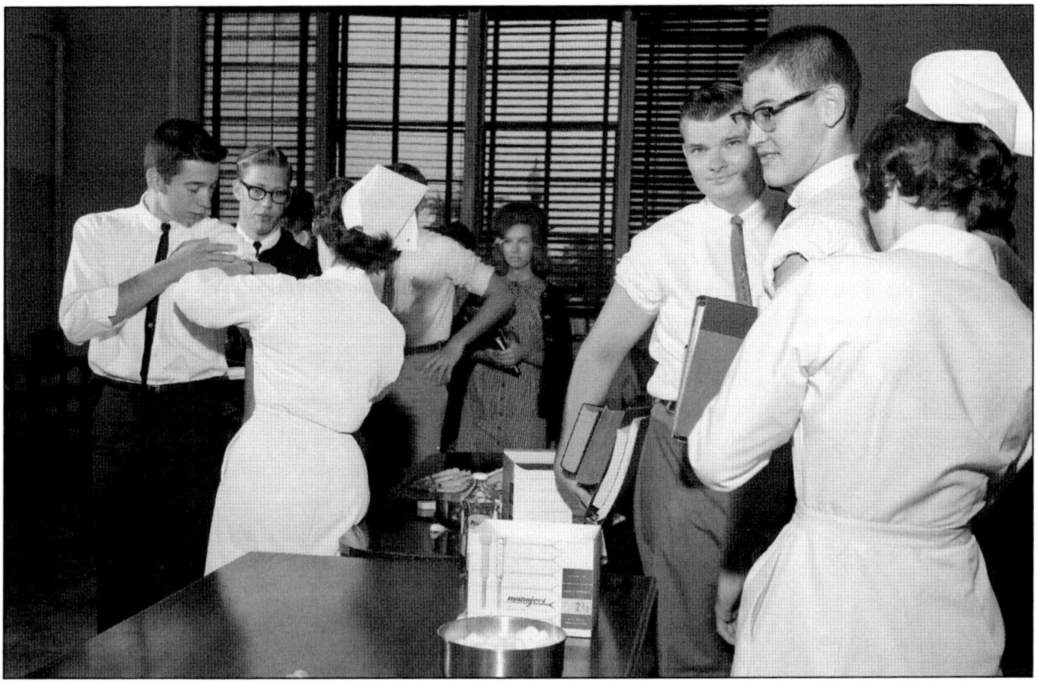

When flu hit the campus in the late 1960s, health service personnel swung into action and got the needles out. Today University Health Services at W. J. Barge Memorial Hospital and University Medical Associates take care of the university family's health needs.

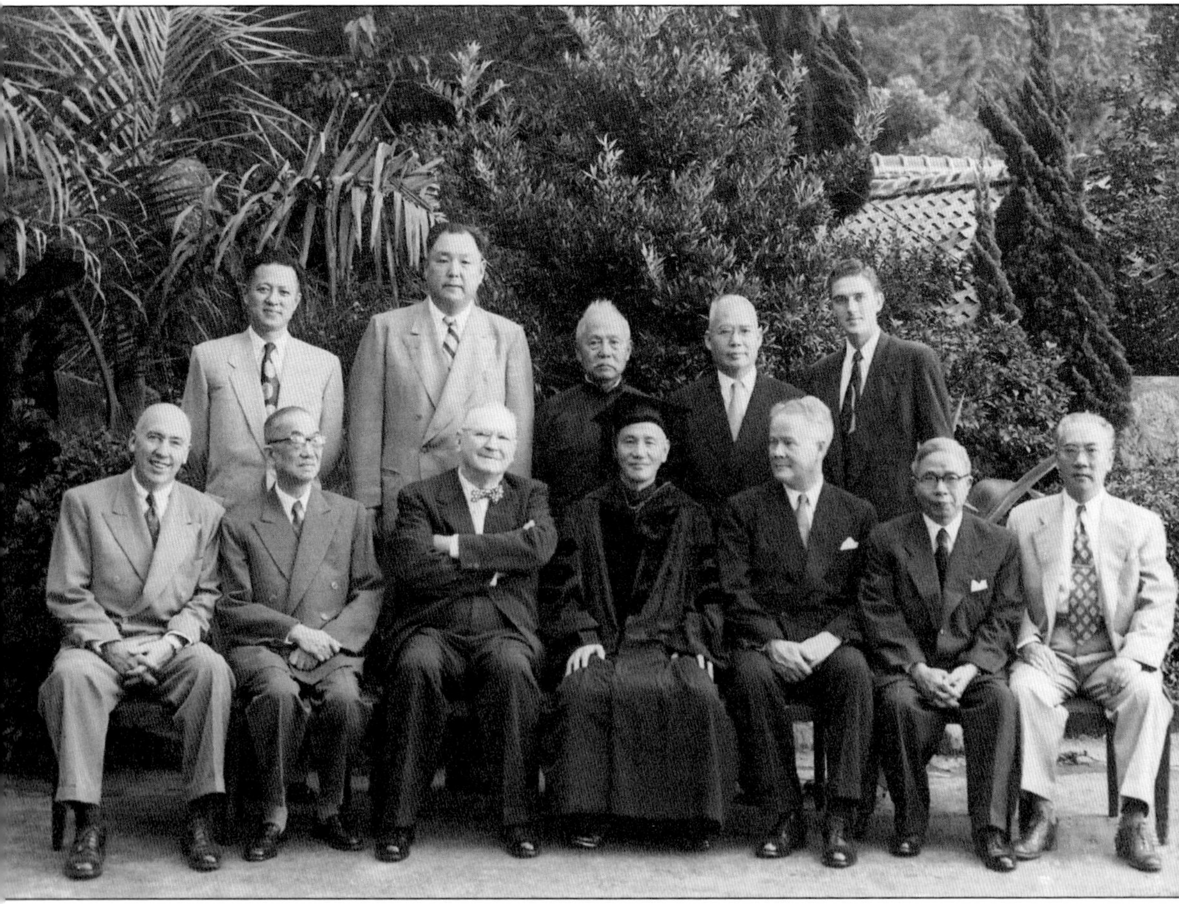

In October 1952, Dr. Bob Jones Sr. (first row, third from left) flew to Tapei, Taiwan, to present an honorary doctorate to Free China's president, Generalissimo Chiang Kai-Shek (first row, center). The ceremony was held in the garden of the president's home. Others attending included the U.S. Charge d'Affairs in Formosa, Karl Rankin, on the Generalissimo's left; Dr. Wei Peng, the Generalissimo's pastor (second row, center); Chinese evangelist Leland Wang (second row, second from right); and Bob Shelton, a 1952 BJU graduate who was serving at the time with the Formosa Gospel Crusade (second row, far right).

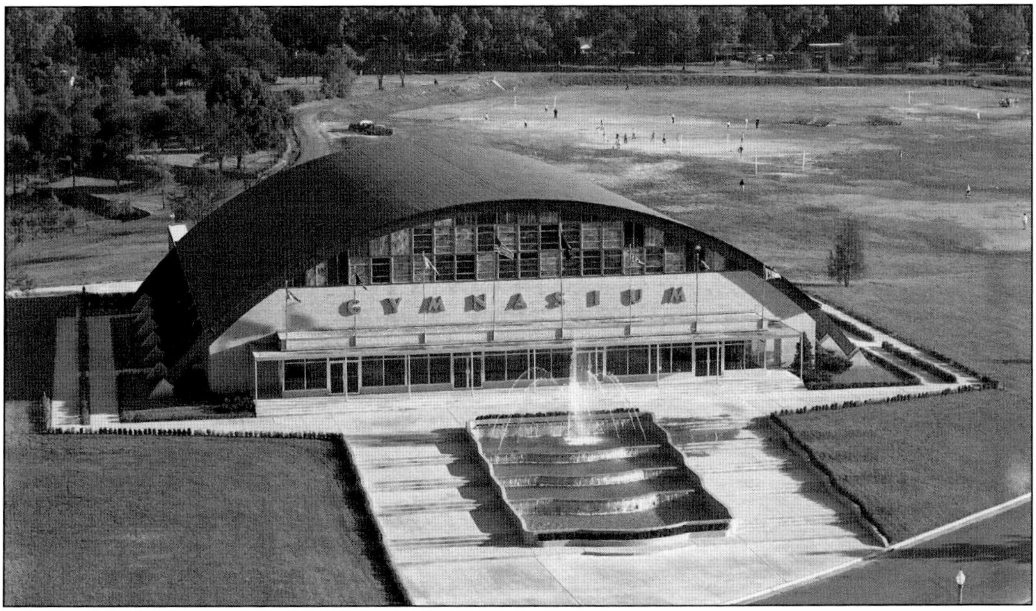

Built in 1959, this gymnasium featured an Olympic-sized swimming pool and one regular-sized basketball court, which could be divided into two small courts or two volleyball courts. On the main level were two faculty offices, three classrooms, and a general room used for karate, judo, fencing, and cheerleading. The pool, two locker rooms, and an exercise room were located on the bottom level. This gym served the university until the Davis Field House was constructed in 2004.

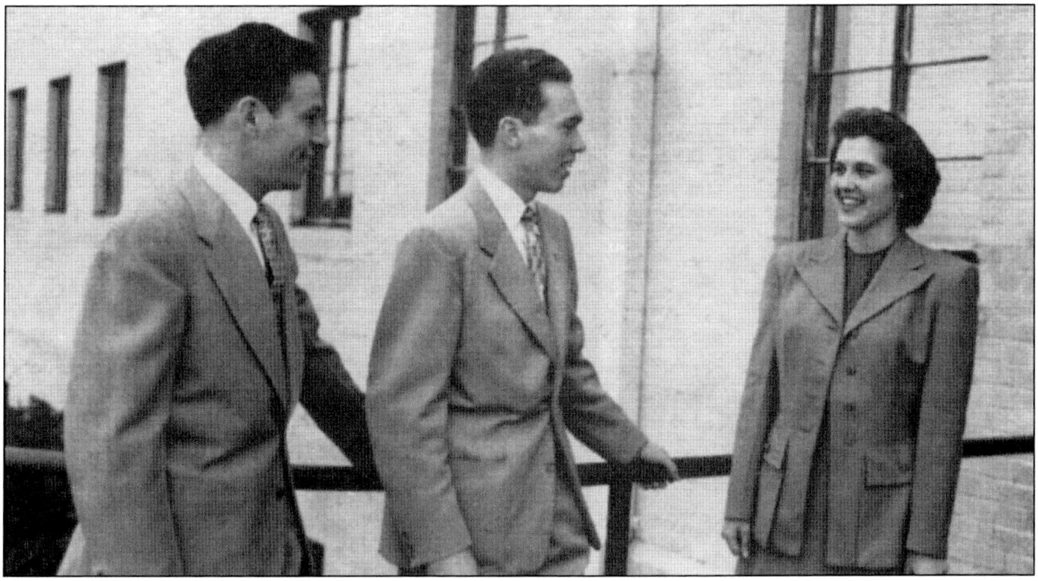

In the second semester of the 1952–1953 school year, Earl Radmacher (center) served as the Baptist Student Union (BSU) president. With him are Lloyd Jones, men's vice president, and Betty Nestor, pianist. At that time, four young people's societies met after Vespers on Sunday afternoons to provide informal fellowship. Other groups included the Methodist Youth Fellowship, the Inter-denominational Student Union, and the Christian Endeavor. Radmacher later served as president of Western Baptist Seminary in Portland, Oregon.

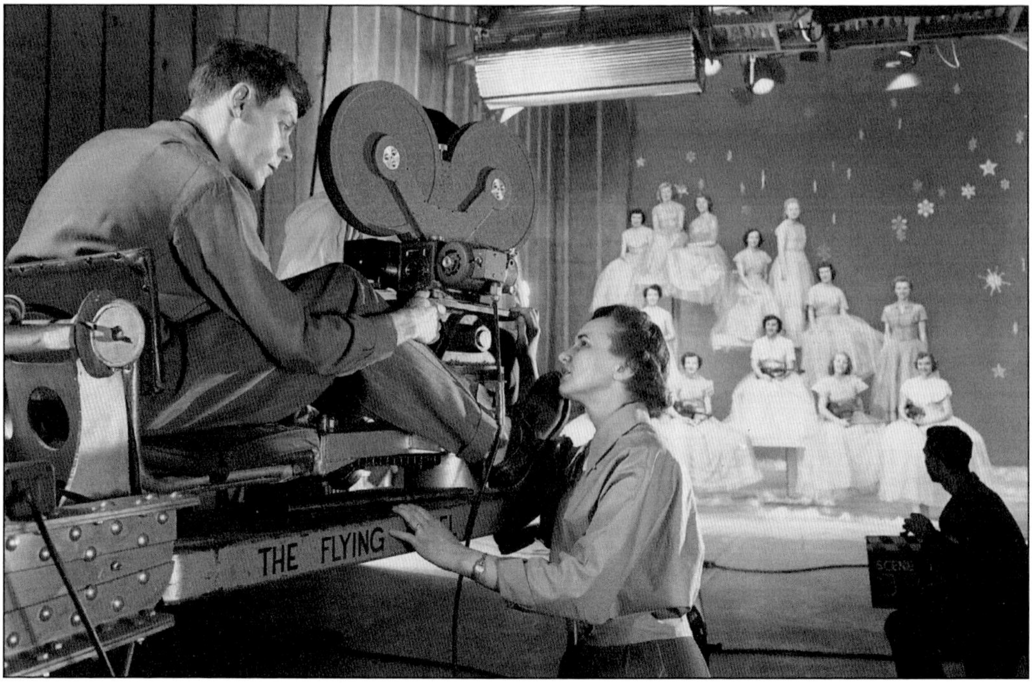

Katherine Stenholm, director, talks with the cameraman during the filming of *Heavenly Harmonies*, the second musical film produced by Unusual Films. The first musical film, *Vesper Melodies*, won the award for the best Christian musical film from Christian Youth Cinema, Inc., in 1951.

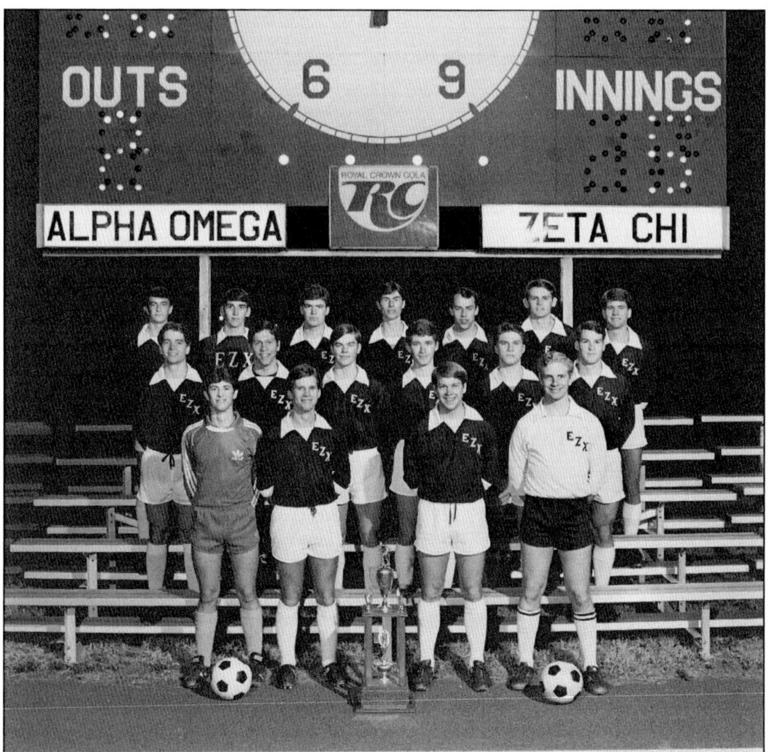

The Turkey Bowl, the men's soccer championship, is a BJU Thanksgiving tradition. In 1980, Zeta Chi defeated its rival, Alpha Omega, 5-2 to win the annual crown. The players are, from left to right, (first row) Brady Camp, Scott Camp, Steve Seaman, and John Wetzel; (second row) Brent Yokely, Ken German, Dave Smith, Ron Ruse, Brian Weiss, and Layton Talbert; (third row) Louis Walthers, Ron Hoffman, Mark Idler, Brad Bell, Gary Seaman, Glen Wimpe, and Doug Knight.

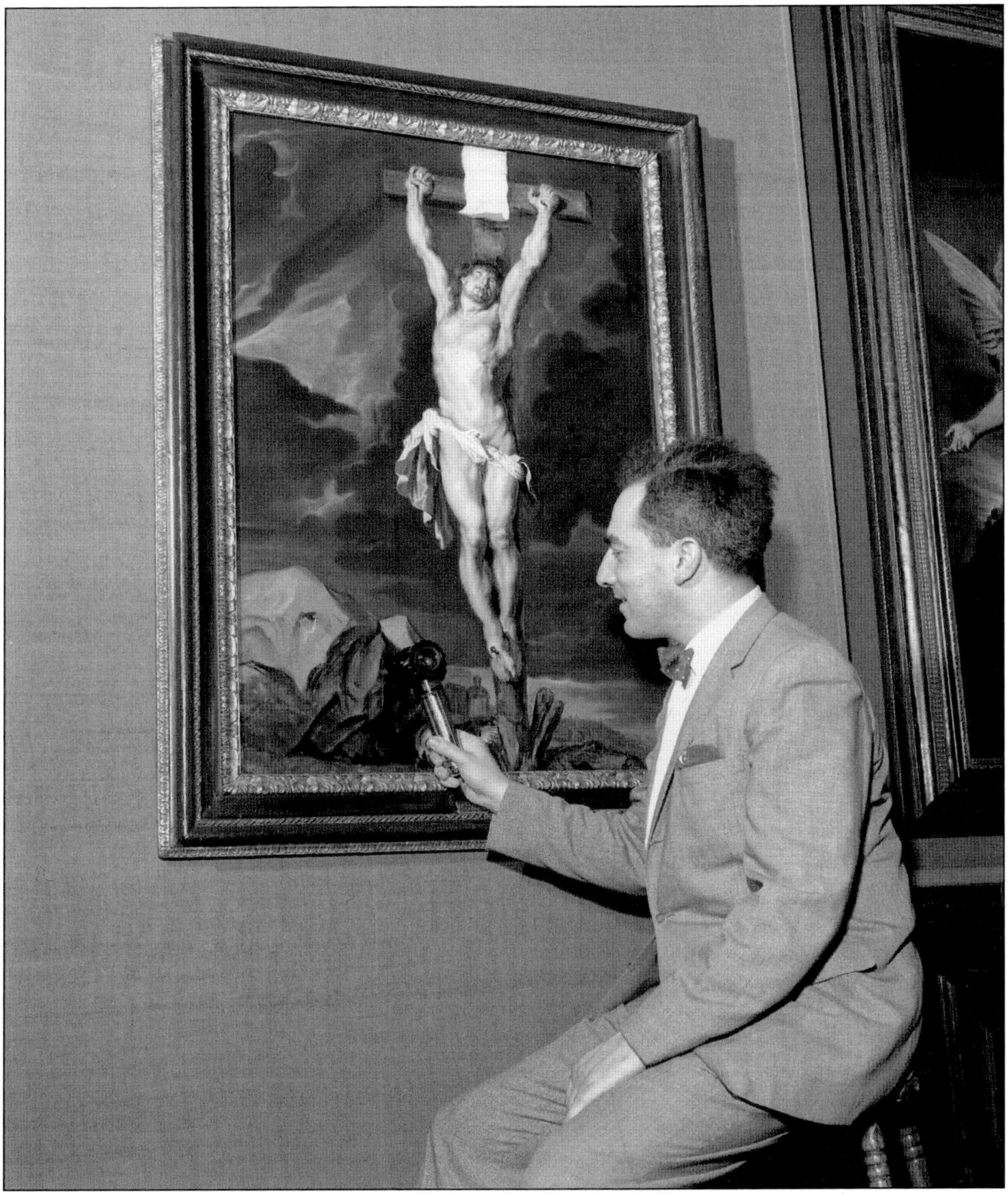

British art historian Andrew Michael Jaffe, a Rubens scholar and director of the Fitzwilliam Museum at Cambridge University from 1973 to 1990, visited the Museum and Gallery at Bob Jones University during the 1960s. Recognized as one of the great authorities on Peter Paul Rubens, Jaffe considered Rubens's *Christ on the Cross* to be the modello that the artist completed for his students to copy and enlarge. Jaffe was a visiting professor at Washington University in St. Louis, Missouri, during the 1960–1961 school year. The Museum and Gallery has 25 galleries displaying Italian, Spanish, French, English, Flemish, and German sacred art from the 14th to 19th centuries. The BJU galleries offer the public an opportunity to see the most extensive of the great Italian Baroque collections in the United States. Erin Jones, wife of Bob Jones University president Dr. Stephen Jones, is the present director.

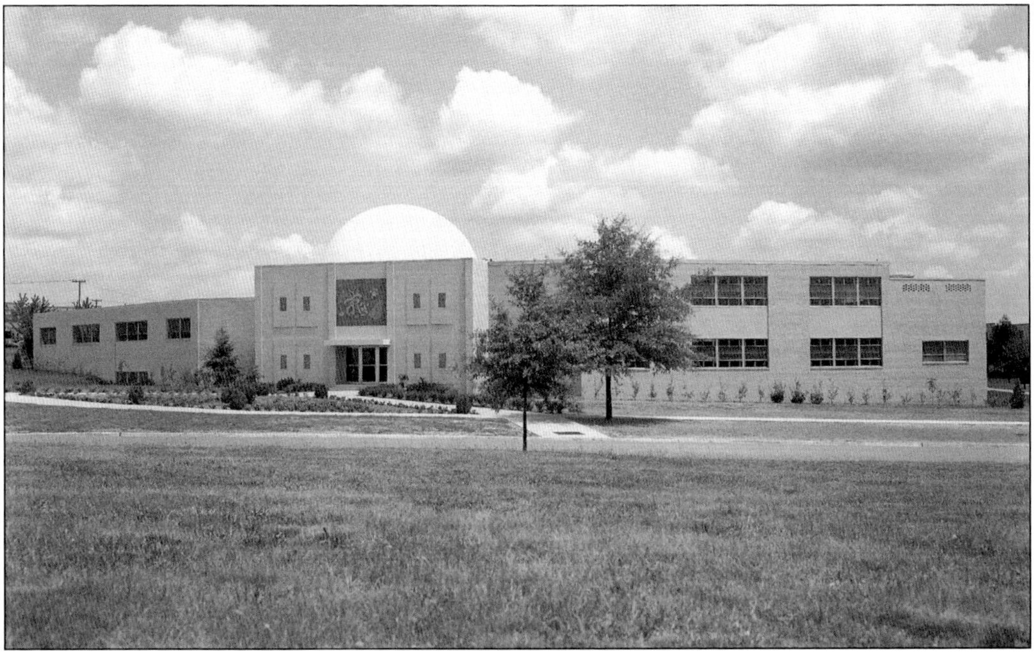

The Howell Memorial Science Building and planetarium were completed in 1960, through the generosity of Lillian Howell of Bridgeport, Connecticut. She heard Dr. Bob Jones Sr. speak on a New York City radio station and bequeathed a significant portion of her estate to Bob Jones University because she believed in what the school was doing to train young people to live for Christ.

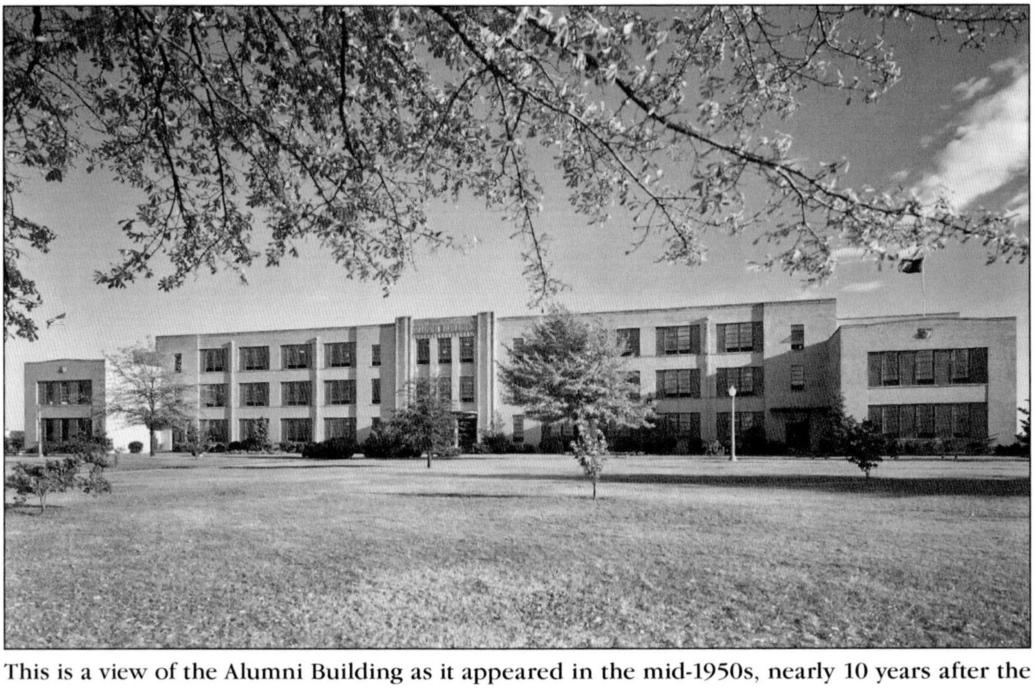

This is a view of the Alumni Building as it appeared in the mid-1950s, nearly 10 years after the Greenville campus opened. Now, more than 60 years later, the building has been upgraded and classrooms and office space added onto the back. With the exception of the covered sidewalks, the front of the building appears much the same as when it was constructed.

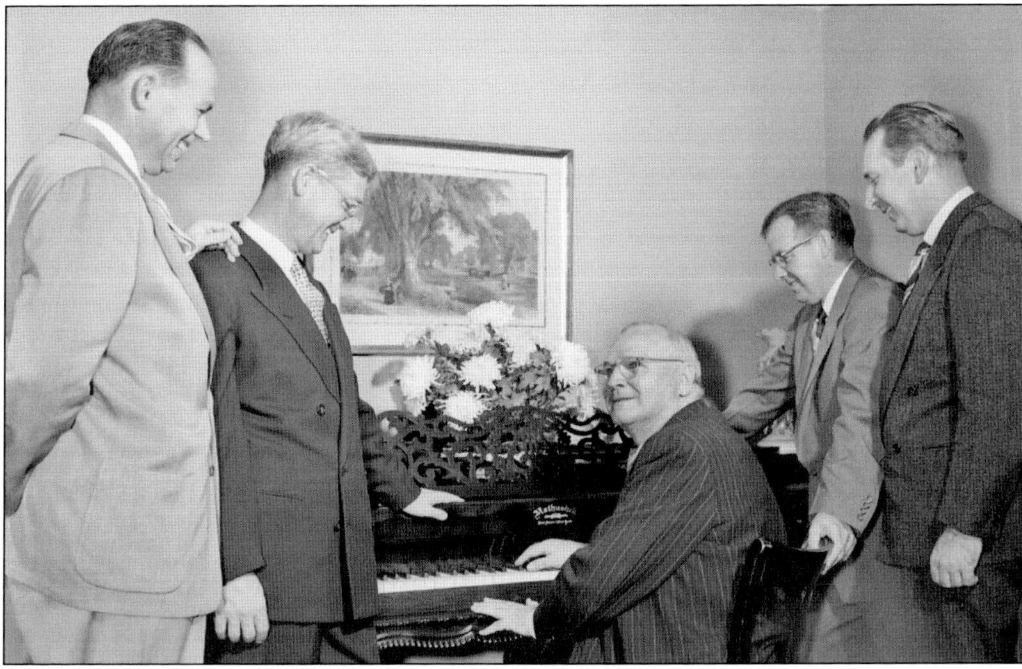

Seen in this photograph from left to right, with Dr. Bob Jones Sr. at the keyboard, are four administrators who played key roles in the operation of Bob Jones University in the early Greenville years—Dr. Marvin Lewis, a 1936 graduate who served as director of religious activities; Robert K. "Lefty" Johnson, a 1935 graduate who served as business manager until his death in 1971; Dr. Gilbert Stenholm, a 1938 graduate who served as dean of the School of Religion, director of extension, and staff evangelist before his death in 1989; and Dr. James Edwards, a 1936 graduate who served as dean of men, history instructor, and dean of administration from 1953 until his death in 1981.

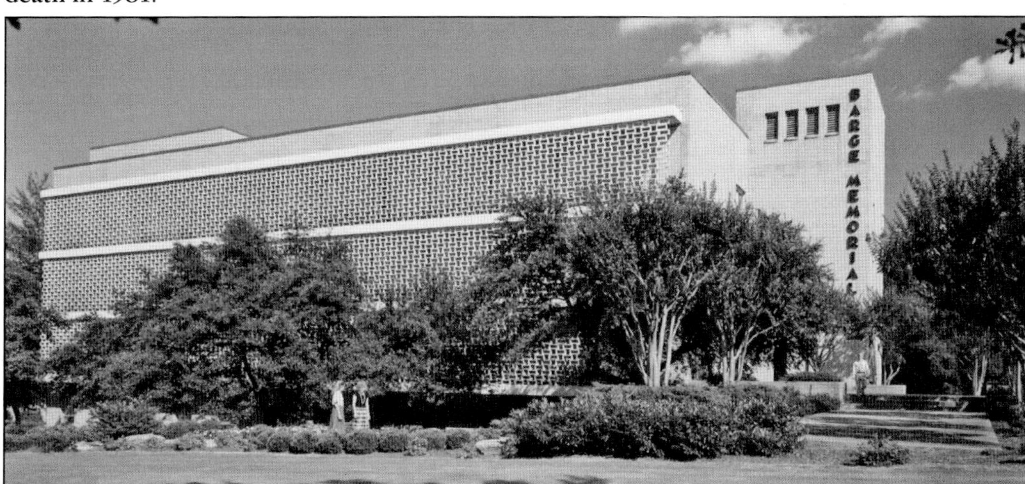

The William J. Barge Memorial Hospital opened in 1969 and replaced the original hospital structure that had served the campus since 1947. When it opened, the hospital had 79 beds, an operating room, a delivery room, a physiotherapy department, an X-ray room, a full obstetrical facility, six examination rooms, a clinical laboratory, and a pharmacy. Today it serves primarily as an infirmary for students too sick to attend class.

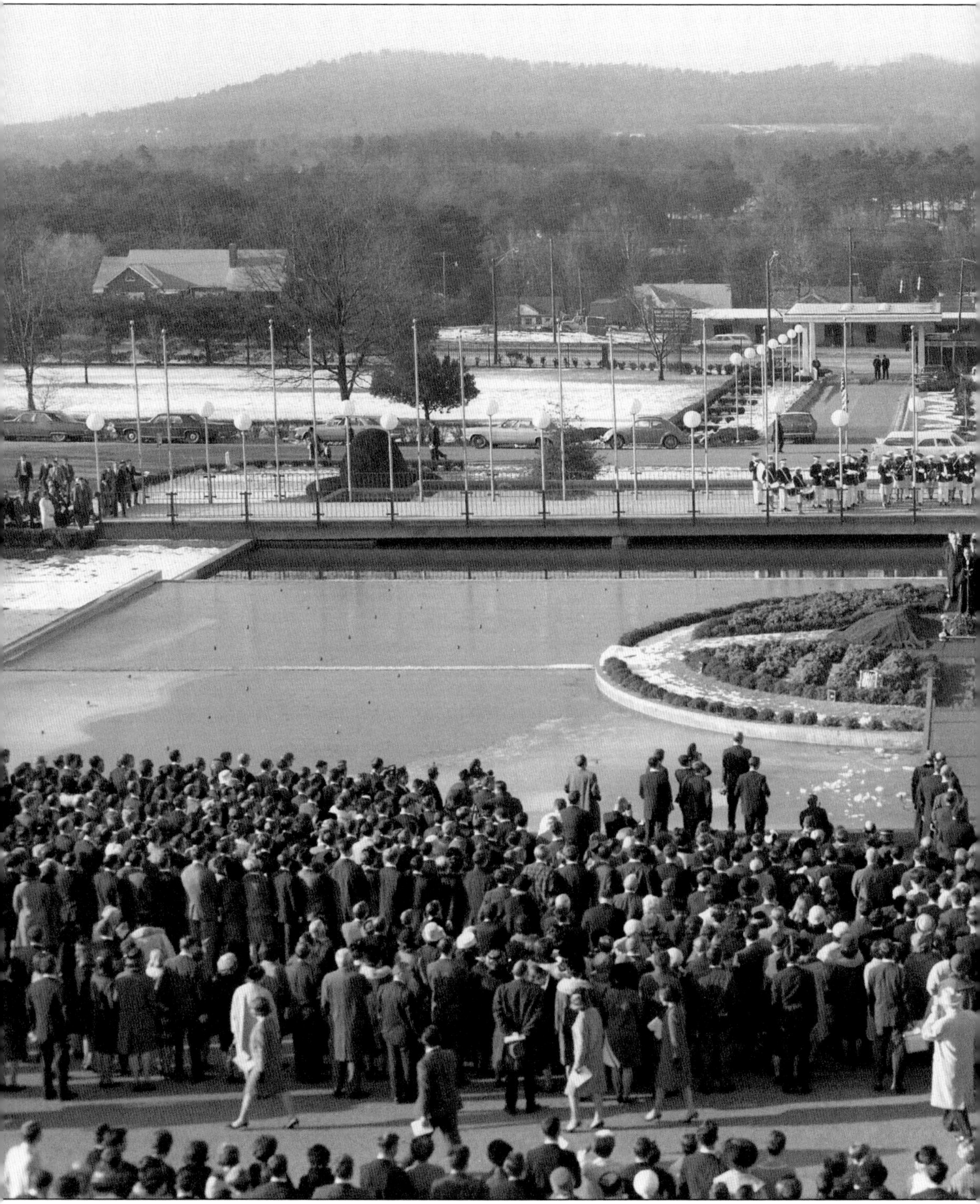

The funeral for Dr. Bob Jones Sr. was held on January 17, 1968, the day following his home-going. His interment took place on a small island in the fountain in front of Rodeheaver Auditorium. Thousands of the university family and others who loved him from all over the Southeast came

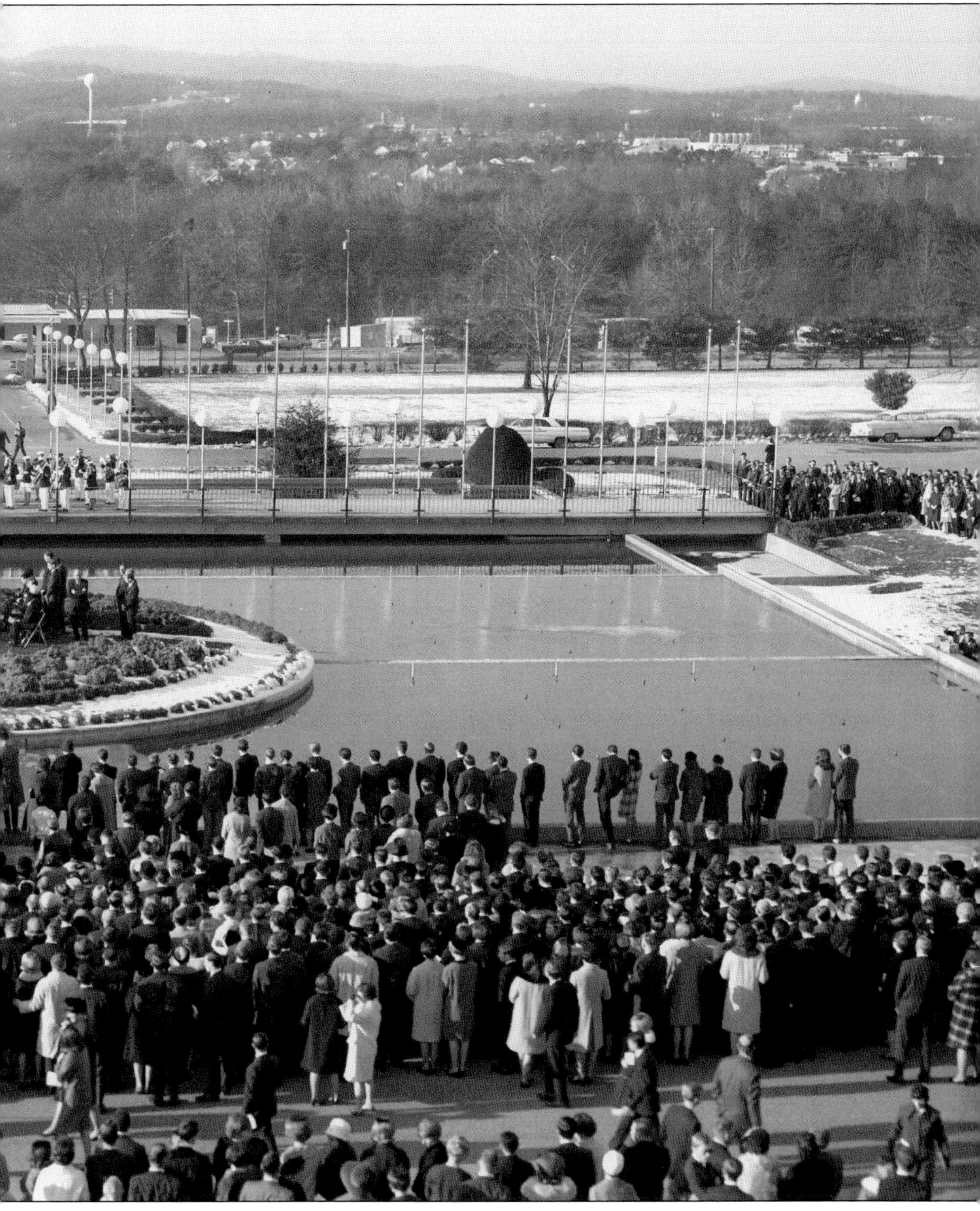

to pay their respects to the man with unflinching allegiance to the Lord and the Word of God. The epitaph on his grave reads, "A fight well fought. A course well run. A faith well kept. A crown well won."

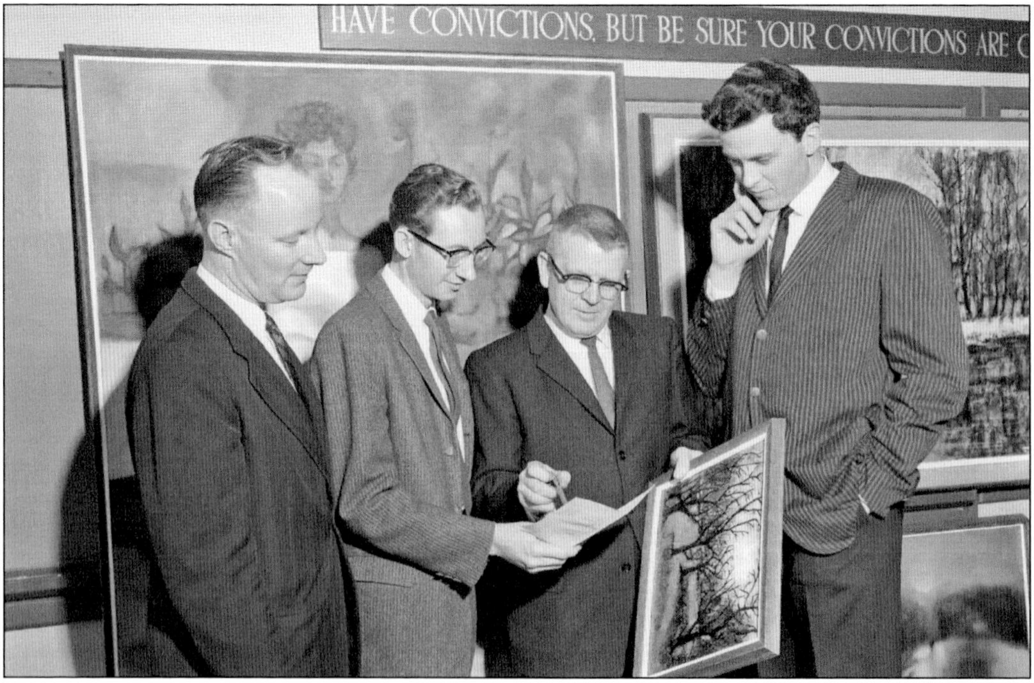

These four men—(from left to right) Emery Bopp, Carl Blair, Darrell Koons, and Lance Schade—played key roles on the art faculty in the mid-1960s. Koons, known especially for his acclaimed paintings of old barns, is holding one of his pastoral scenes of an aging orchard. Dr. Bob Jones Jr.—always one with a sense of humor—liked to call Schade "High Pockets." His towering height seemed to justify that moniker.

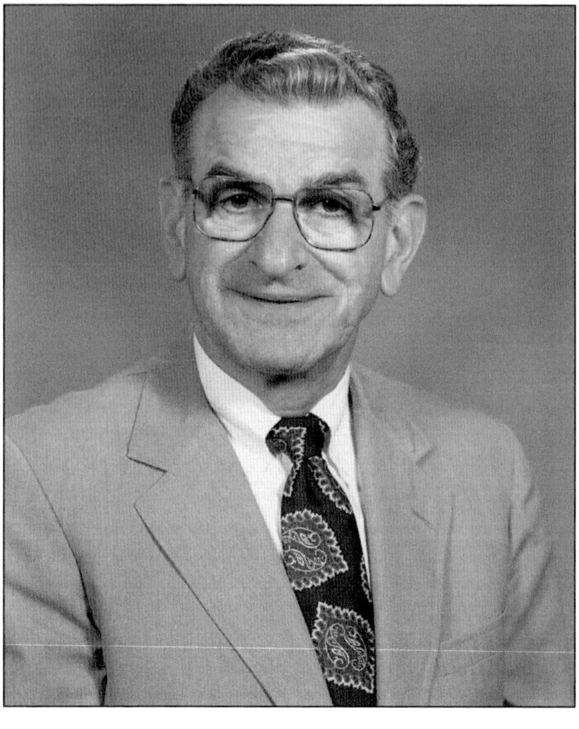

Dr. Edward Panosian served at BJU for over 50 years, teaching history and helping mold students' lives into conformity to Jesus Christ. Dr. Panosian graduated with a double major from BJU in 1952, earned a Ph.D. in 1959, and did postgraduate work at Tulane University and the University of Chicago. He is considered to be among the nation's foremost church historians. Teaching the History of Civilization for 48 years, Dr. Panosian taught more individual students than any other BJU professor. He is beloved by thousands of BJU graduates for his godly testimony and academic acumen. With a deep, resonant voice, he is also well known for film, radio, and stage performances. Dr. Panosian retired from the faculty in 2004.

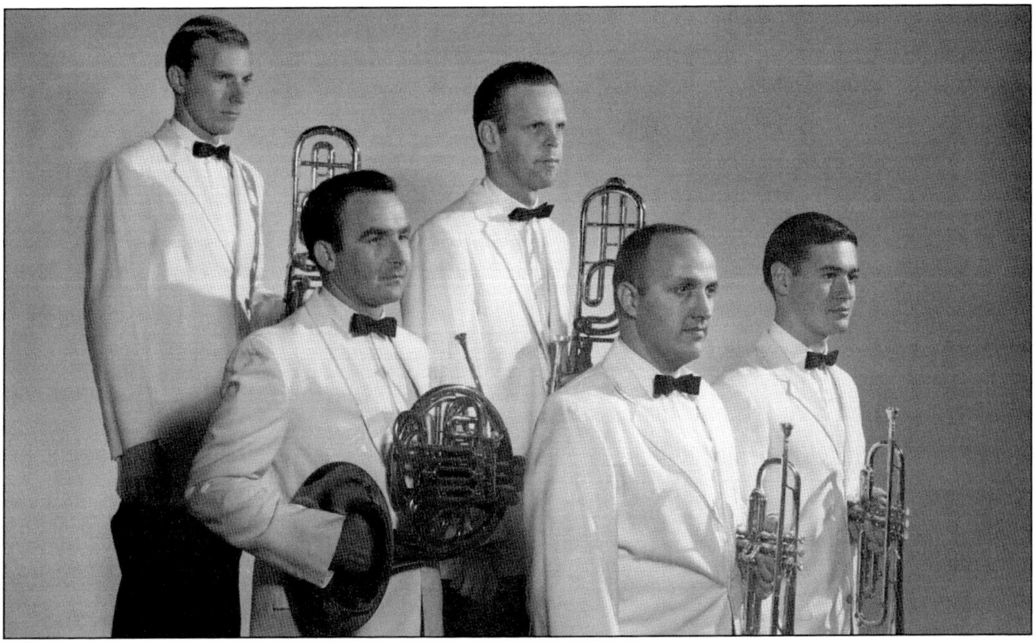

These five brass musicians—three faculty members and two students—formed a brass ensemble in 1965 that played at the Music Educators Conference in Louisville, Kentucky. From left to right, they are Don Harwood, trombone; Jim Conley, French horn; Frank Garlock, trombone; Argyle Paddock, trumpet; and Fred Rice, trumpet. Conley, Garlock, and Paddock were on the music faculty.

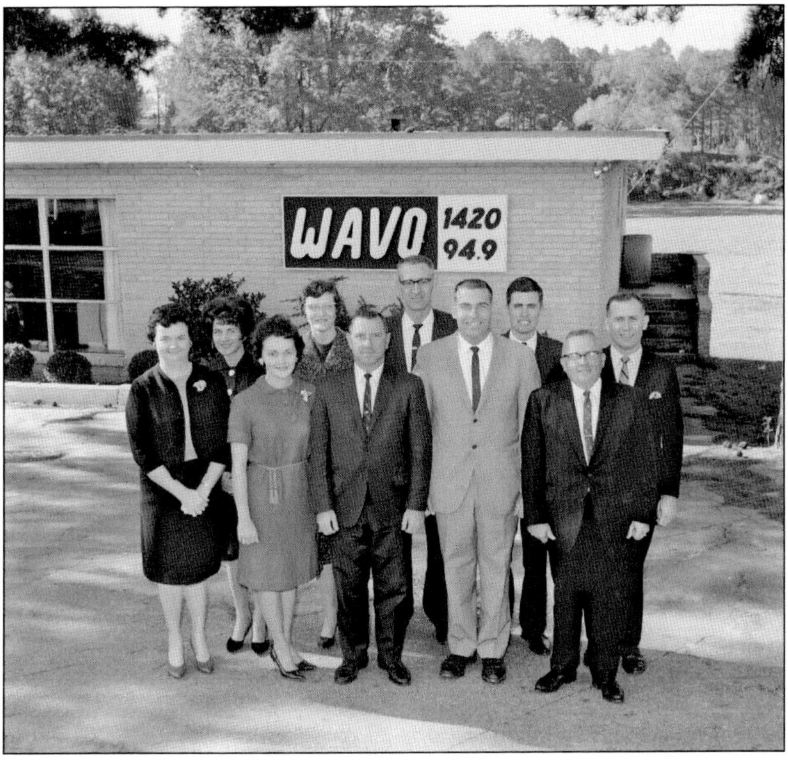

In 1963, BJU purchased WAVO, an Atlanta-area radio station. For nearly nine years, the station operated in conjunction with the Greenville-based WMUU and featured a format of news, music, and BJU programming. Pictured is the staff of WAVO, with Elmer Rumminger, station manager, in the center of the second row.

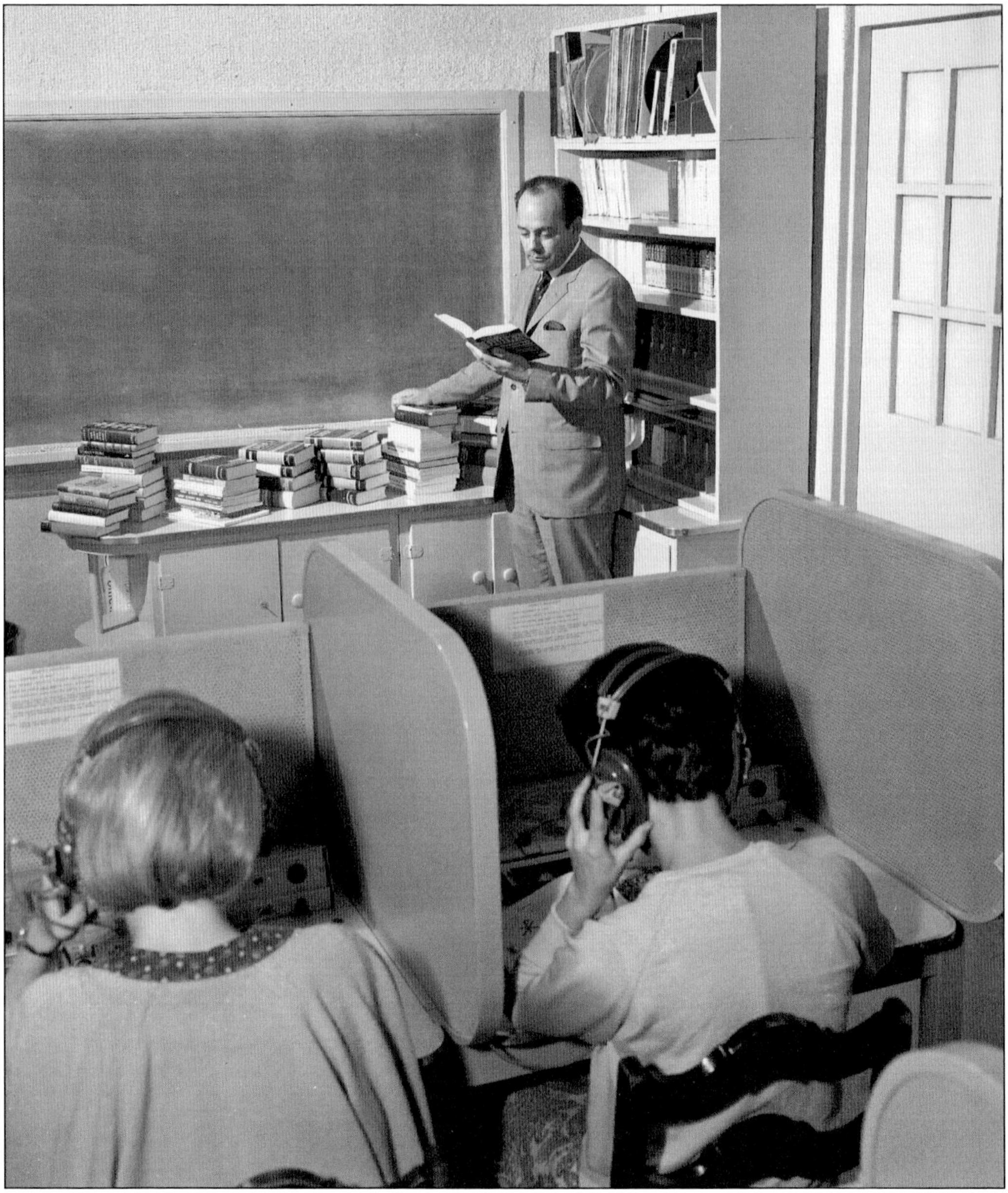

Dr. Guenter Salter, who first joined the faculty as an instructor in 1967, conducts a German language lab. Shortly after coming to BJU, he was appointed department chairman and in 1971 dean of the College of Arts and Science, a position he served in for more than 30 years. Dr. Salter, a native of Germany, completed his Ph.D. at Vanderbilt University after joining the BJU faculty.

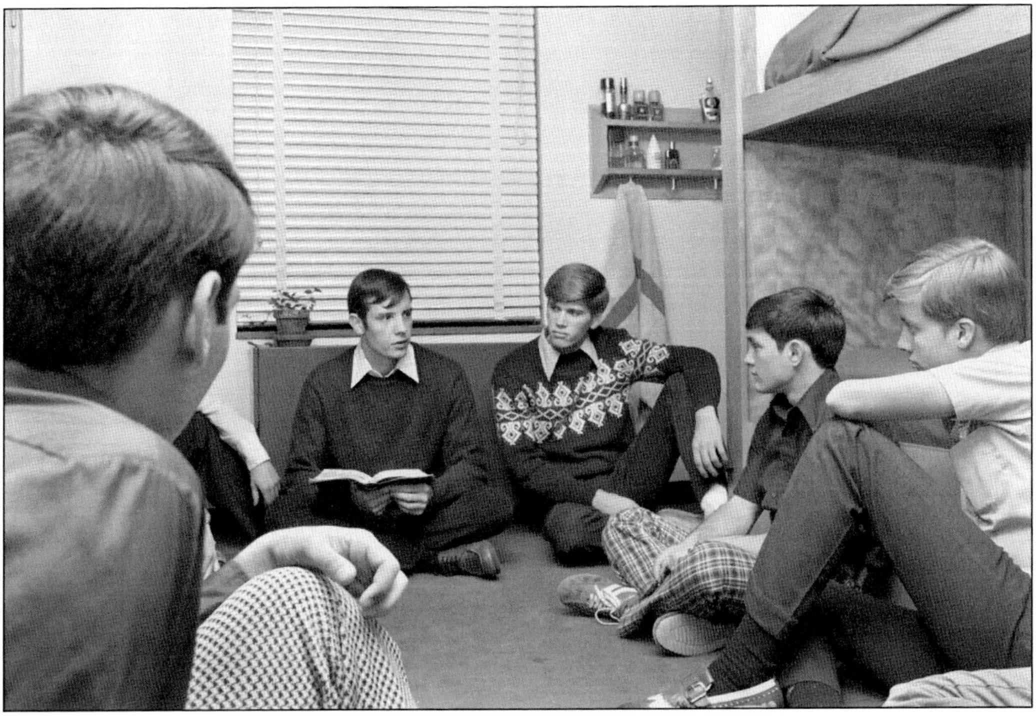

Every night, BJU students have devotions together in their residence halls with their prayer group or their own roommates. In each room, one student is appointed prayer captain or assistant prayer captain. Looking to the Lord at the end of an activity-filled day helps students in their spiritual and educational challenges. These young men were students in the 1977–1978 school year.

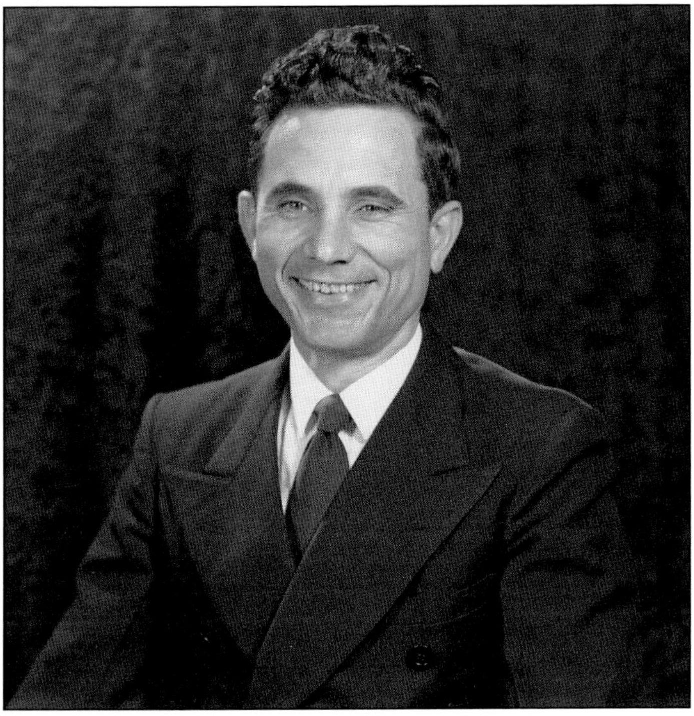

In addition to his over 30 years as general manager of the WMUU radio station, Jim Ryerson sang in university choirs and at other musical performances, including operas with guest artists. He also counseled many students as campus pastor. The call letters "WMUU" reflect the description of BJU as "the world's most unusual university."

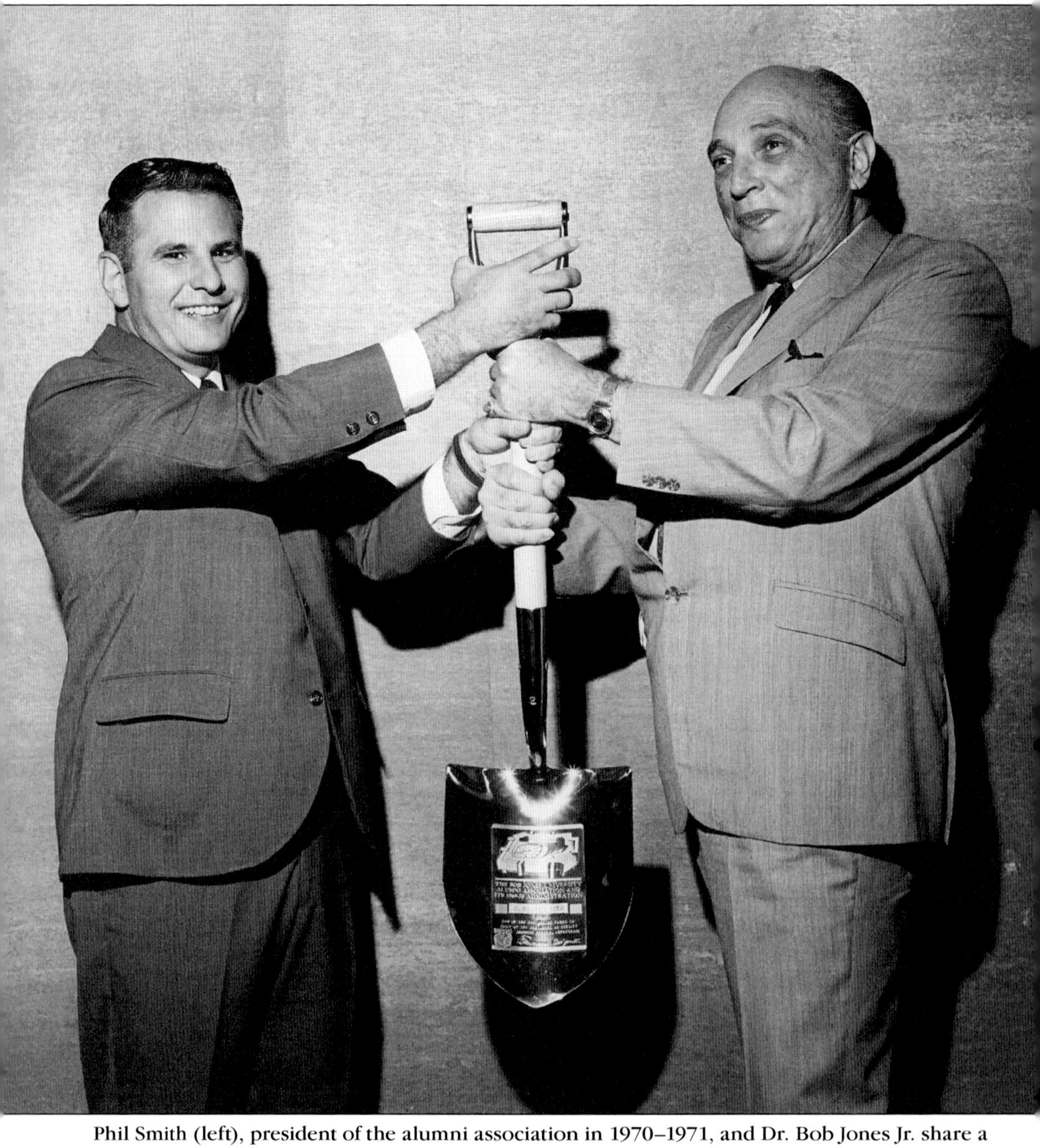

Phil Smith (left), president of the alumni association in 1970–1971, and Dr. Bob Jones Jr. share a shovel handle in 1970 to mark the beginning of a three-year drive to raise funds for the 7,000 seats in Founder's Memorial Amphitorium. The amphitorium was dedicated in 1973 and continues as the school's largest venue.

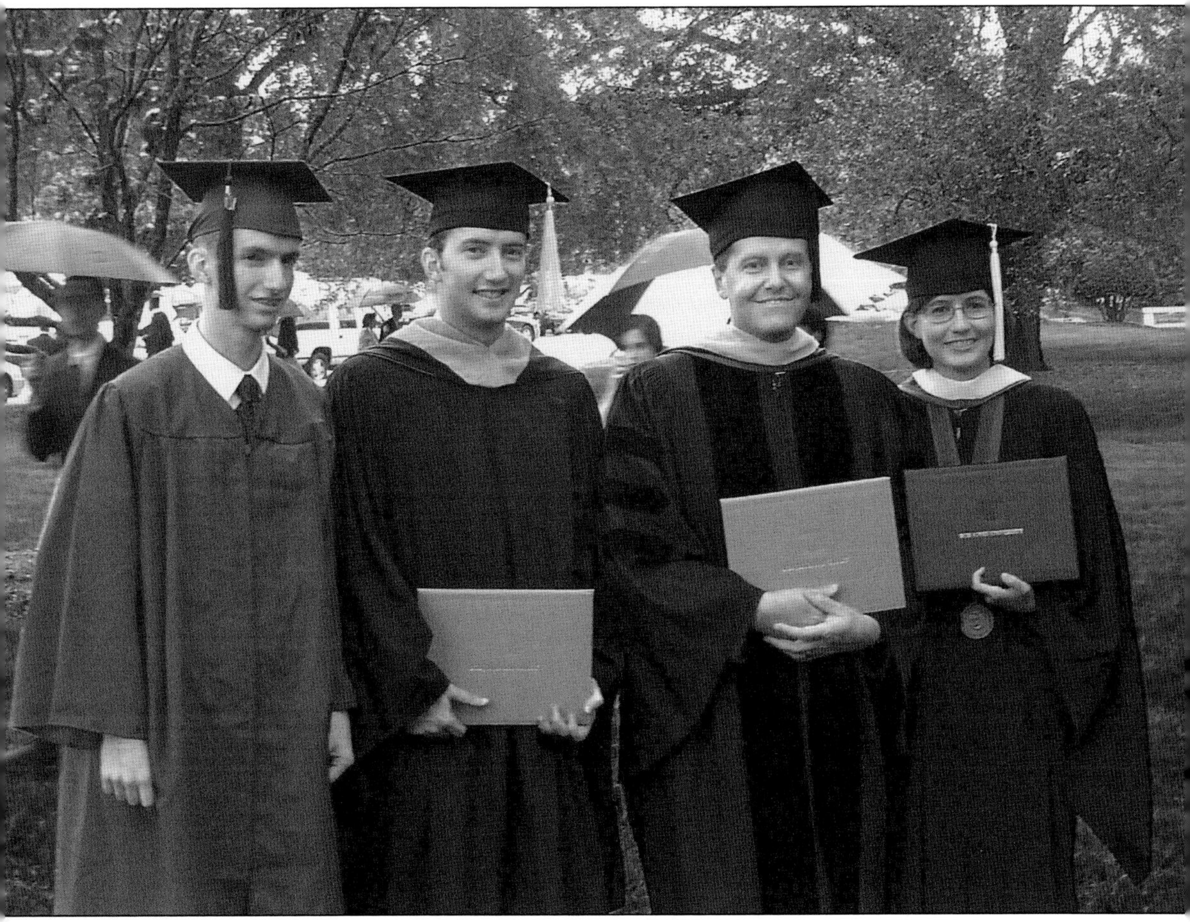

Attending BJU was a family affair for the Doug Garland family, which celebrated four diplomas received during the 2007 commencement week. Anthony (far left) earned a diploma from Bob Jones Academy; Andrew (second from left) earned a master's in mathematics education; Abby (far right) earned a bachelor's in humanities; and their father, Doug (third from left), a current faculty member in the School of Applied Studies, received his doctor of education in curriculum and instruction.

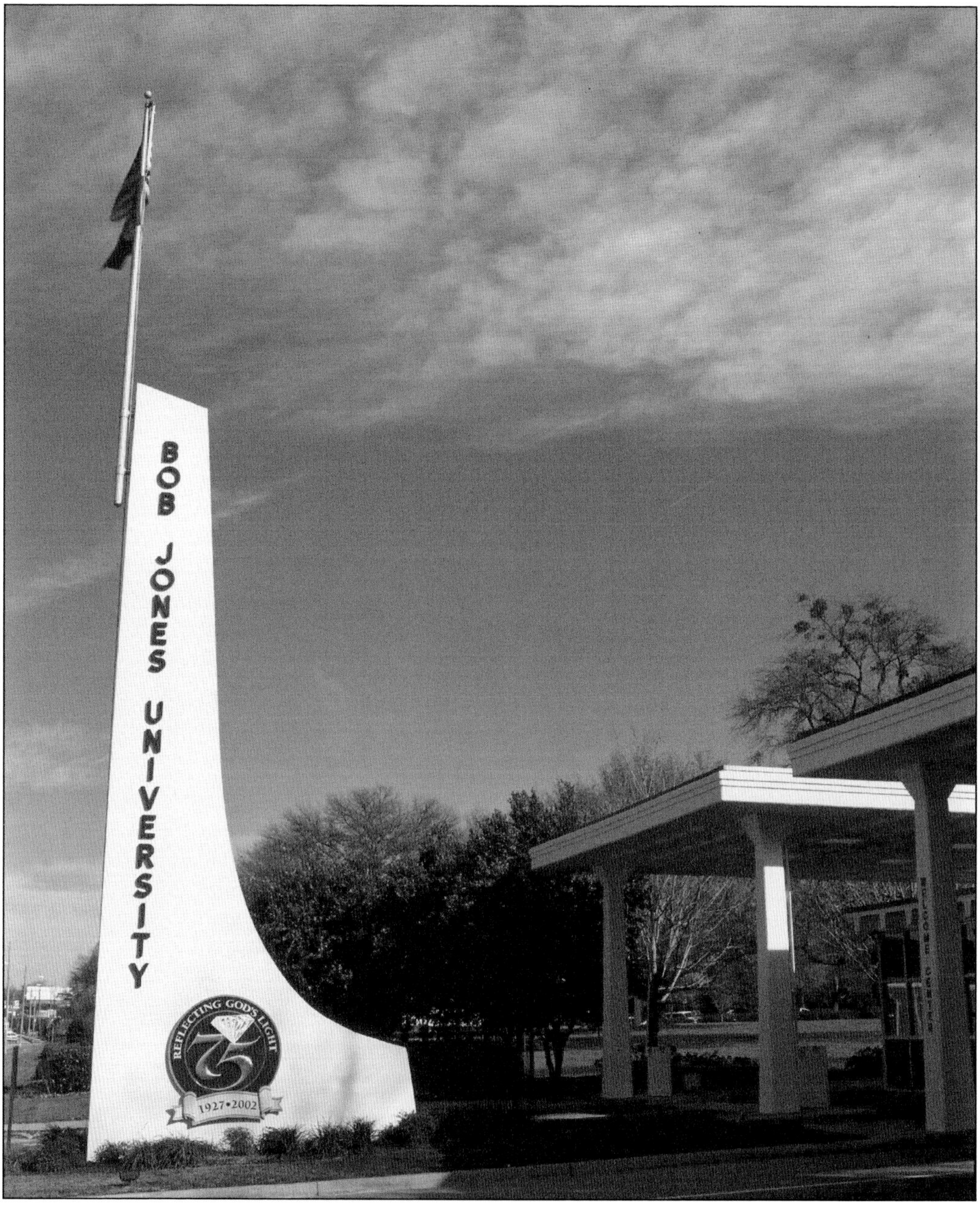

In early summer of 2007, motorists driving by the front of the university on Wade Hampton Boulevard noticed that "the giraffe" had vanished. The white pylon that had marked the university's entrance for 42 of its 60 years in Greenville was removed and replaced with a lower-profile marker when the new Welcome Center was constructed. Remnants of the "giraffe," constructed in 1965, have become souvenirs.

Four

THE SOUTH CAROLINA YEARS 1977–2007

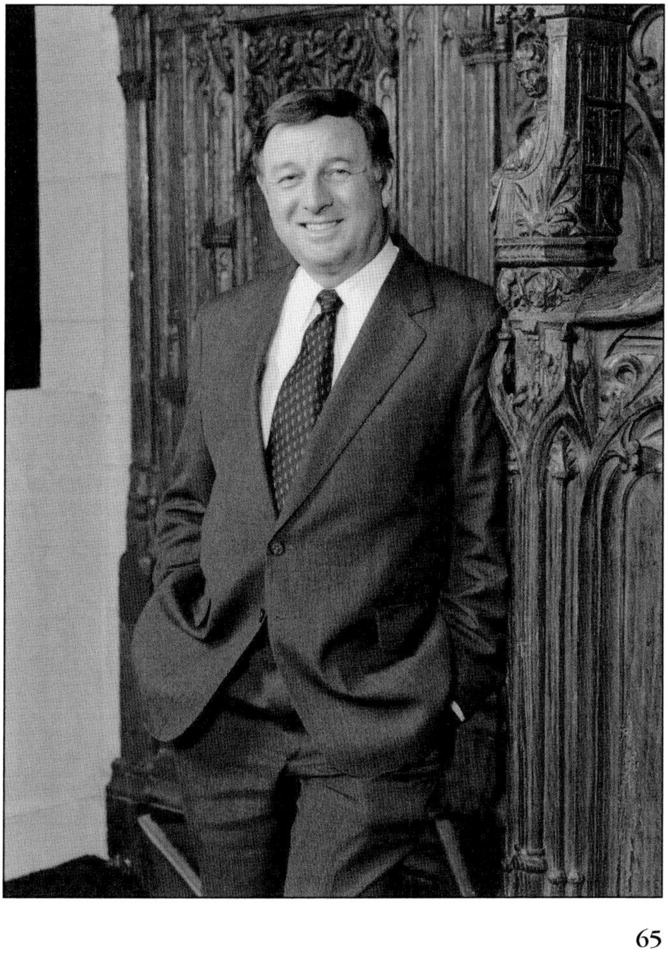

Dr. Bob Wood joined the BJU administrative staff as executive vice president in January 1977. For nearly three decades, he managed the operations of the university. He created ancillary businesses to increase revenue, provided oversight of the formation of the business structure of BJU Press, strongly supported the growth of BJ HomeSat and BJ LINC, and was the driving force behind the formation of University Medical Associates—all while compassionately counseling students, faculty, and staff. Before joining BJU, Dr. Wood was pastor of Killian Hills Baptist Church in Lilburn, Georgia, and served as vice president of the Brown Transportation Company in Atlanta. Currently executive vice president emeritus, he is a frequent speaker at chapel and Sunday morning services, and continues to assist with university operations.

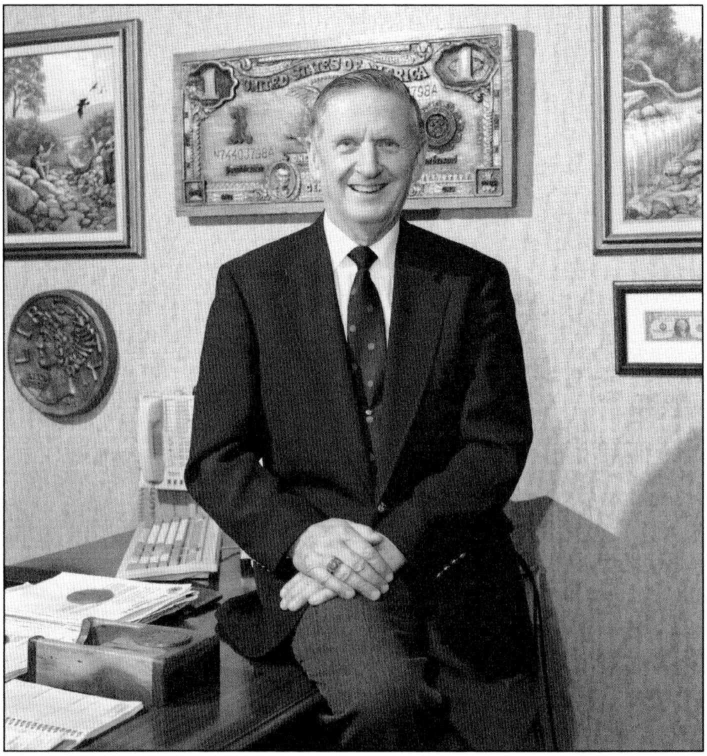

Roy Barton, a 1953 graduate of BJU, served as a bank vice president in Maine before Dr. Bob Jones III persuaded him to come to the university in 1974, where he became director of financial affairs and later the chief financial officer. For more than 30 years, Dr. Barton managed the university's financial affairs and, even after his retirement, continues to assist with various projects in the development office.

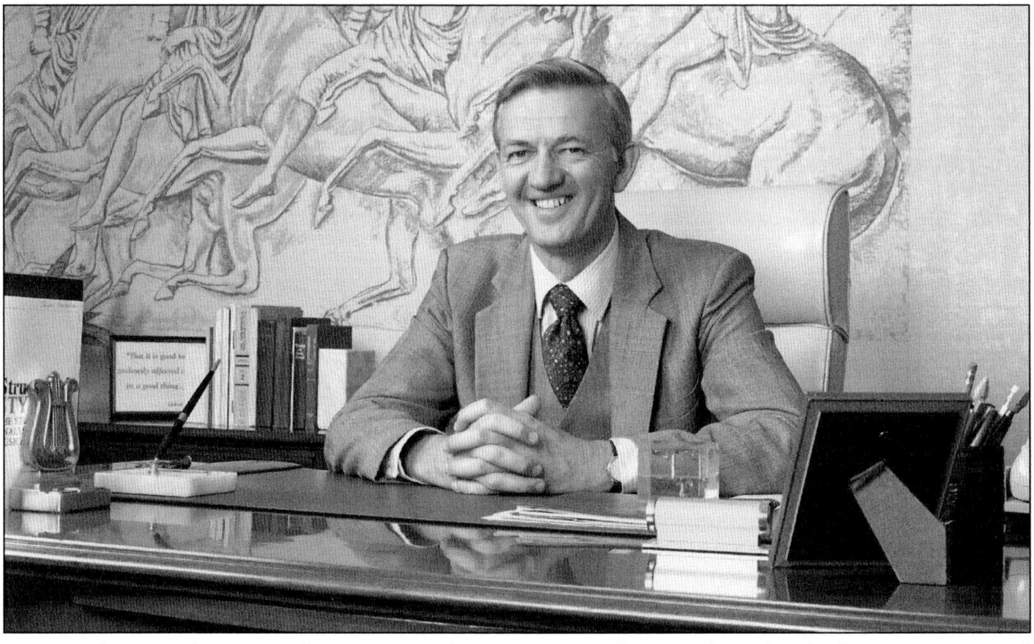

Dr. Dwight Gustafson, seen here in 1982, became acting dean of the School of Fine Arts in 1954 when he was 24 years old. He served as dean from 1955 to 1997, when he was succeeded by Dr. Darren P. Lawson. Having served for 43 years, he is the longest-serving dean in BJU history. He is a conductor and well-known composer who received his doctorate from Florida State University after earning his bachelor and master of arts degrees at Bob Jones University.

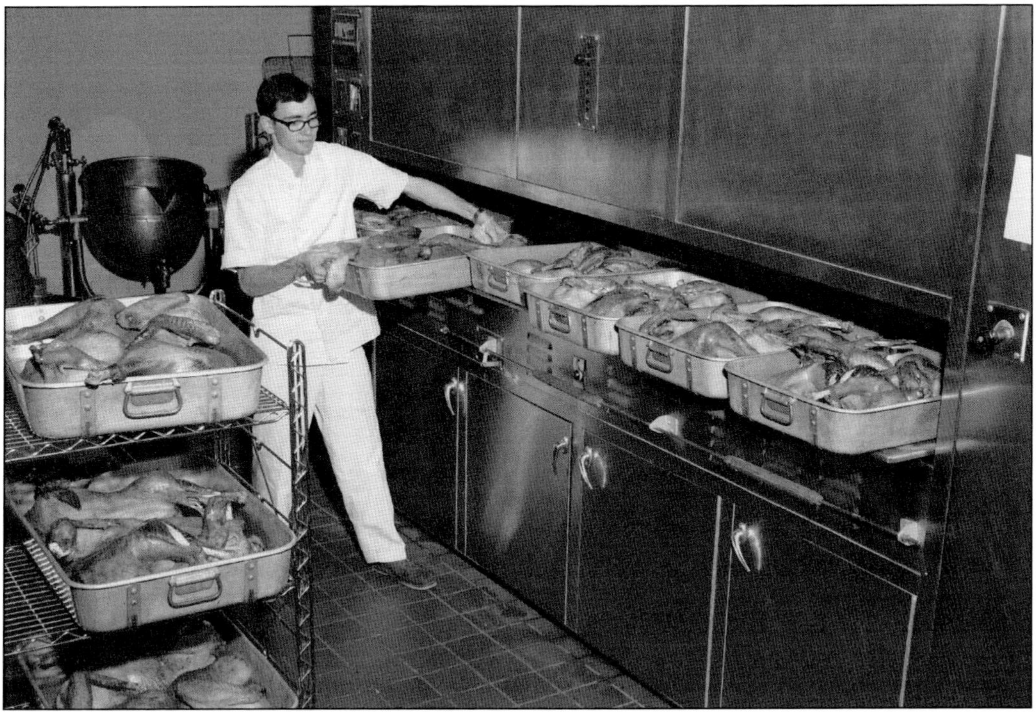

Before BJU gave students a Thanksgiving holiday, the dining common prepared about 300 turkeys weighing over 6,000 pounds for the Thanksgiving dinner. The dining common employs 60 full-time staff and 400 students who work part-time.

The Information Desk in the Administration Building is the place where visitors to campus can find a friendly face to assist them, whether they want information about the time and location of various events or information about the university's many academic or cultural programs. Campus visitors also may purchase tickets there to eat in the dining common.

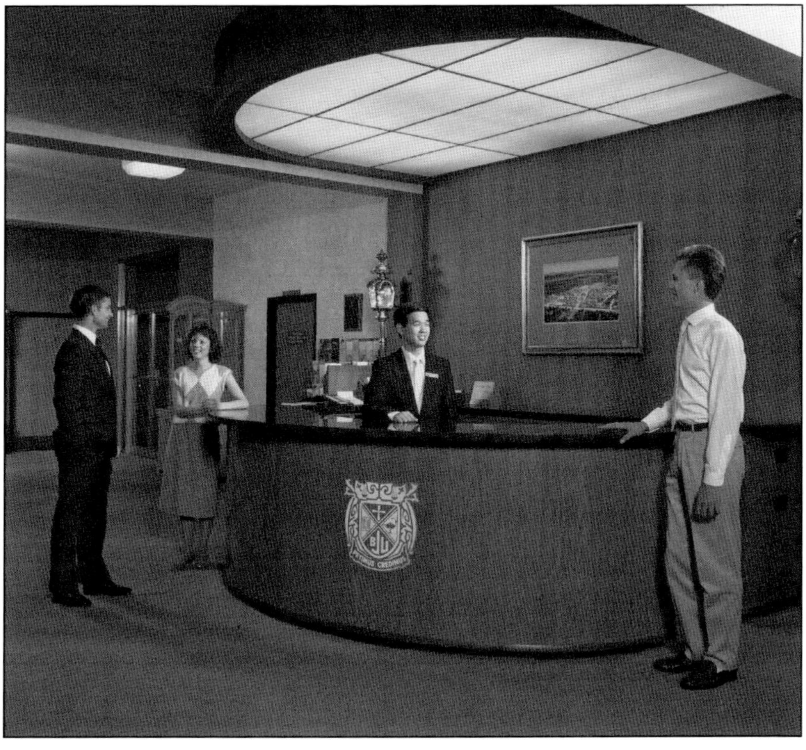

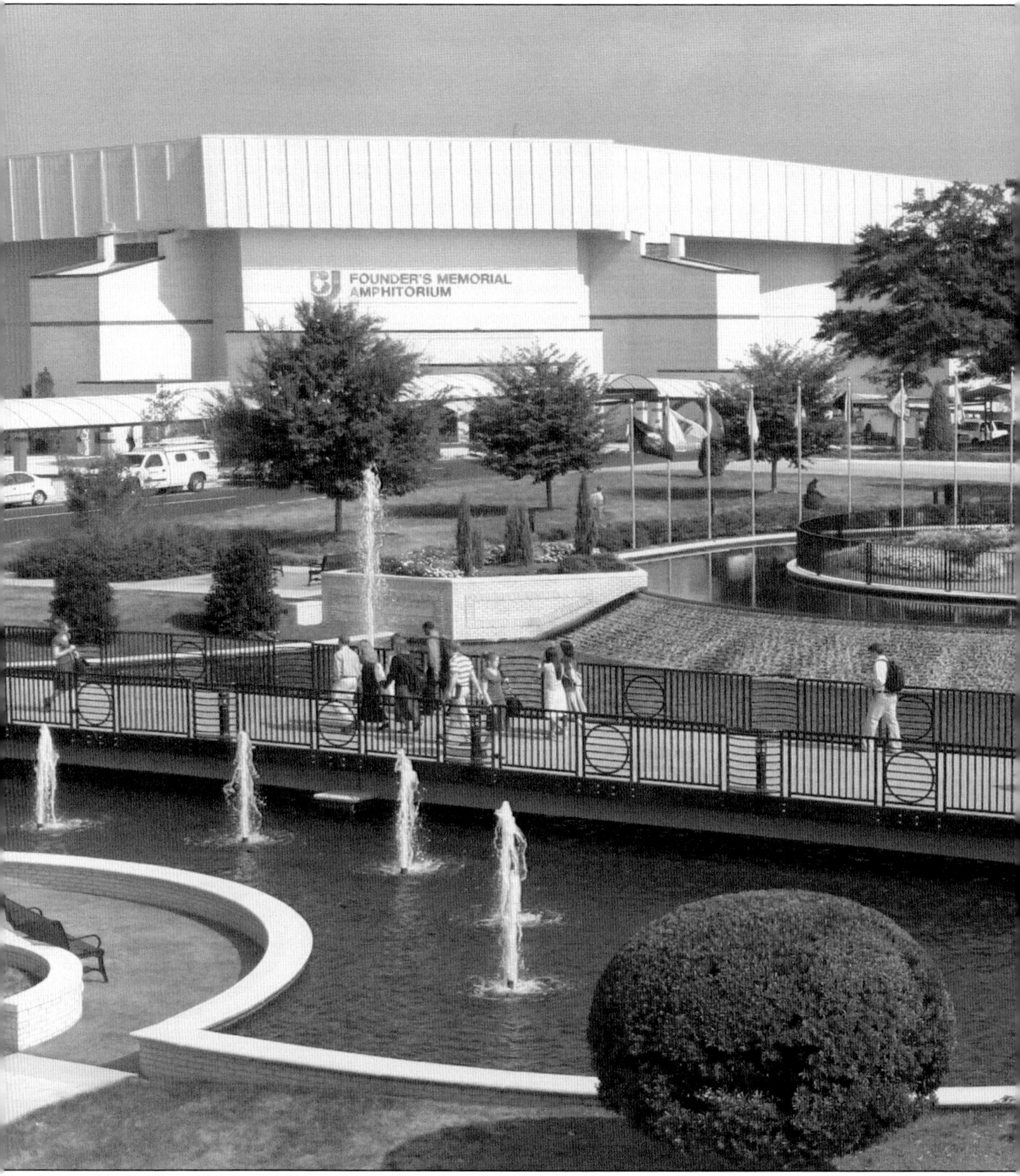

This panoramic view of the front campus in 2006 coming in from Wade Hampton Boulevard shows the 2,600-seat Rodeheaver Auditorium on the right and the 7,000-seat Founder's Memorial Amphitorium (FMA), which Dr. Bob Jones Jr. modeled after a Greek amphitheater, on the left. Constructed in the shape of a giant megaphone, Rodeheaver is considered to be one of the best-equipped collegiate auditoriums in the nation and is used primarily for musical and dramatic productions. FMA is the setting for daily chapel and other events that assemble the entire student

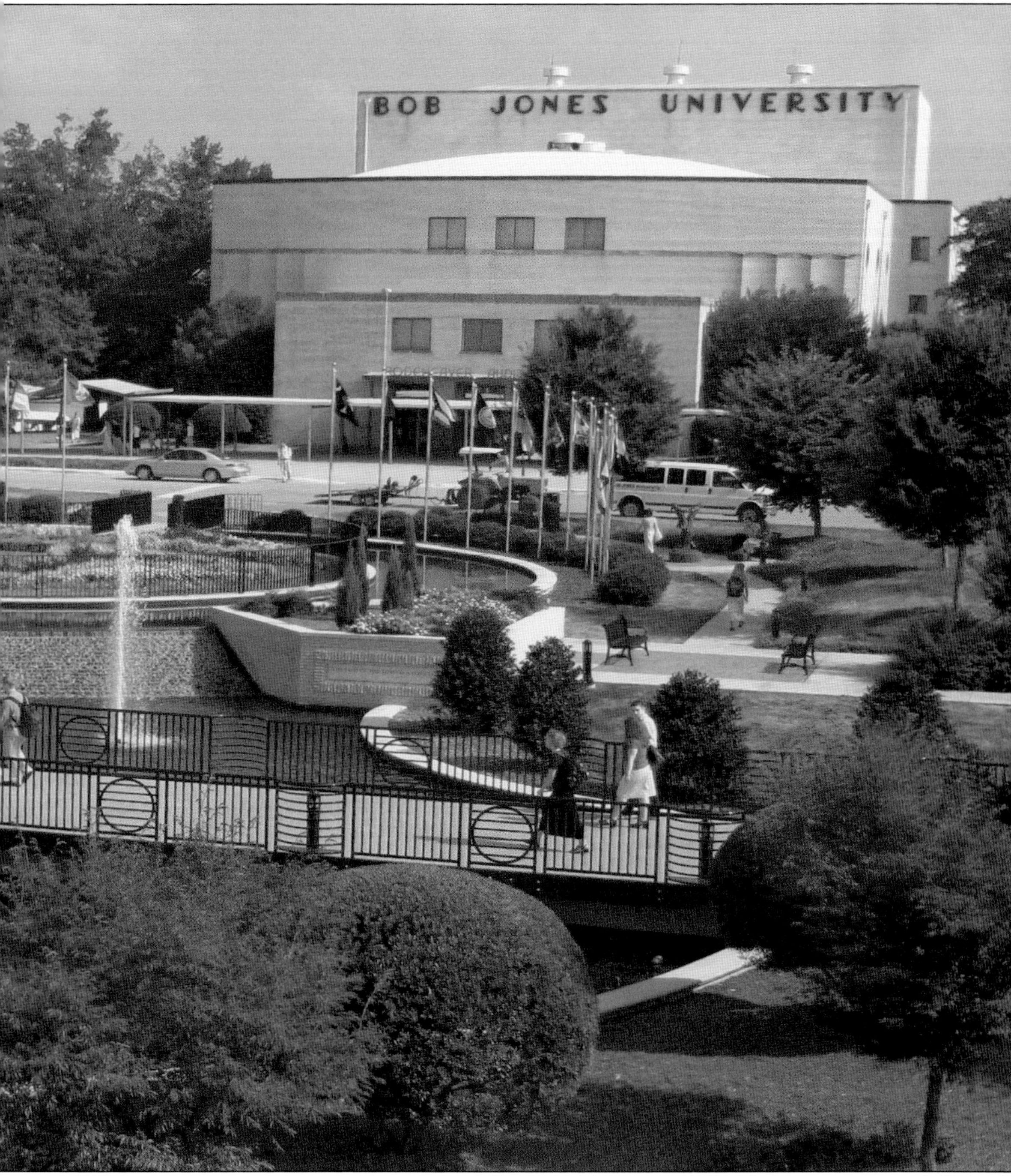

body, faculty, and staff at one time. The bridge in the foreground crosses the fountain and gets an abundance of foot traffic between the Student Center and the Alumni Building every day. Covered walks that eliminate the constant use of umbrellas on rainy days are extended over much of the campus and can be seen in front of both Founder's Memorial Amphitorium and Rodeheaver Auditorium.

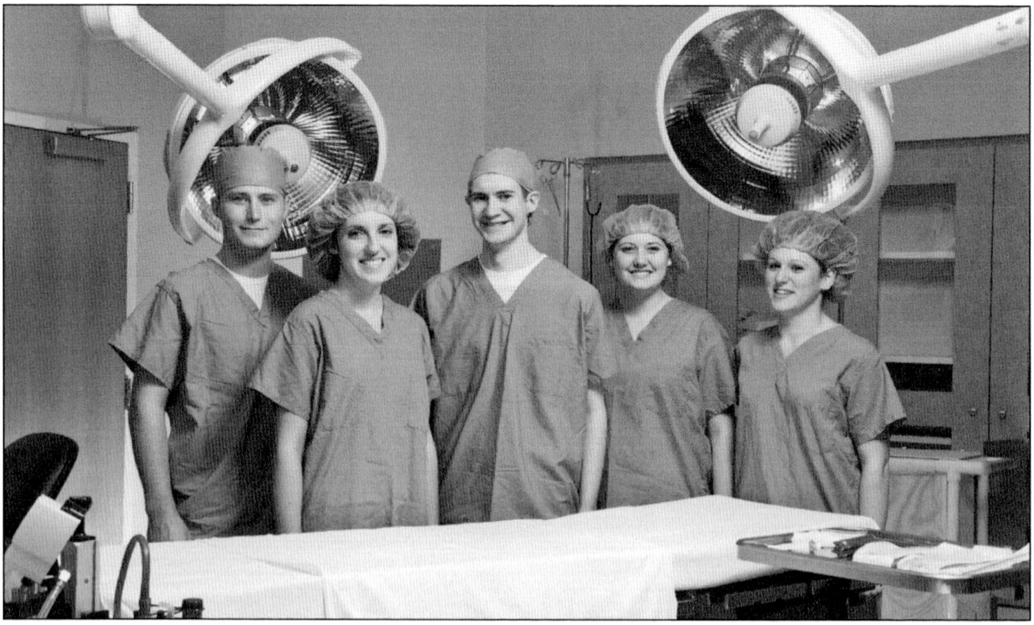

From its inception in 2000, the University Nursing Association has had as its aim "To be the servants of Christ, doing the will of God from the heart, with good will, doing service as to the Lord and not to men." In an operating room at St. Francis Hospital are the 2006 officers: (from left to right) Aaron Gfeller, senior representative; Danielle Fisher, president; Donald Jacobs, vice president; Kelly Drake, junior representative; and Elizabeth Mullens, sophomore representative.

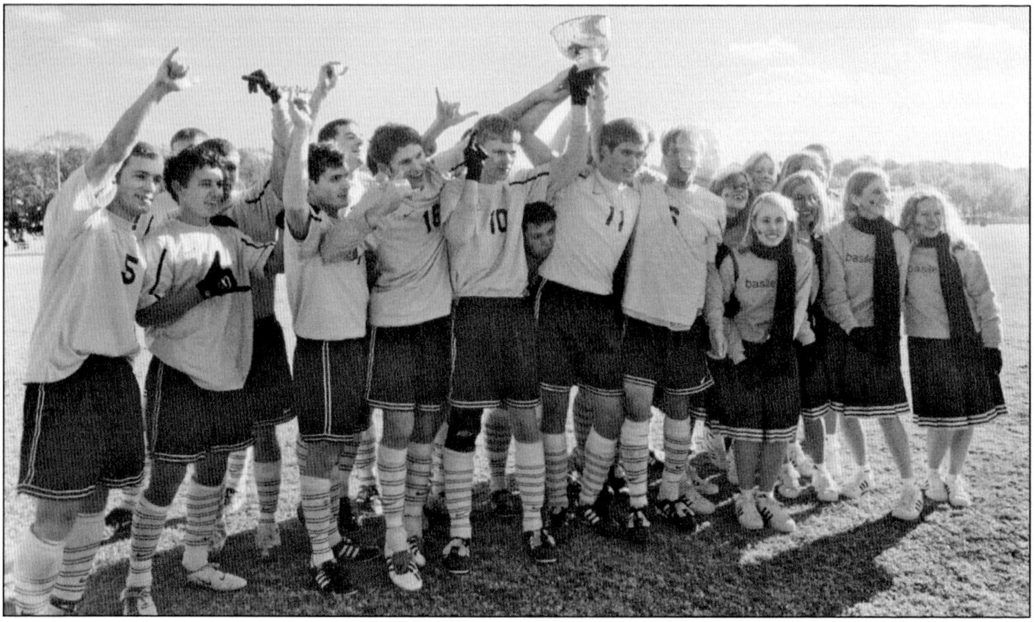

Not as Emily Dickinson said, but rather, "Success is counted sweetest to those who *e'er* succeed"—at least, that is the way the 2002 Basilean soccer team and cheerleaders feel about their third consecutive championship in five years. Basilean scored twice in the first half, and their goalie, Will Parker, blocked a barrage of kicks in the second half to preserve the margin of victory over Beta Gamma in the annual Turkey Bowl Game held in Alumni Stadium.

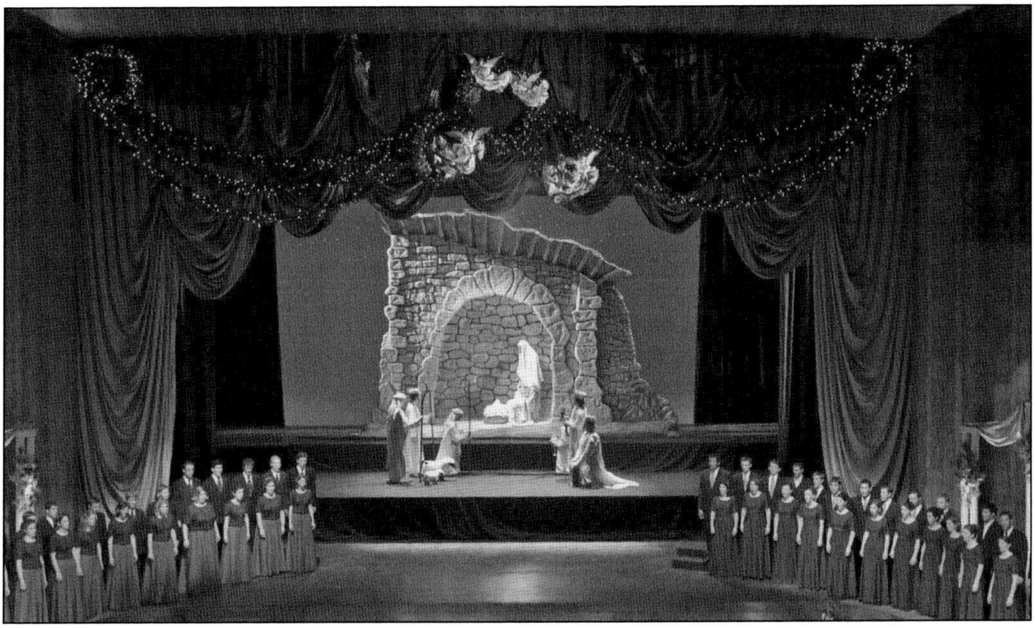

Each year, Christmas Vespers features choral groups and dramatic scenes that focus on the true meaning of Christmas, the birth of the Savior. *Tidings of Comfort and Joy* was the title of the 2004 program under the direction of Dr. Lonnie Polson. Drs. Warren Cook, Beth Eubank, and Christopher Gilliam directed this combined choir.

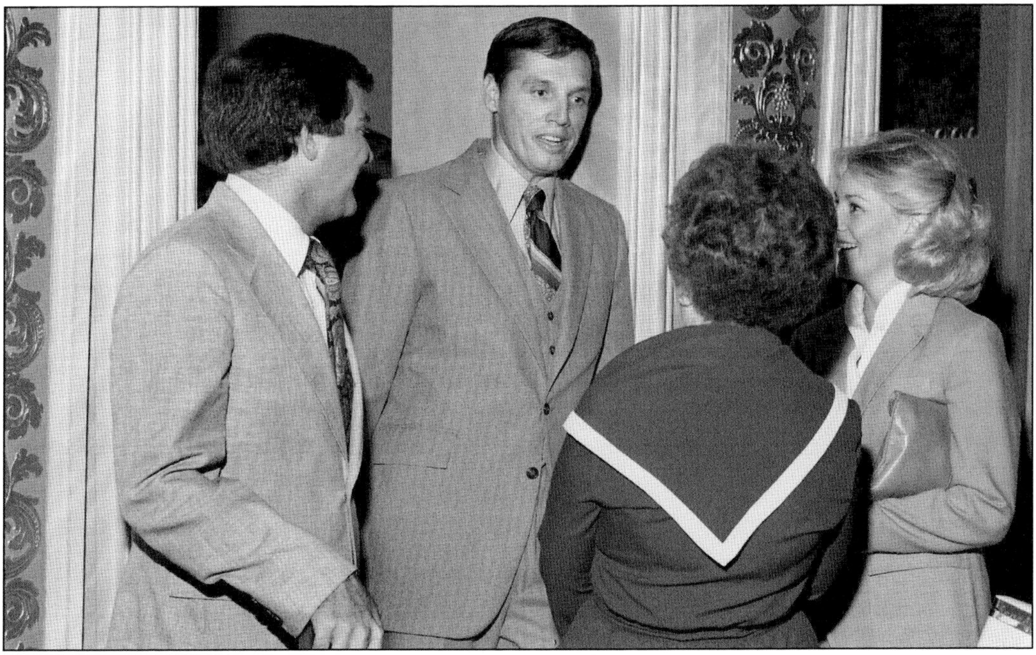

Dr. Bob Jones III, president, talks with visitors at the dedication of the addition to the J. S. Mack Library on September 6, 1980. Nearly 60,000 square feet were added to the original building in a $2.8-million expansion project that took 16 months to complete. Prior to beginning tours of the new facility, Mary Gaston Jones shared a brief history of the growth of BJU's library, and Dr. Bob Jones Jr., chancellor, delivered a dedication message.

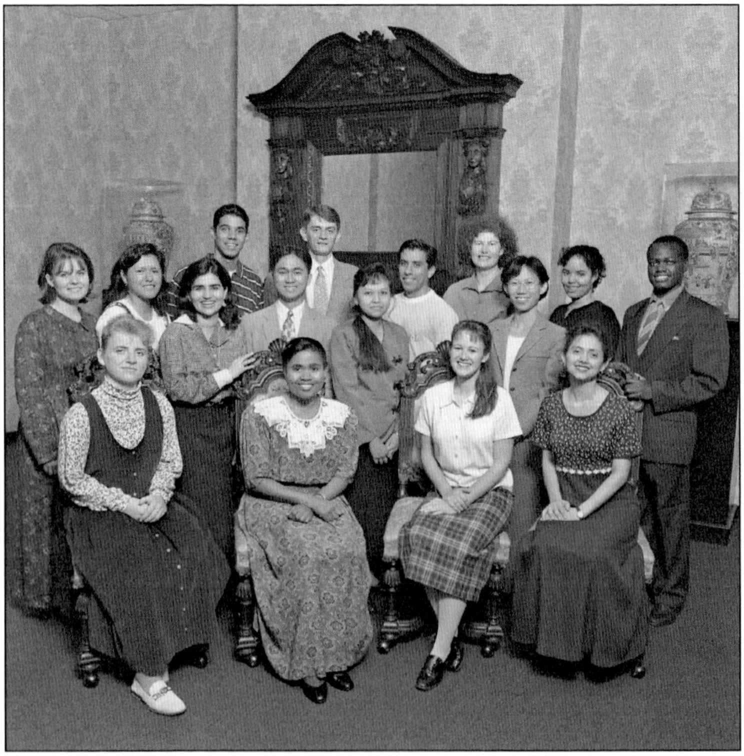

Dr. Bob Jones III established the World and Timothy Funds in 1984 to make Christian training for foreign students a reality. These students were enrolled in the programs in 1998: Ela Kryston, Cecilia Torres, Yadin Rodriguez, Sasha Kruchkov, Milthon Martinez-Jiminez, Elaine Goodchild, Rebecca Dinzey-Genao, Joash Kendagor, Miriam Lara-Acosta, Eliezer Yanson, Claudia Hernandez-Grande, Jenny Ho, Agnieszka Augustyniak, Yolette Ermont, Damans Sanchez, and Renata dos Santos.

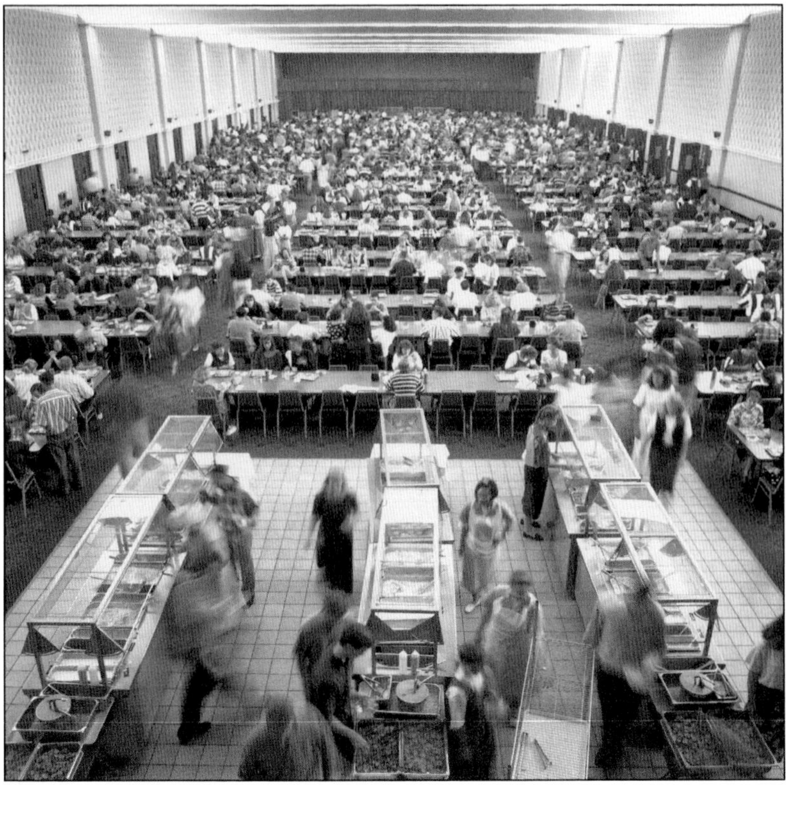

Buffet lines keep people moving in the Dixon-McKenzie Dining Common, which has been in service since 1965. The main seating area is longer than a regulation football field and today accommodates 1,750 students at one time.

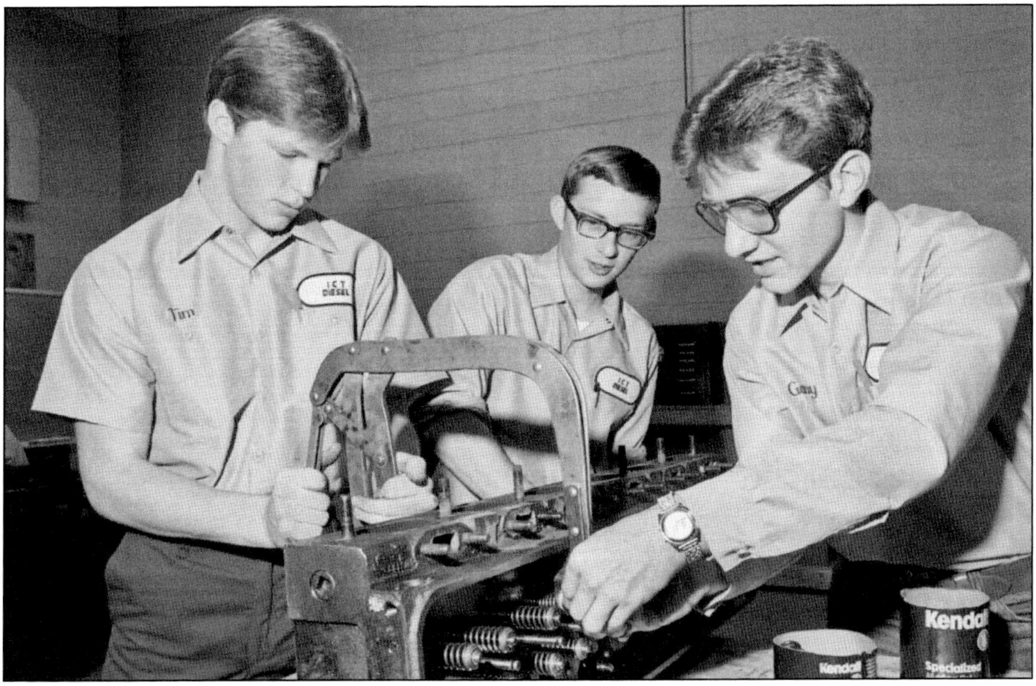

School of Applied Studies (SAS) students are learning what it takes to be a good mechanic. Along with helping students develop Christlike character and grow in their knowledge of the Word of God, the SAS has a twofold purpose: to train students to effectively serve the Lord and to equip them for careers in ministry or trade professions. SAS offers three-year associate degrees, with opportunities to earn a four-year bachelor's degree from the School of Business.

Dr. Phil Smith served the Lord at BJU for nearly half a century as dean of the College of Arts and Science, registrar, provost, and chief academic officer. He holds a bachelor of science in secondary education from BJU, a master of science in educational administration from Miami University of Ohio, and a Ph.D. from Pennsylvania State University. Under his leadership, BJU became one of the largest Christian colleges, with one of the broadest academic offerings in the world. He expanded the academic programs from 37 majors in 1965 to 128 in 2005. He provided oversight for the hiring of university faculty; provided academic oversight for Bob Jones Elementary School, Junior High, and Academy; provided direction for BJU Press curriculum development that has impacted the education of thousands in Christian schools and home schools; helped initiate both the Office of Career Development and Placement, and the Office of Extended Education; and guided the university through the process of becoming accredited. He retired in 2005.

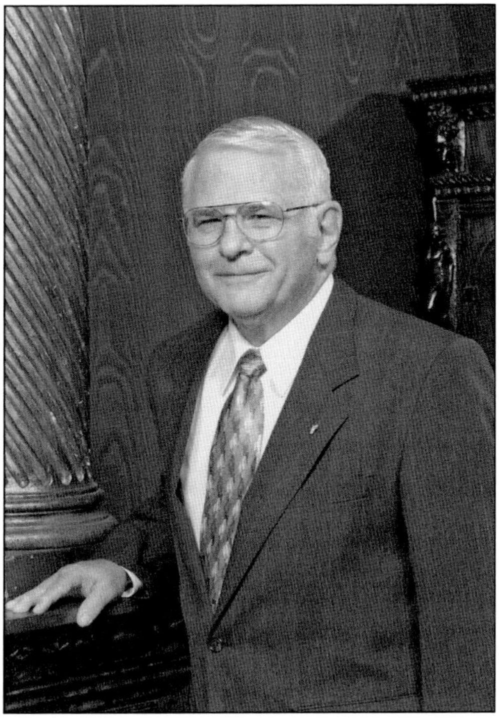

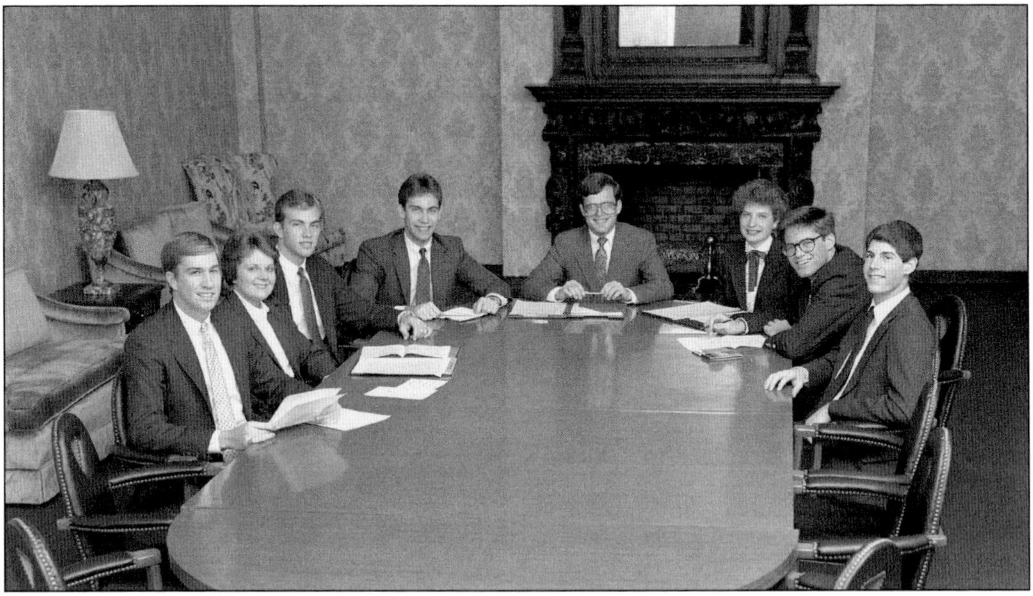

Pictured are the 1983–1984 officers of the University Business Association: (from left to right) Jim McCrudden, treasurer–investment club; Janet Willoughby, vice president–office administration; Jon Sparkman, vice president–accounting; Dave Sparkman, president–investment club; Tony Bryson, president; Gina Edwards, secretary; John Spencer, vice president–management; and Steve Sanders, vice president–community service. The University Business Association seeks to provide students with practical instruction and to expose them to the guidance and experiences of successful businesspeople.

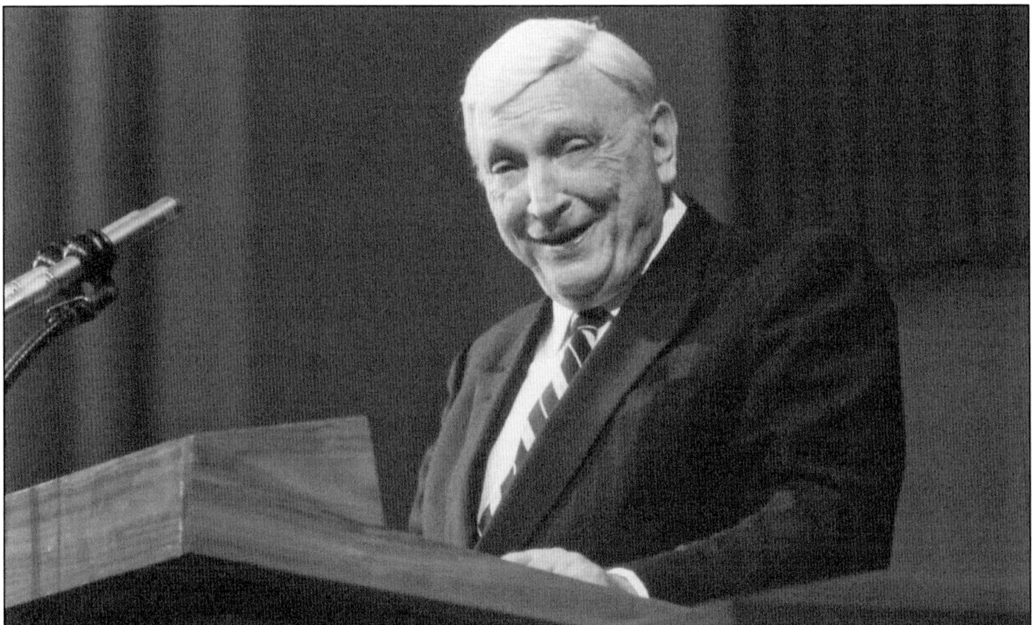

Dr. Bob Jones Jr. was a multitalented man: educator, actor, evangelist, scholar, cultural advocate, and apologist for Fundamentalism. Often a chapel speaker until his death on November 12, 1997, he frequently exhibited his sense of humor on the chapel platform.

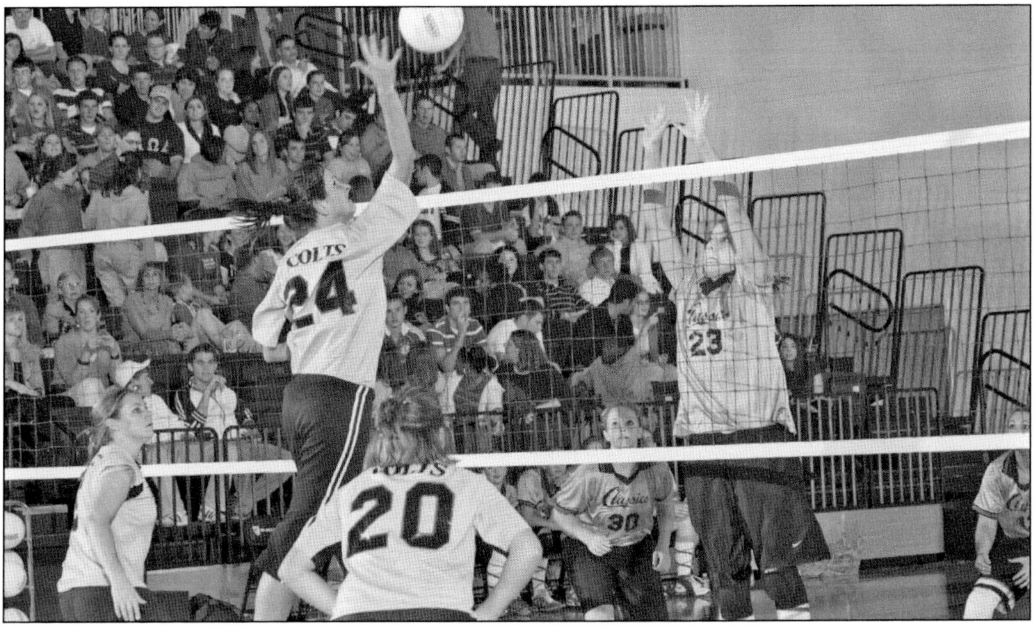

Bob Jones University provides plenty of athletic action for women students. Competition is especially intense in volleyball, as indicated by these players from the Pi Delta Classics and the Theta Sigma Colts, battling for the 2007 volleyball championship. In this photograph, Theta Sigma's Susan Ross spikes the ball as Lauren Lehman goes up to block.

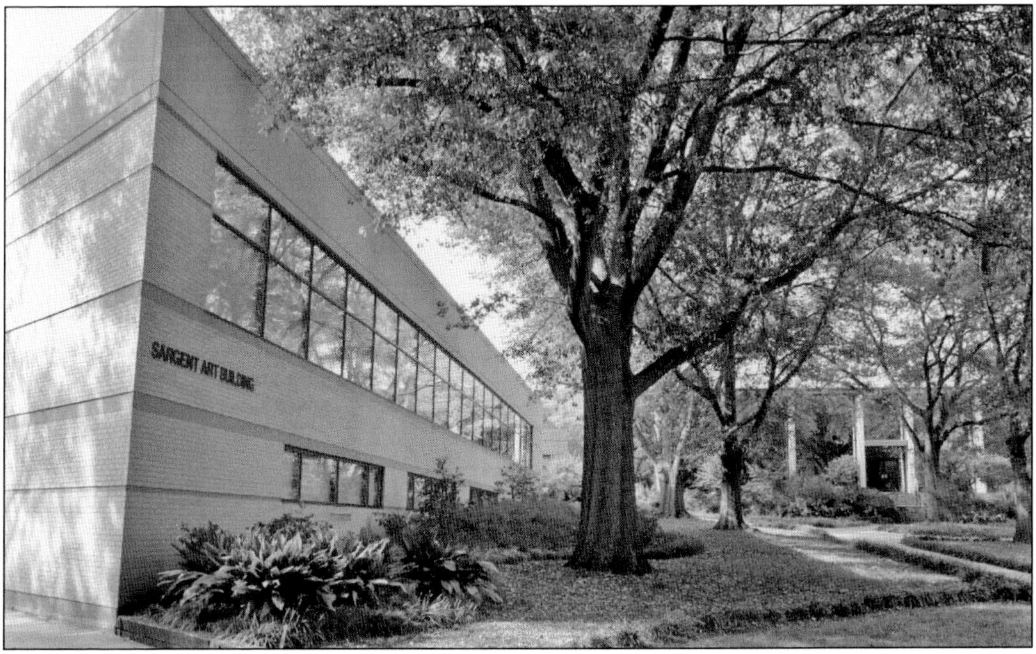

Earl Wheaton Sargent (1898–1978) and Eleanor Greene Sargent (1899–1990), Greenville industrialists and philanthropists, generously contributed to the needs of Bob Jones University. The Sargent Foundation was established in 1954 to support student scholarships and contribute to community needs. The Sargent Art Building, part of the Gustafson Fine Arts Center, was named for the couple in 1998. It houses offices, classrooms, studios, and seminar and conference rooms.

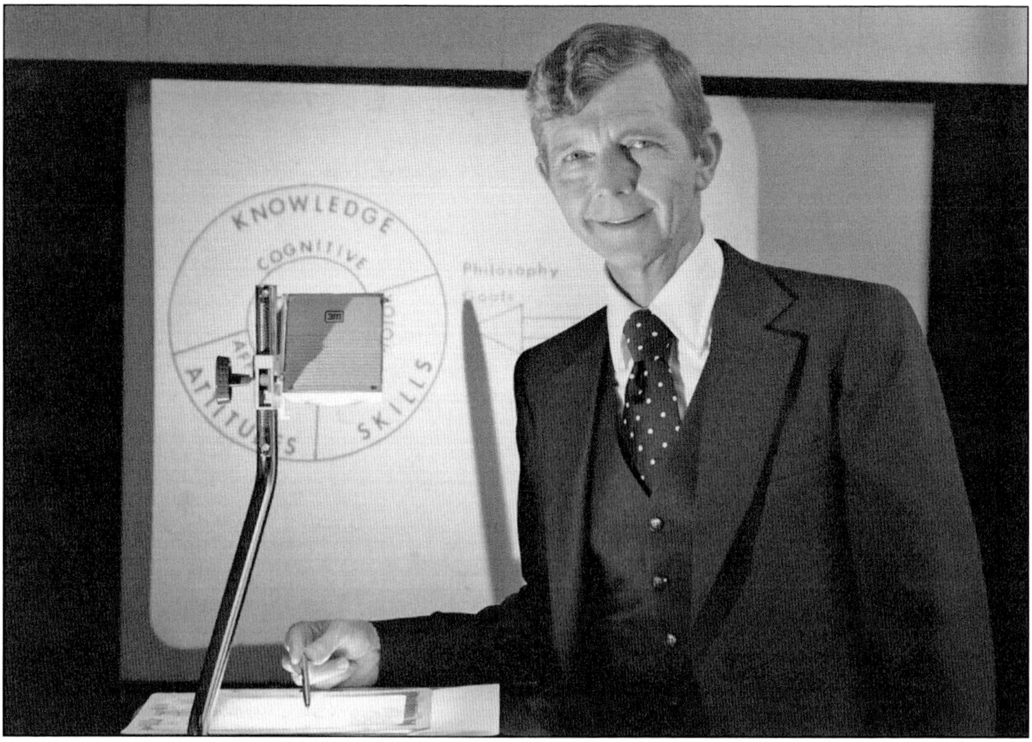

Students who sat in Dr. Walter Fremont's psychology classes rarely fell asleep. His animated sessions and friendly personality contributed to his effectiveness in conveying biblical truths as they related to his subject matter. Studying at the University of Dayton, the University of Wisconsin, and Penn State University, where he earned his Ph.D., he came to BJU in 1950 because he wanted to take a one-year Bible course. Dr. James Edwards persuaded him to teach part-time and later full-time. In 1953, he became dean of the School of Education, where he served for more than four decades until he was forced to relinquish his responsibilities when stricken with Lou Gehrig's disease. To recognize and honor his valuable contributions as a dean and faculty member, the administration named the men's fitness center the Fremont Fitness Center (below). He and his wife, Trudy, coauthored a number of books on education and guidance.

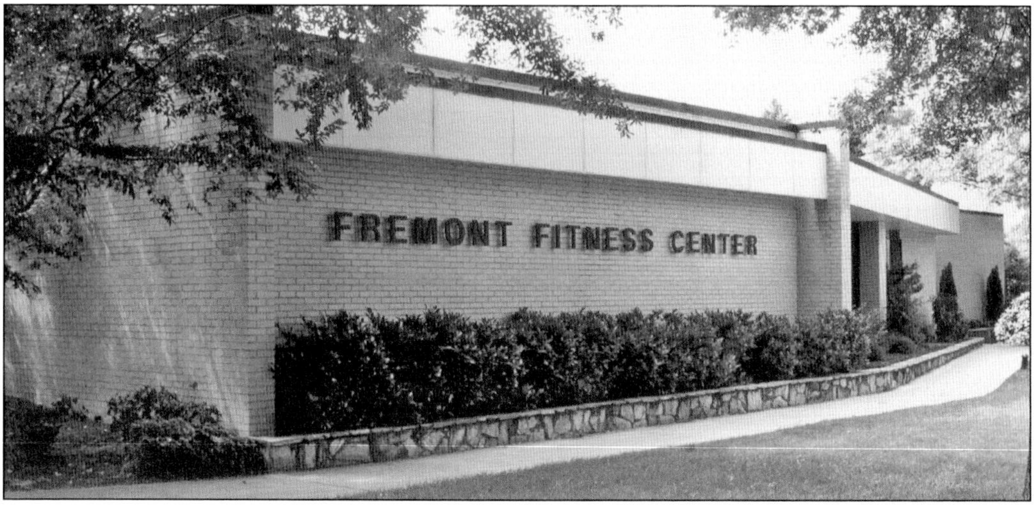

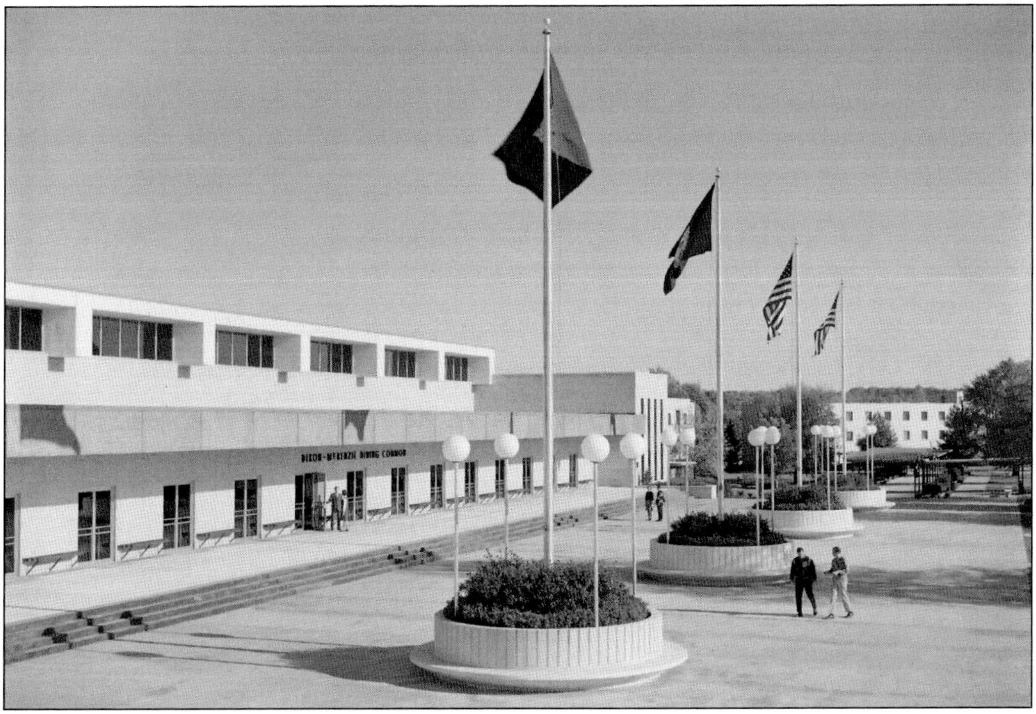

When the Dixon-McKenzie Dining Common was constructed in 1965, the building housing the former Winn-Dixie grocery store on Wade Hampton Boulevard was incorporated into part of the kitchen. In addition to a large student dining area, the dining common has a large dining room for faculty and staff families, and two private dining rooms, one that accommodates up to 200 people and a second that seats approximately 30 people. These rooms are used for special events and to entertain university guests.

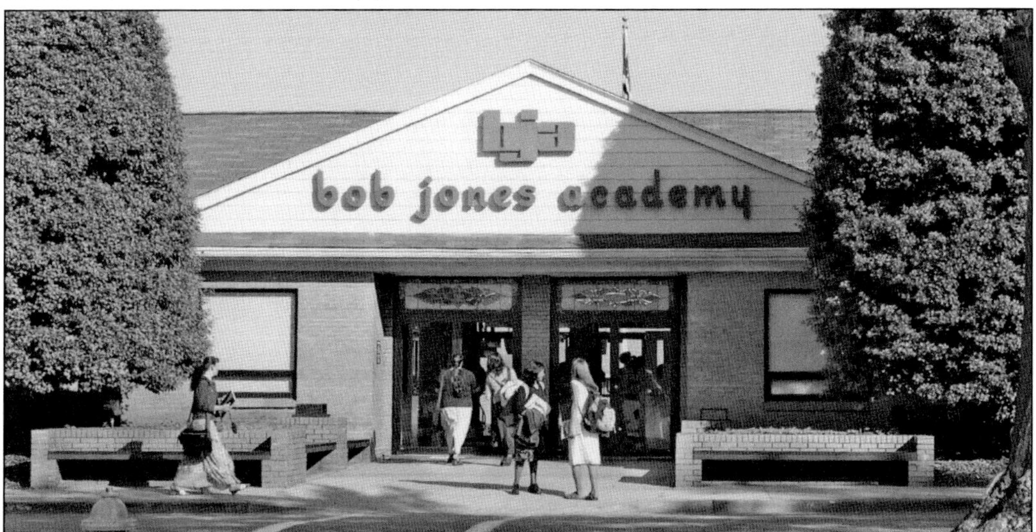

Founded at the same time as the college in 1927, Bob Jones Academy is the oldest of the BJU precollege schools and one of the oldest Christian high schools in the country. Bob Jones Junior High School began in 1952 and Bob Jones Elementary School in 1970.

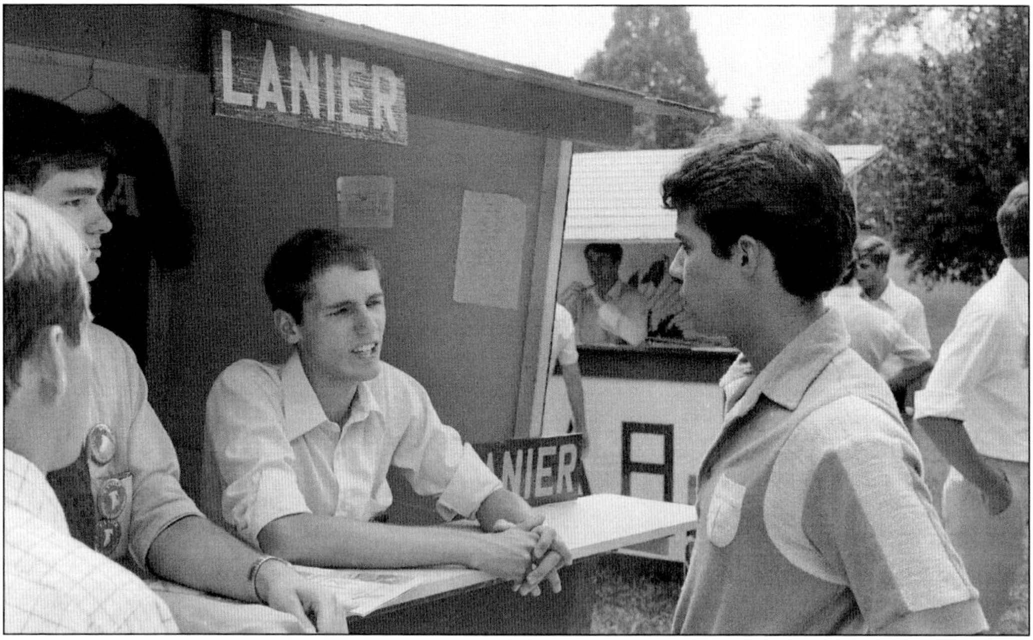

Manning the Lanier literary society's booth during Rush Week in 1980, two young men endeavor to sell incoming students on good reasons to join their organization. Societies compete to enlist new members at the beginning of each semester.

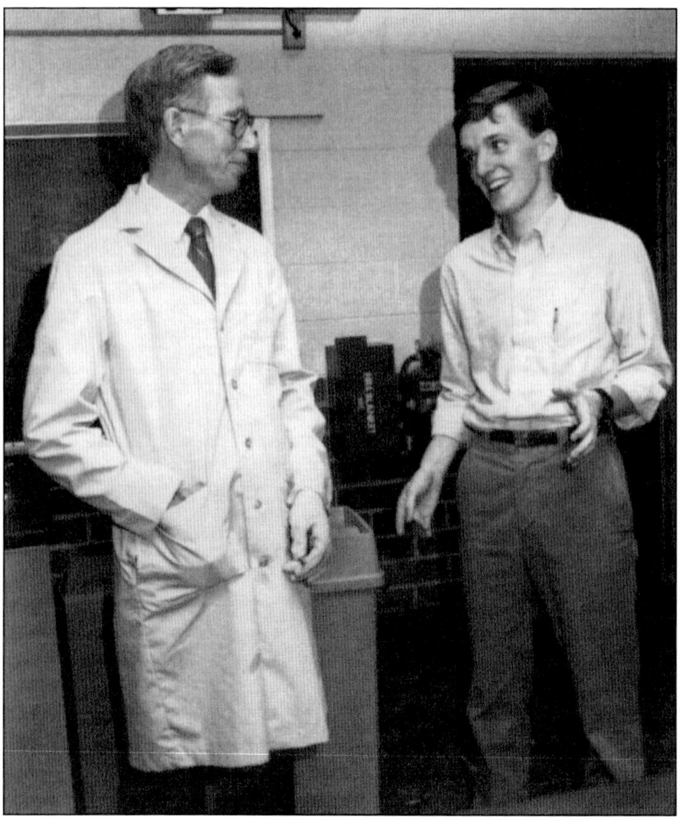

Dr. Al Isaak talks with one of his biology lab students during the 1989 school year. Dr. Isaak, who received his doctorate from Kansas State University, joined the BJU faculty in 1972.

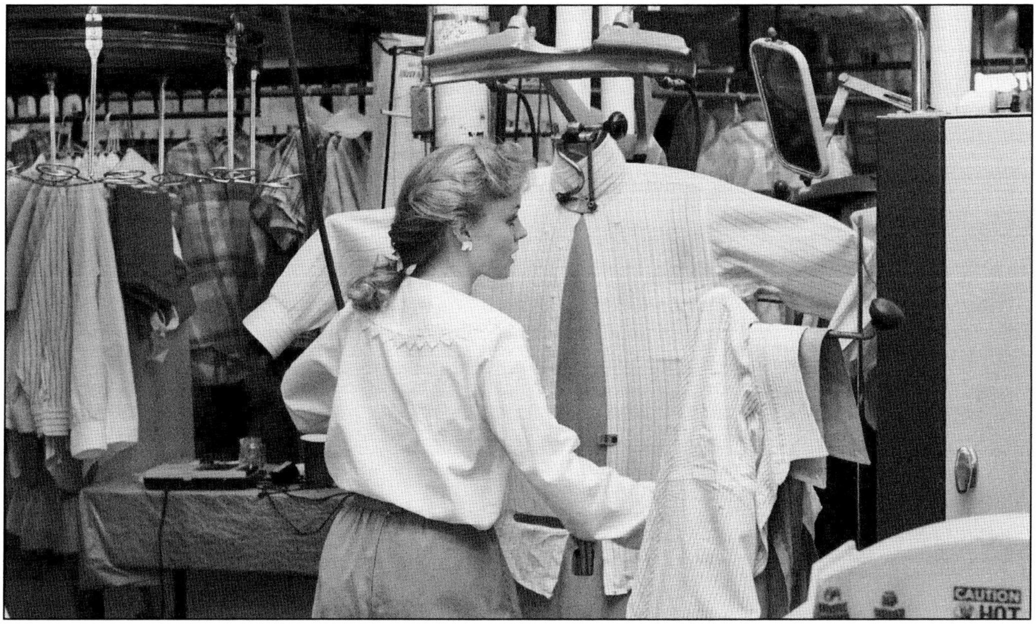

A 1989 work-loan student puts the finishing touches on a shirt at the University Cleaners. Approximately 2,100 students work on campus, and the university benefits from their part in filling many campus responsibilities, such as lifeguarding, day care, piano accompanying, maintenance, laundry, and dining common crew. The students learn self-discipline, which can ultimately lead to a greater appreciation for their spiritual and academic education.

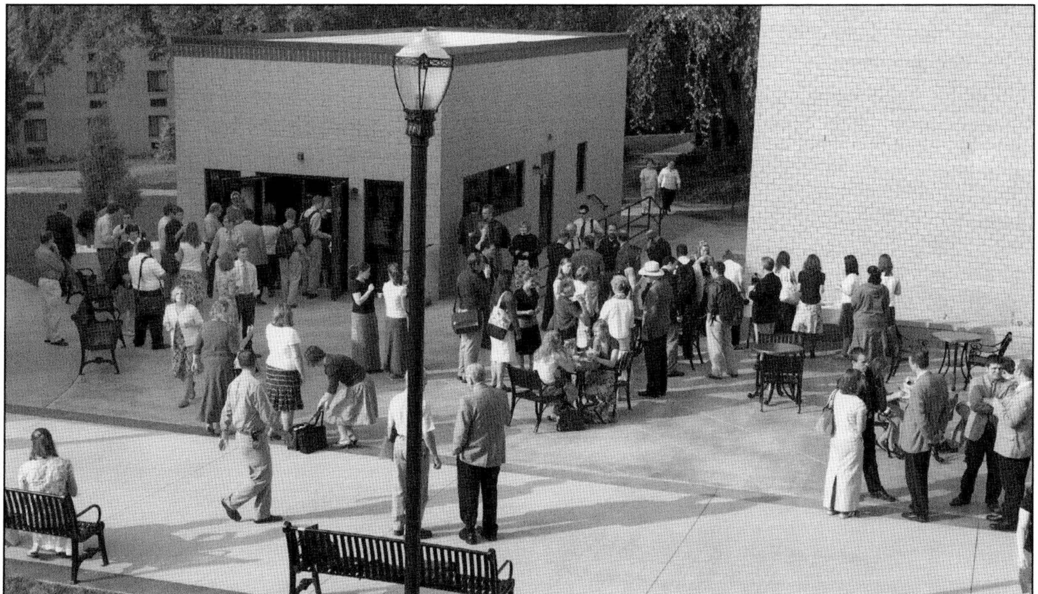

Appropriately called "Cuppa Jones," the new coffee shop opened in the fall of 2007 between the library and the seminary building. Students find it a great place to get a quick cup of java as they are hurrying between classes. The new facility has some inside seating, but the majority of students take their coffee to go and sip it en route to class or enjoy it while relaxing in the adjacent plaza.

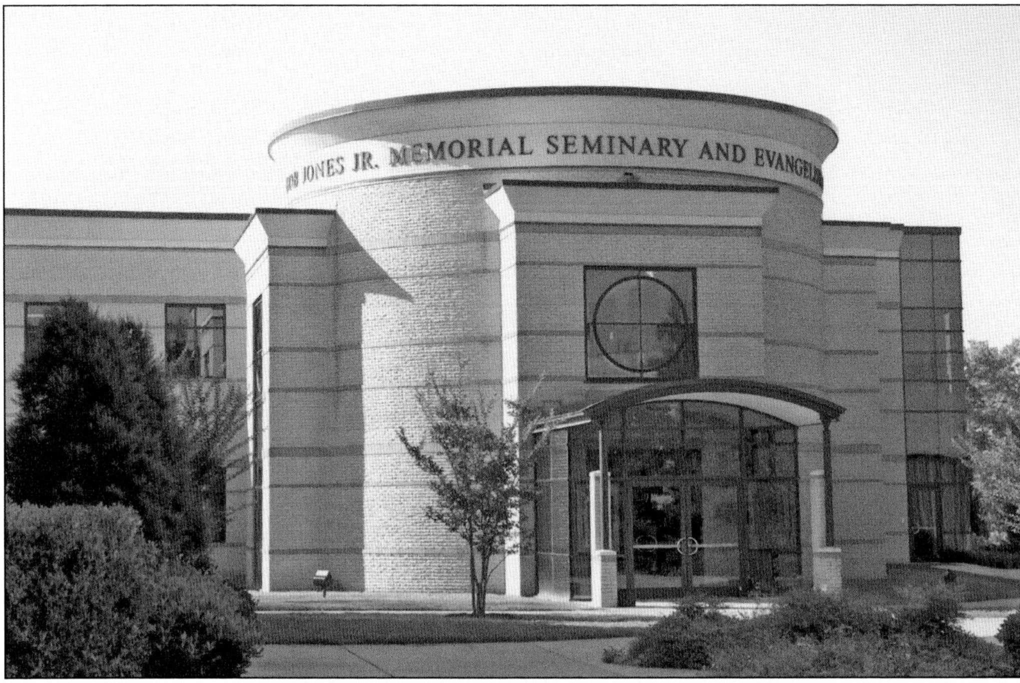

The 16,000-square-foot Bob Jones Jr. Memorial Seminary and Evangelism Center is one of the newest buildings on campus, located between the J. S. Mack Library and the Alumni Building. Honoring the life of the university's second president, the center's rotunda houses multimedia computer presentations and a gallery of memorabilia, including a 20-foot-by-7-foot mural painted by Jim Brooks, featuring 17 evangelists who greatly influenced America and three noted hymn writers (below). The evangelists are, from left to right, Roger Williams, Jonathan Edwards, George Tennant, David Brainerd, George Whitfield, Francis Asbury, Timothy Dwight, John Leland, Asahel Nettleton, Luther Rice, D. L. Moody, J. Wilbur Chapman, R. A. Torry, A. J. Gordon, Billy Sunday, W. B. Riley, and Bob Jones Sr. The three hymn writers (bottom right, from left to right) are Ira Sankey, Fanny Crosby, and P. P. Bliss. The two-story structure features advanced technology resource and research facilities, classrooms, faculty offices, a conference room, and a lecture hall.

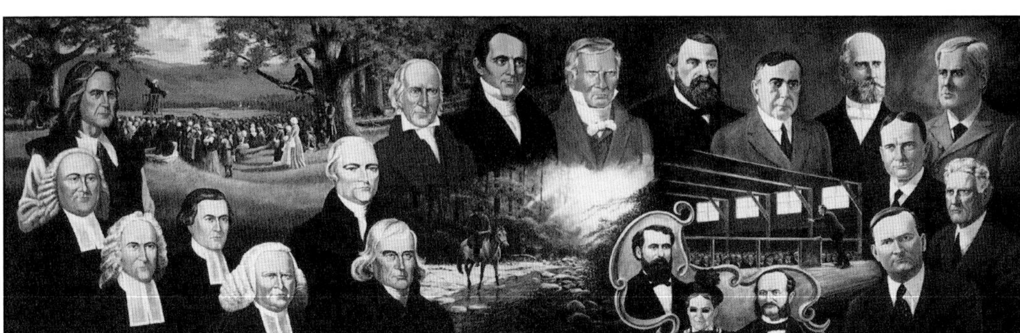

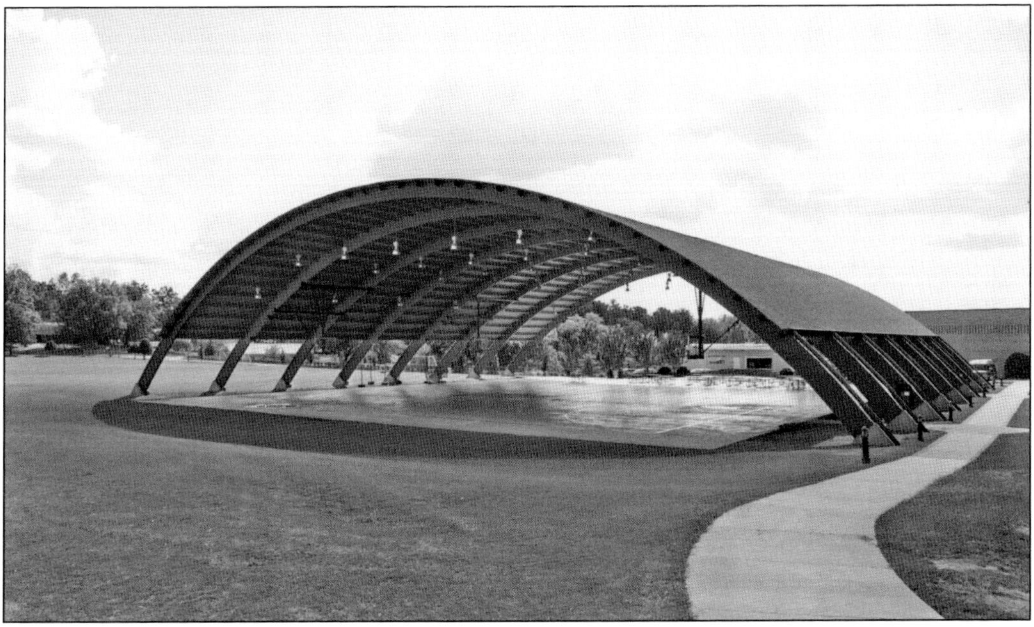

When the Davis Field House replaced the old gym, the roof of the gym was relocated to the far end of the soccer fields across from the Printing Division. It now serves as a sheltered Activity Center where students can shoot basketball hoops and participate in social events—when the weather is good or bad. The center also features a fire pit.

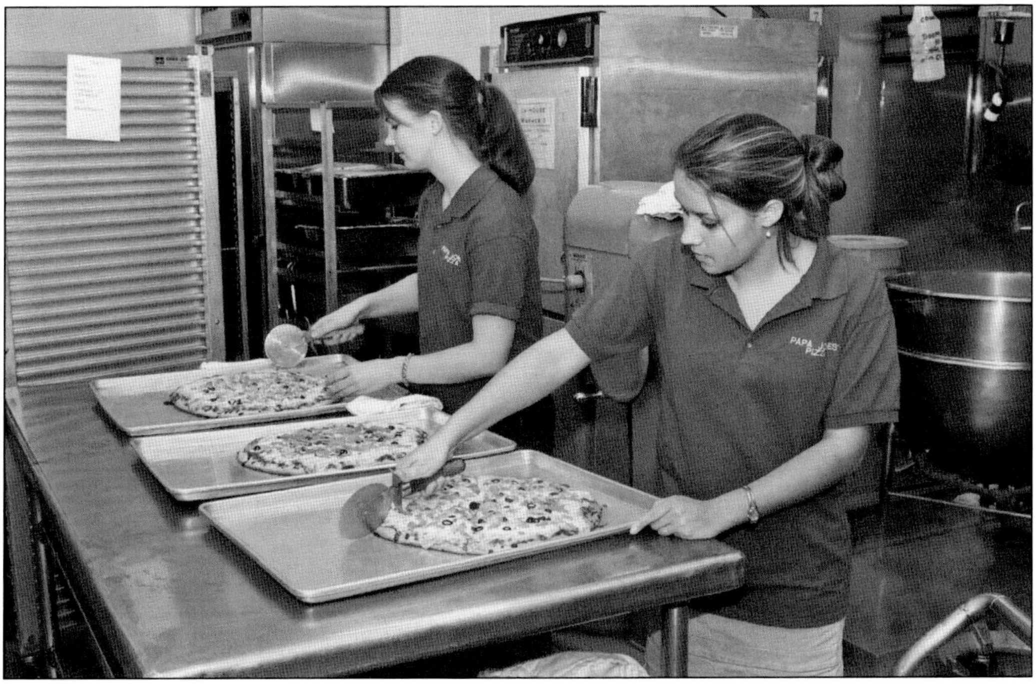

Who doesn't like pizza? It takes a multitude of pizzas to satisfy the appetites of hundreds of students and faculty and staff members who eat at Papa Jones on Friday nights. These two students in the 2005–2006 school year are busily cutting the hot pepperoni and sausage pizzas to keep the buffet line well stocked.

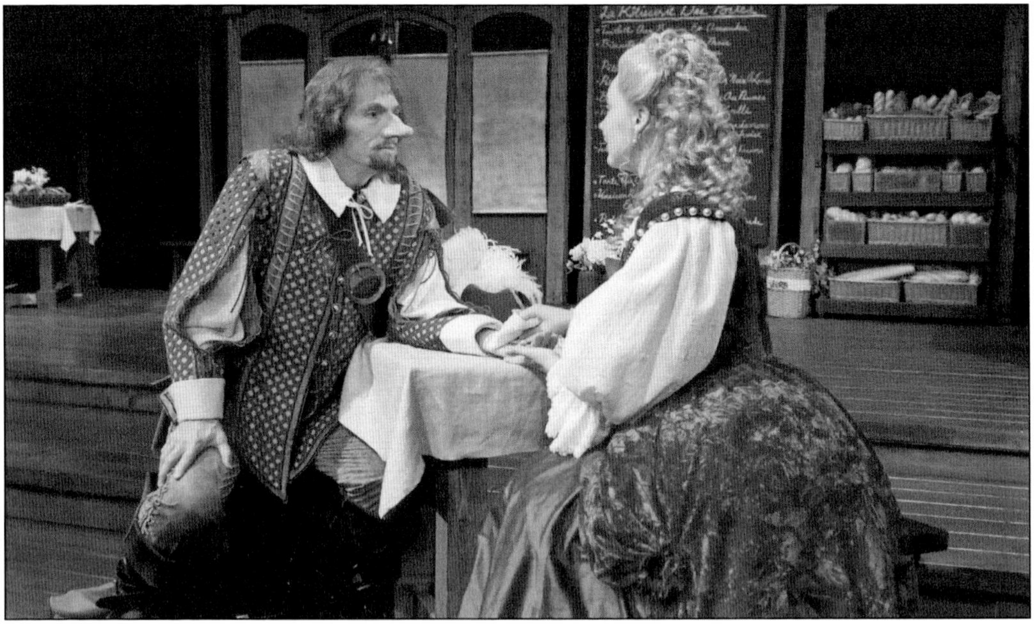

The Classic Players presented Edmond Rostand's *Cyrano de Bergerac* to packed audiences in the fall of 2005. Directed by Beneth Jones, the drama featured Dr. Bob Jones III as Cyrano, the large-nosed poet, and Jennifer Polson as the beautiful Roxanne in the story of true sacrificial love. As described in BJU's 2005 yearbook, the *Vintage*, the play used "an innovative set and impressive staging that included a lovers' balcony and an exploding battlefield."

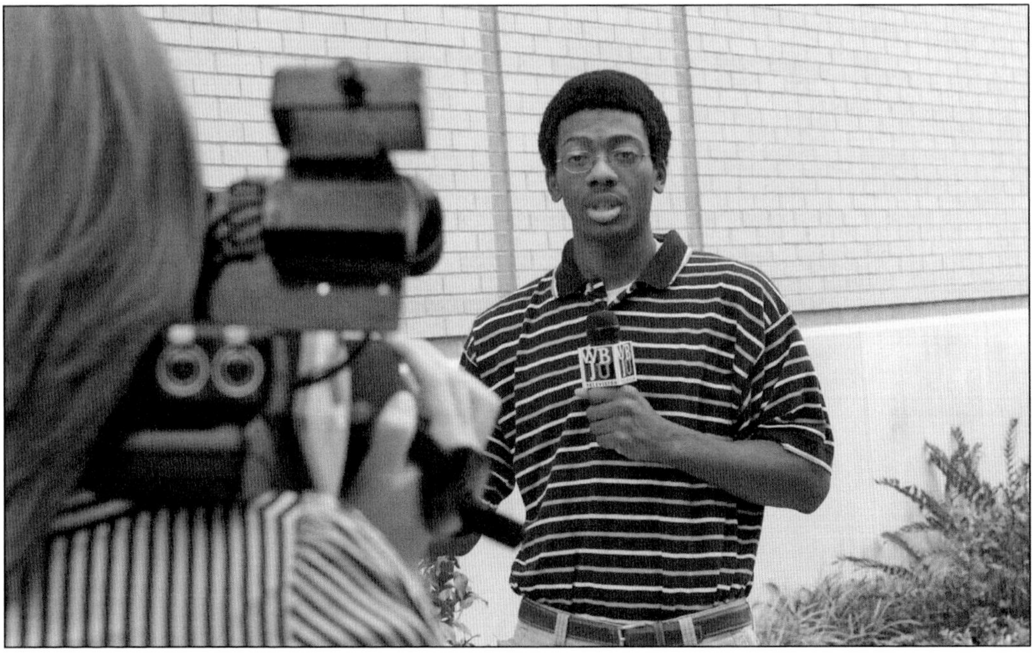

Jeremiah Dew, a member of the WBJU radio and television staff, reports campus news. WBJU-Radio and WBJU-TV are campus stations that broadcast into the residence halls. Radio and television (RTV) majors are strongly encouraged to serve at one of the stations or work in other campus media such as the *Collegian* newspaper.

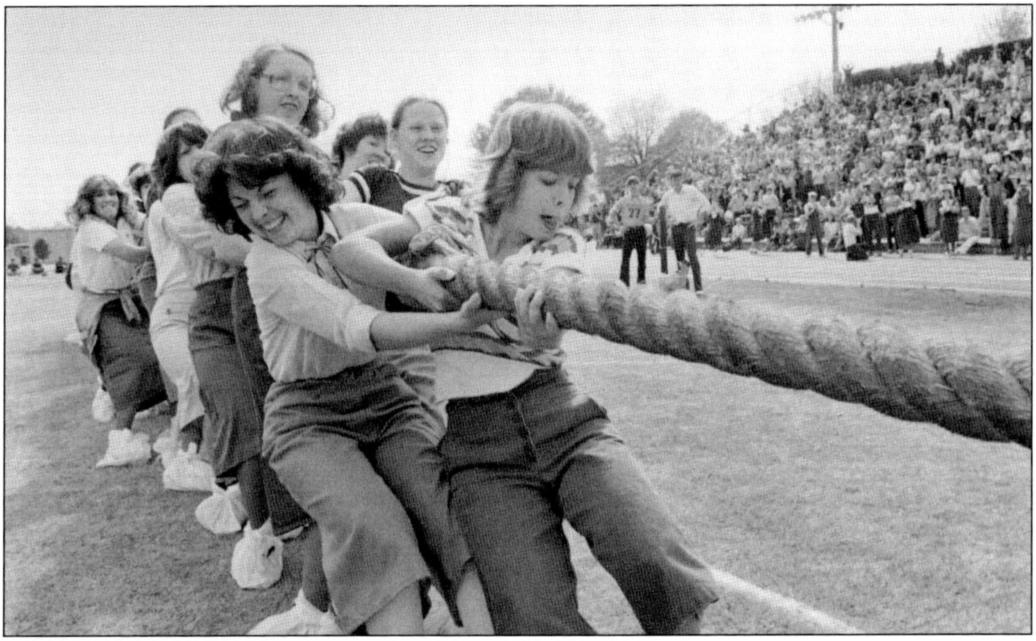

With their feet in plastic bags, BJU girls engage in a classic tug-of-war during Gold Rush Daze in 1982. The cheering spectators in the Alumni Stadium provide the necessary encouragement for the girls to try harder. Gold Rush Daze, held once every four years, gives students and faculty a break from the rigors of academic pursuits and is always highlighted with fun things to do and watch.

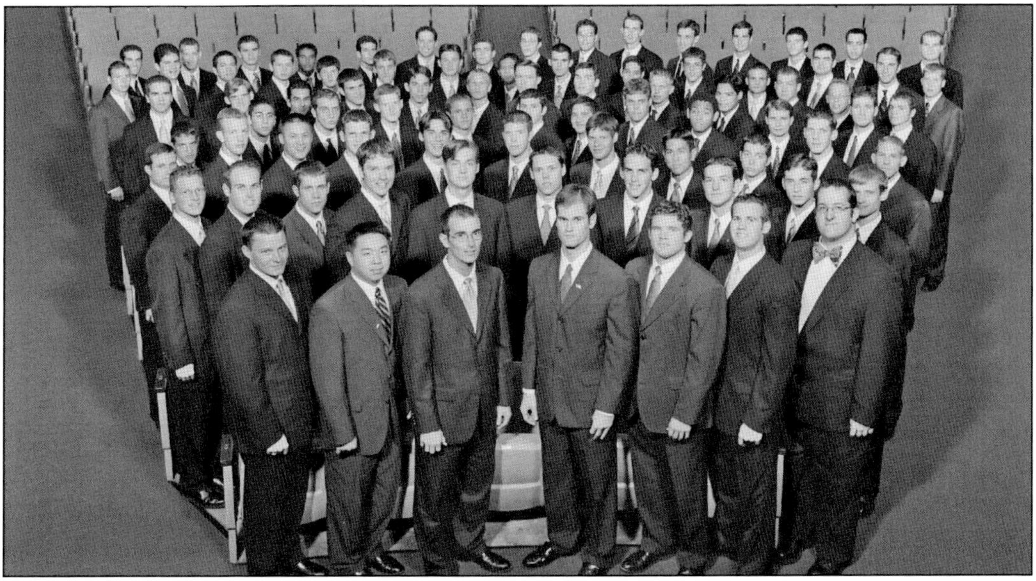

This 82-man Usher Crew in 2002, under the direction of Tom Butts, was responsible for directing audiences in church services, concerts, plays, and special events, such as Bible Conference, whether the events were held in Founder's Memorial Amphitorium, Rodeheaver Auditorium, War Memorial Chapel, or Stratton Hall. The ushers have their own Sunday school class and conduct an outreach to a boys' home, where they play basketball with the boys, as well as serving as counselors to them.

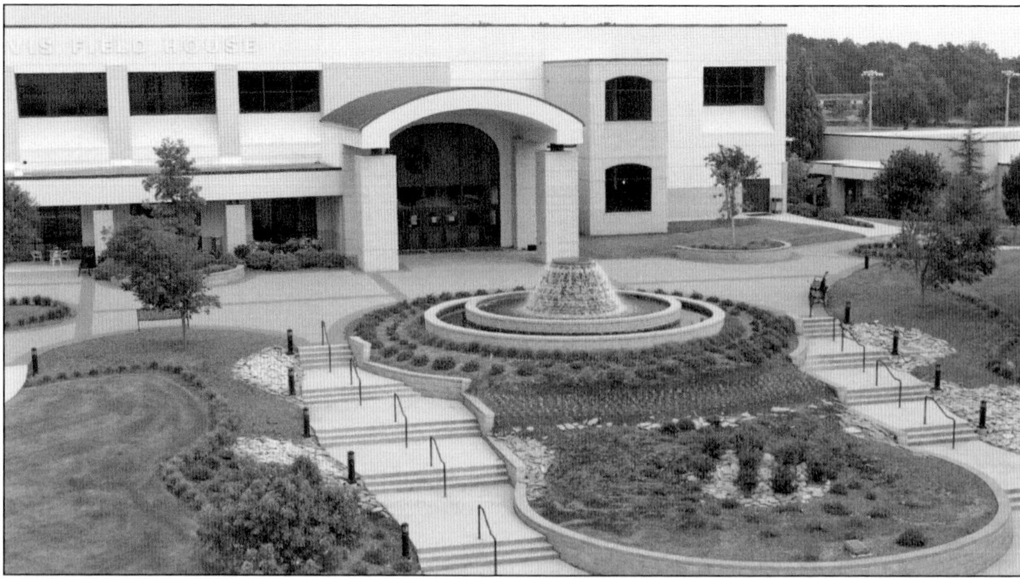

The Davis Field House is a 90,000-square-foot structure that includes a gymnasium seating 3,000 spectators, classrooms, offices, locker rooms, a women's fitness center, an aerobics room, an indoor jogging track, and a swimming pool. Three separate areas can be utilized as four regulation courts for basketball and volleyball, and six courts for badminton. It greatly enhanced BJU's physical education facilities when completed in 2004.

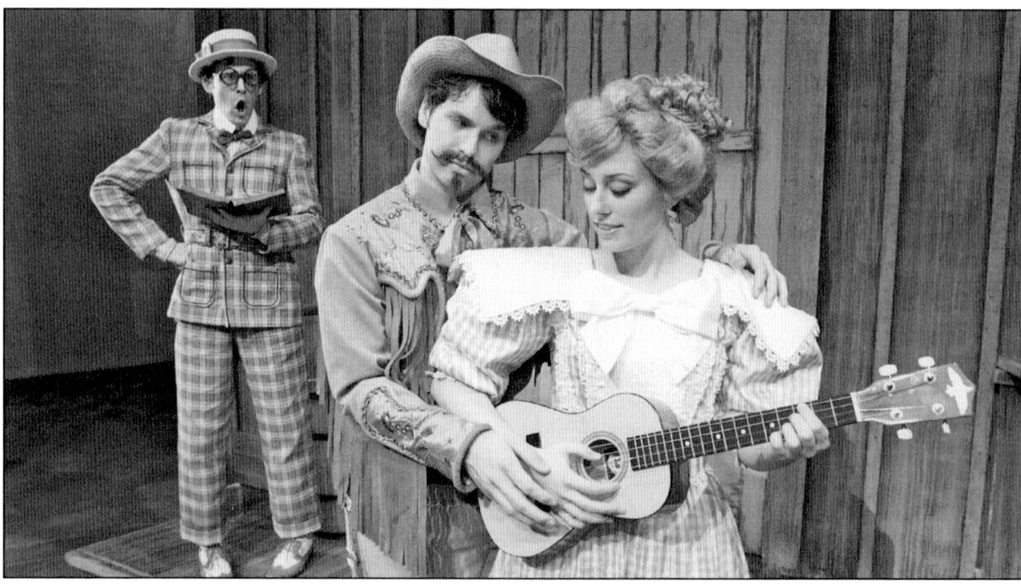

Christi Woodruff, as Bianca, played a key role in the Classic Players' *Taming of the Shrew* set in a 19th-century mining town. Presented during Thanksgiving week 2006, the drama is the story of Kate Minola, the shrew, and Bianca, her flirtatious younger sister who has many suitors, one of whom was played by Josh Innerst. Lead roles were played by Drs. David and Charlotte Burke, he as Petruchio, and she as the shrew—the older sister, who is bad-tempered and aggressively assertive but who ultimately marries and is tamed by her husband, Petruchio. Director Jeff Stegall called the Burkes "the dynamic duo." Pictured from left to right are Philip Eoute (as Lucentio), Innerst (as Hortensio), and Woodruff (as Bianca).

Dr. Bob Jones Jr. developed a love for drama at an early age and gained the attention of the American theater with his one-man-show, *Curtain Calls*, which toured the United States from 1937 to 1945. Over the years, he played many roles in BJU dramatic and film productions, at least one and sometimes two times a year. He is shown here portraying Macbeth in 1950.

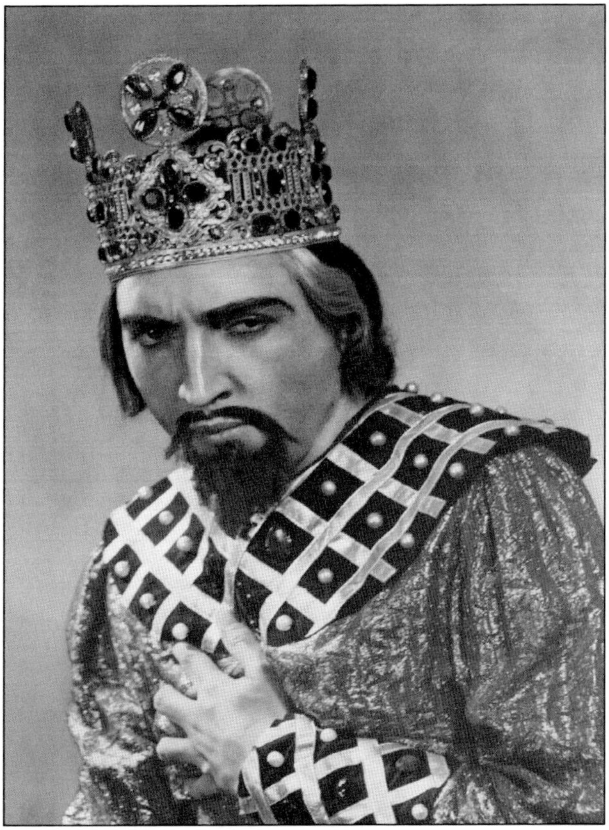

Students clamor around Republican Ronald Reagan in the fall of 1979 when he visited the campus during his campaign for president of the United States. Accompanied by his wife, Nancy, the former California governor spoke during the morning chapel service and found a warm reception from students and faculty alike.

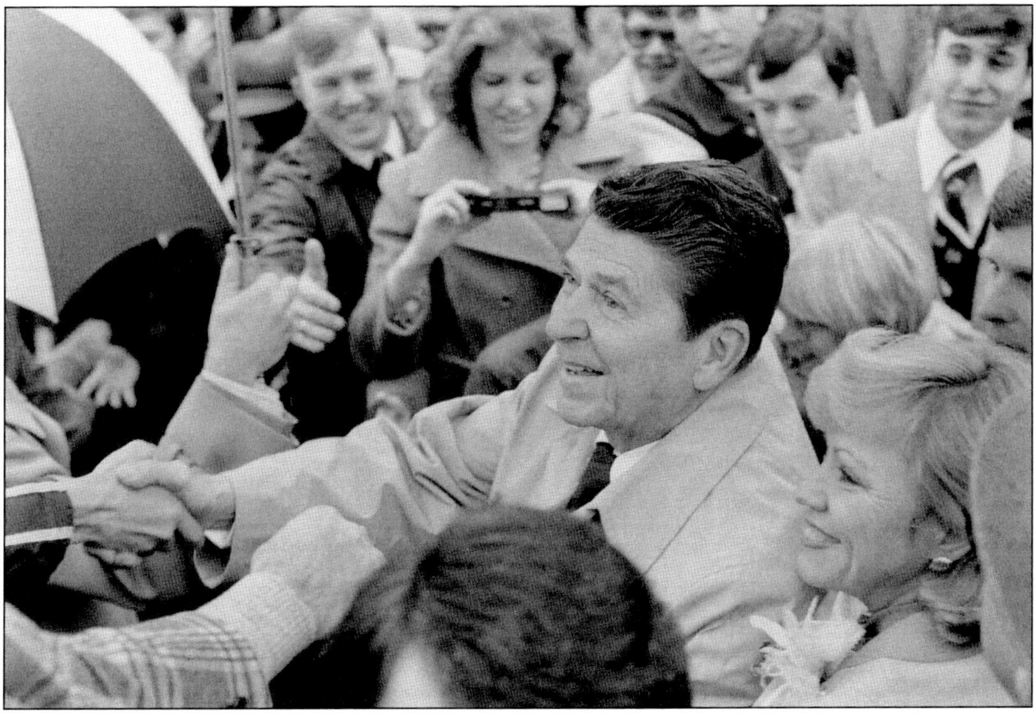

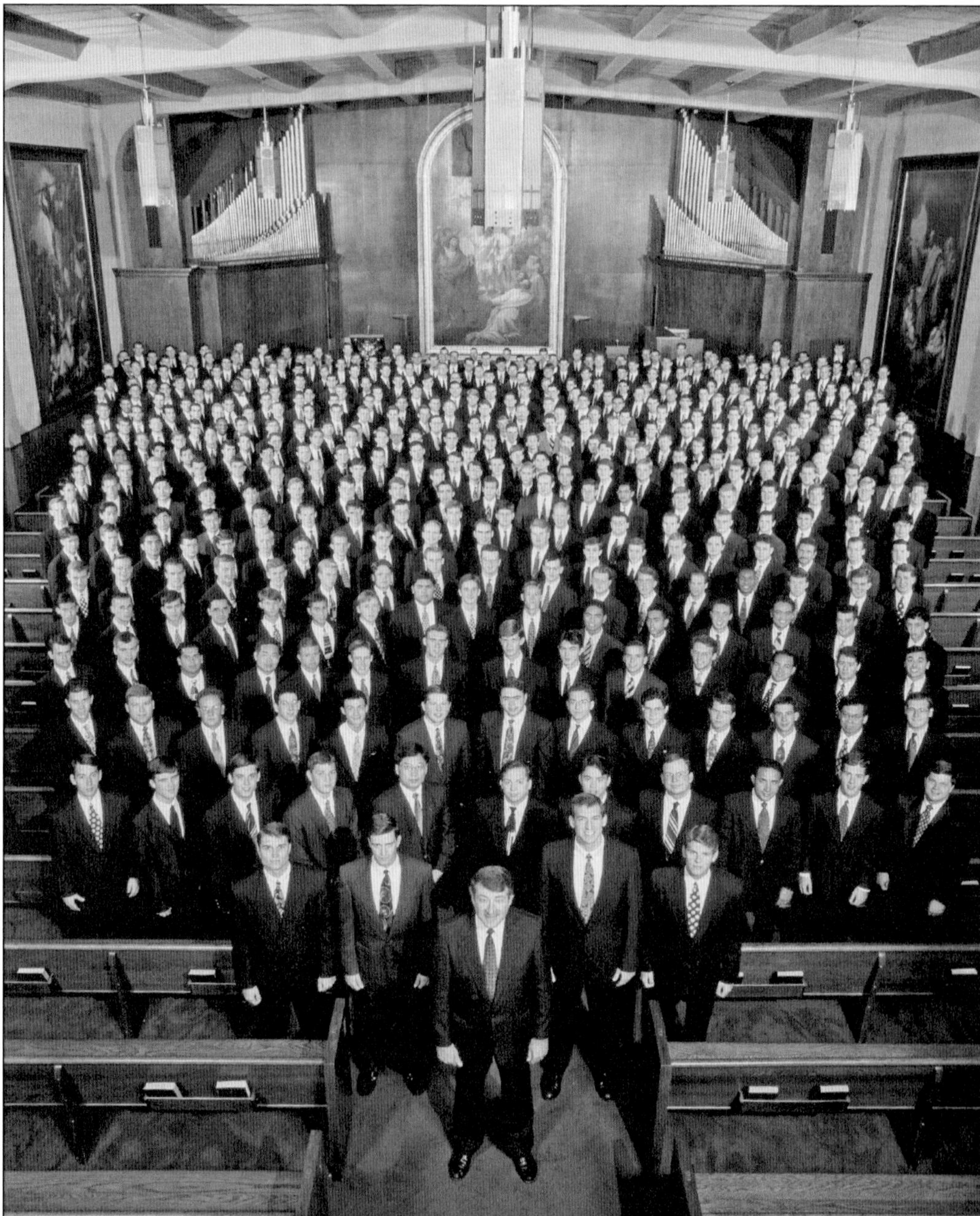

Since BJU's founding in 1927, thousands of young men have been trained for the ministry and mission field in the ministerial classes at the university. Each year, hundreds of men are enrolled in the program. The 1996–1997 class is shown above. Officers of this class were (second row, from left to right) Dave Saxton, president; Matt Collier, vice president; Jonathan Stertzbach, secretary; and Mark McKellen, treasurer.

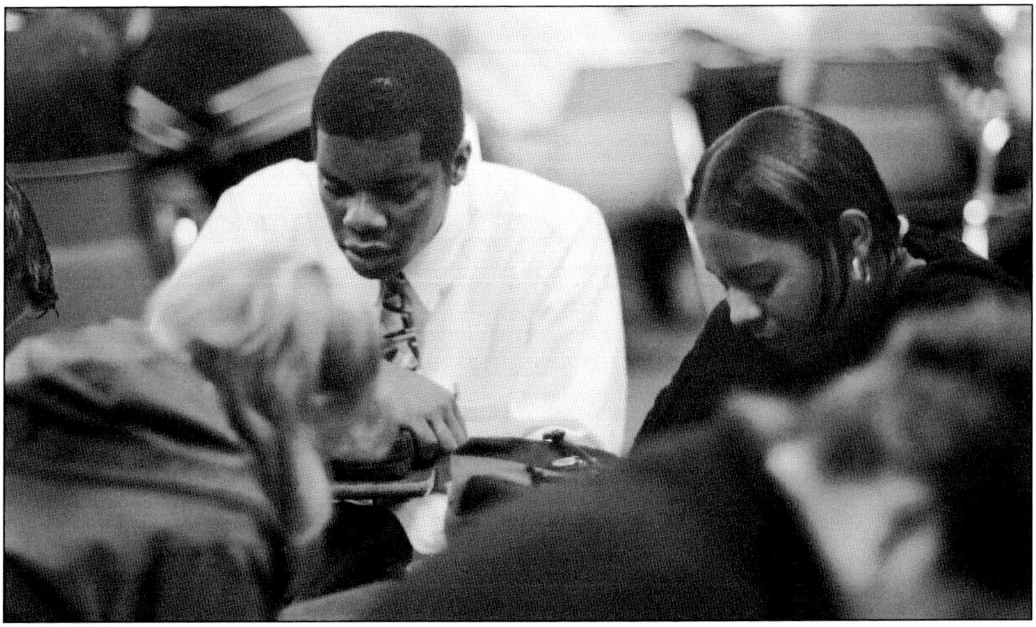

The school's leadership has included prayer in every aspect of campus life: in the residence halls, in the classrooms, in the gymnasium, on the athletic field, and at cultural events, such as plays and concerts. In 1991, the administration chose to set a day apart from the normal classroom activity and dedicate it to prayer. Now the Day of Prayer, which is a distinguishing feature of life at BJU, is held each semester.

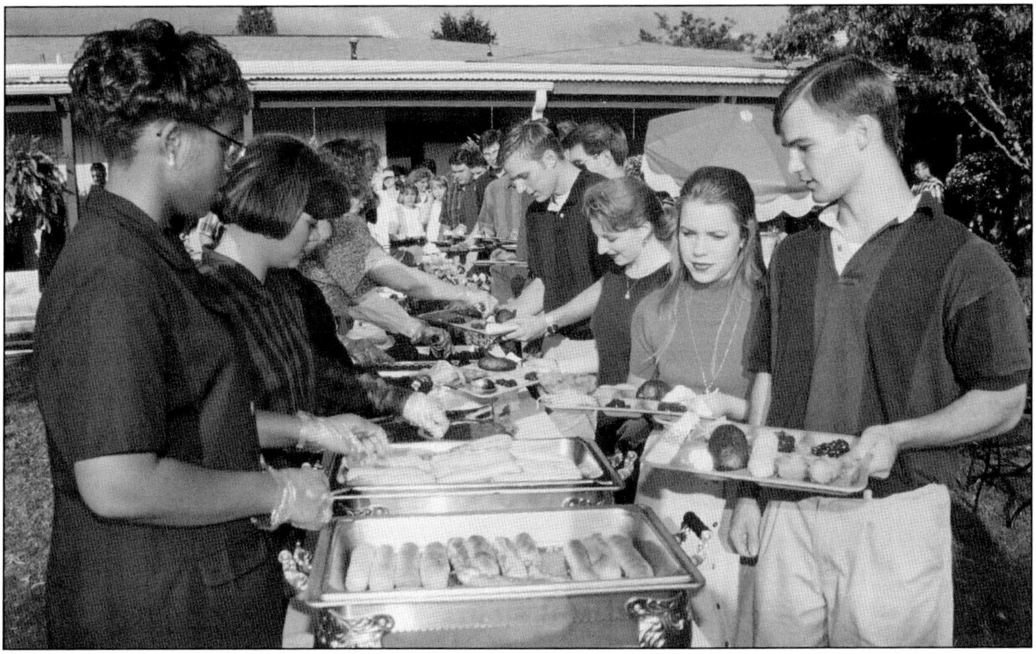

A time BJU seniors always look forward to is the reception that the university president and his wife stage on their lawn for those about to graduate. Good food, good friends, and good manners are always characteristic of this special time. Undergraduate students assist with serving the food during the 1996 reception at the home of Dr. Bob Jones III and Beneth Jones.

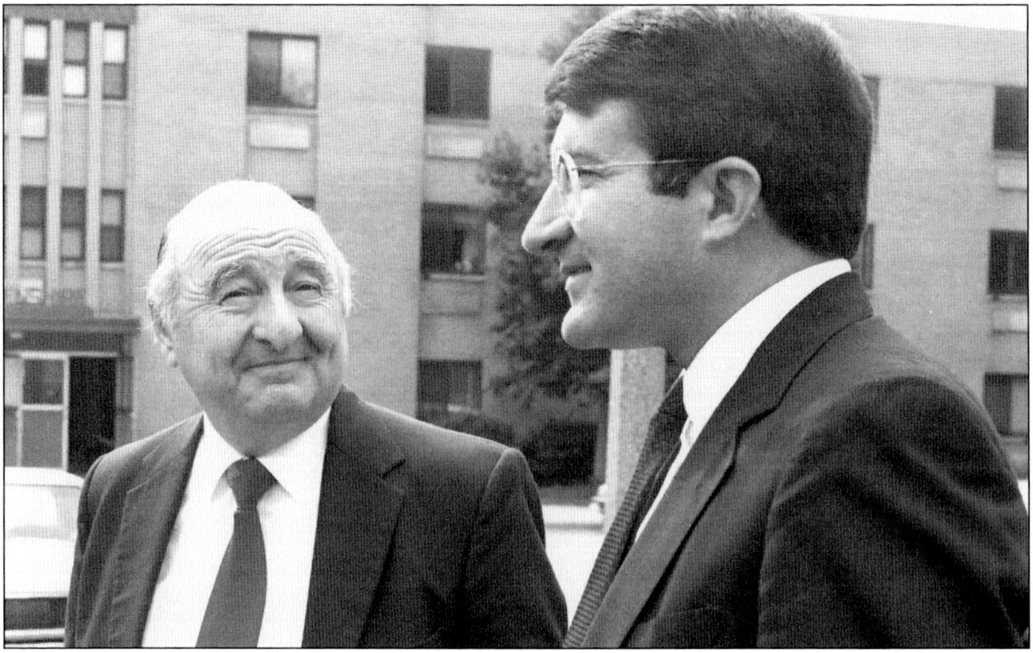

Dr. Richard Rupp (left), director of the Ministerial Training and Extension, and Dr. Bruce McAllister, then his assistant director, talk in front of Brokenshire Residence Hall. Dr. Rupp followed Dr. Gilbert Stenholm, who headed the program from 1965 to 1980 as the program director, and in 1991, McAllister succeeded Dr. Rupp as head of the "preacher boys."

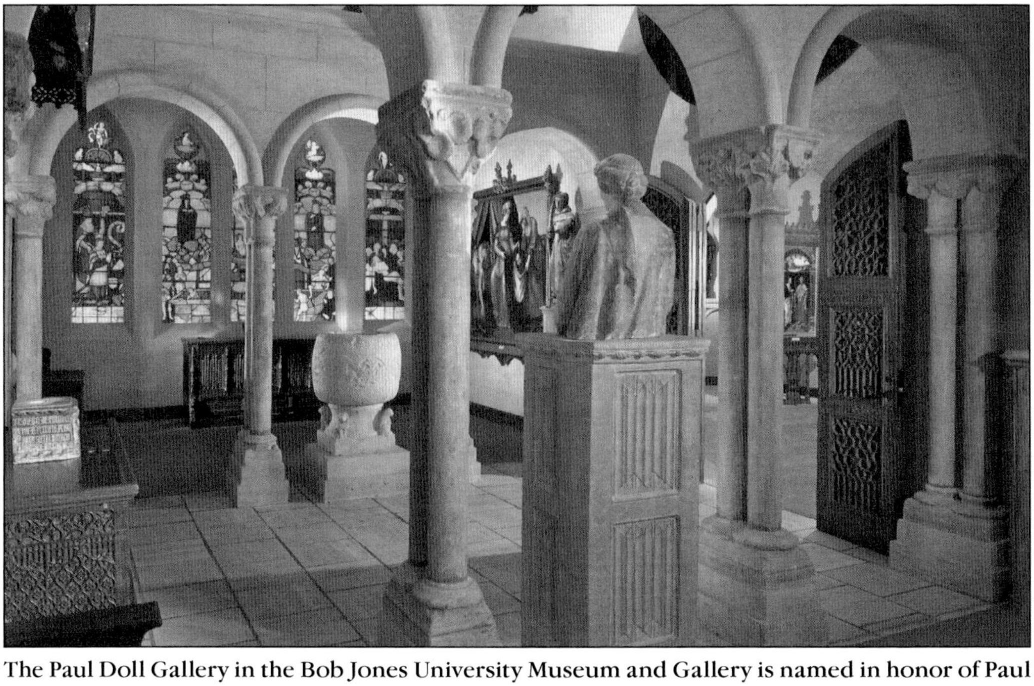

The Paul Doll Gallery in the Bob Jones University Museum and Gallery is named in honor of Paul Doll of Lake Toxaway, North Carolina, a collector of art who has donated a number of items to the university. The cloistered room gallery and stained-glass windows contribute to the attractiveness of the setting for the primarily 12th-century French and Flemish medieval works of art.

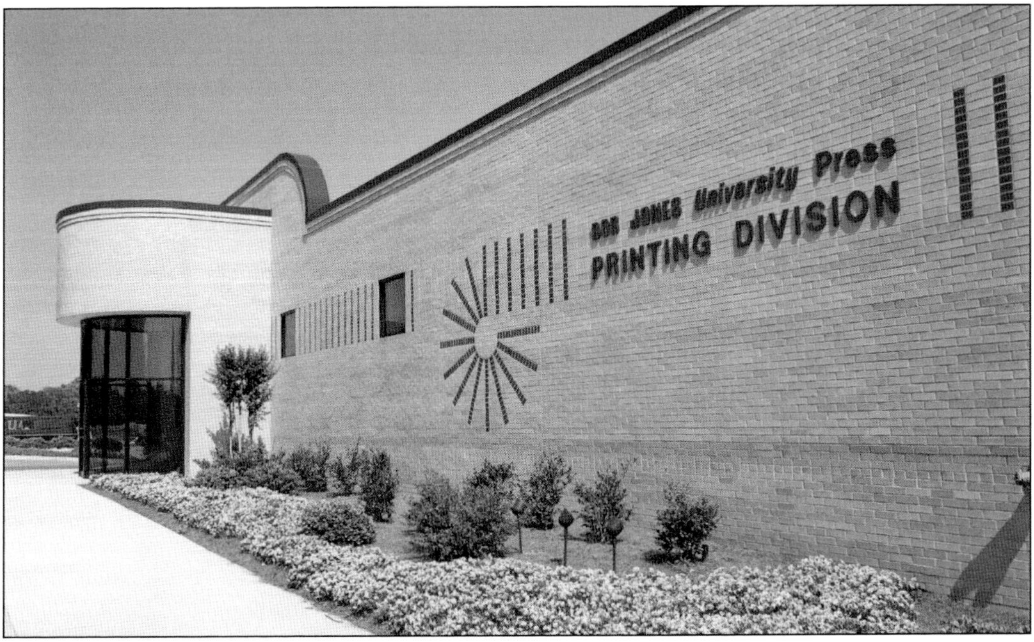

The printing division of the BJU Press is housed in this 100,000-square-foot building. The press room accounts for 40,000 square feet, and the distribution area occupies another 60,000 square feet. Jim Golla, operations manager, said that currently about 675 million pages are printed annually. The building was enlarged in 1995 and has over 70 full-time and part-time employees.

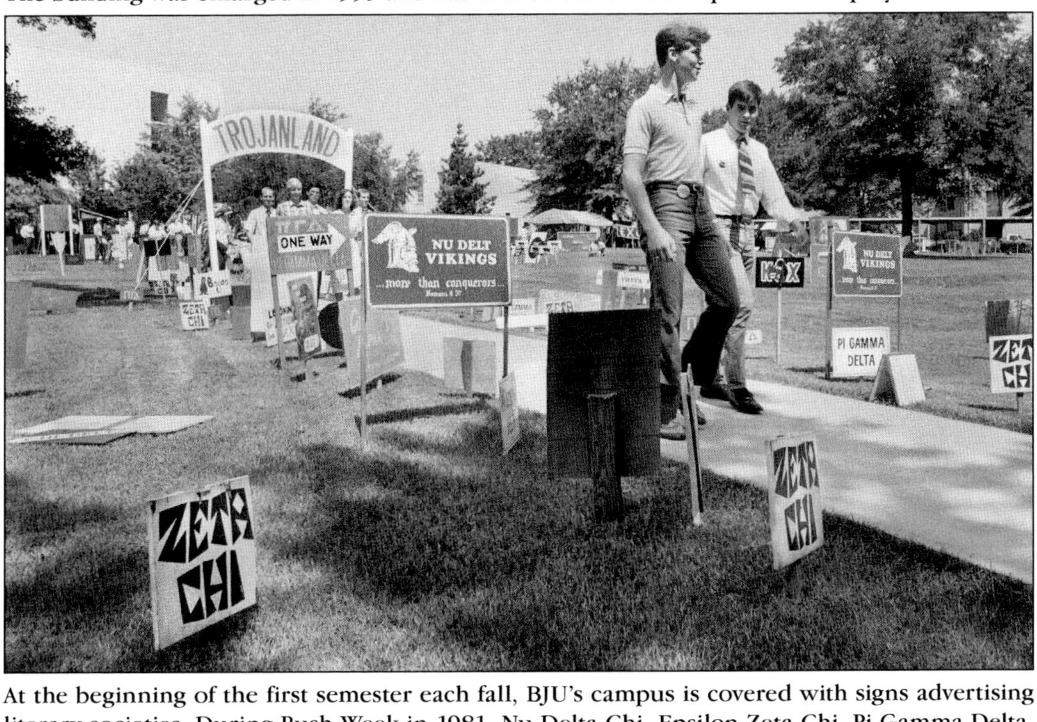

At the beginning of the first semester each fall, BJU's campus is covered with signs advertising literary societies. During Rush Week in 1981, Nu Delta Chi, Epsilon Zeta Chi, Pi Gamma Delta, Alpha Omega Delta, and the other men's societies—as well as all of the women's societies—went all out to lure new students to became a part of their organizations.

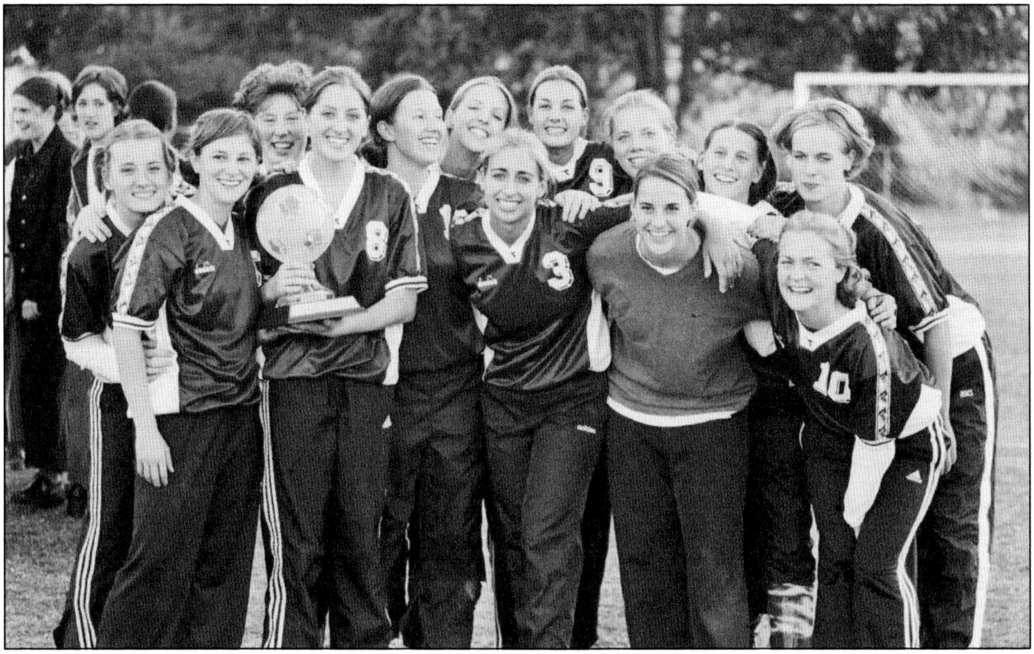

This contingent of 13 women on the Nu Alpha Phi soccer team won the 2006 championship. In addition to spiritual food for the soul, Bob Jones University offers all its students many opportunities for wholesome physical exercise that contribute to healthy bodies.

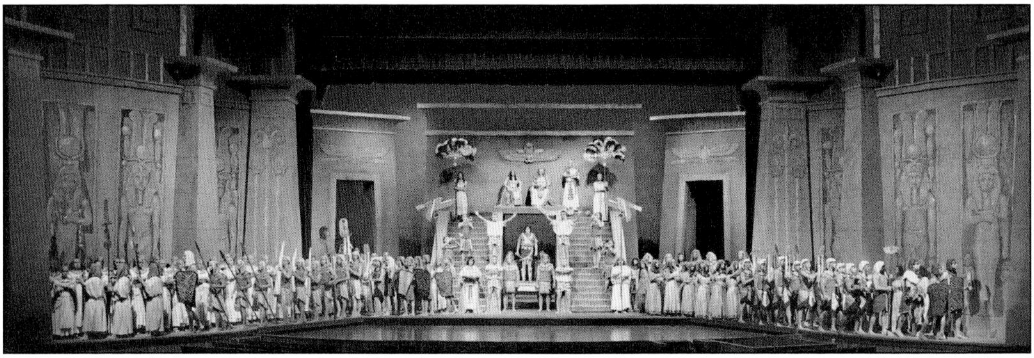

The last time the Bob Jones University Opera Association presented Verdi's *Aida* in March 2000, some 200 people were in the cast—the largest cast of any BJU opera to date. The opera was staged by Dr. William McCauley and conducted by Dr. Dwight Gustafson. In addition to other special guests, the cast included Lily Zhang as Aida. She is a graduate of the Giuseppe Verdi Conservatory of Music in Milan and the China Conservatory of Music in Beijing.

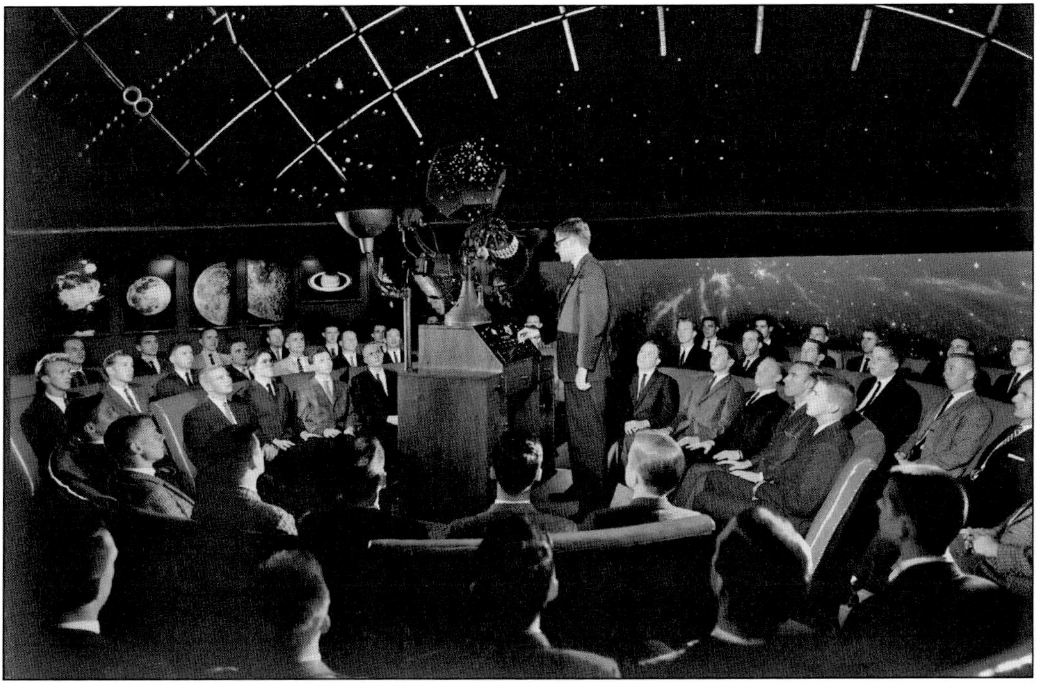

Dr. Stewart Custer, a member of the Bible faculty who has a special interest in astronomy, gives ministerial students a lecture about the constellations in the Howell Memorial Science Building planetarium in the 1960s.

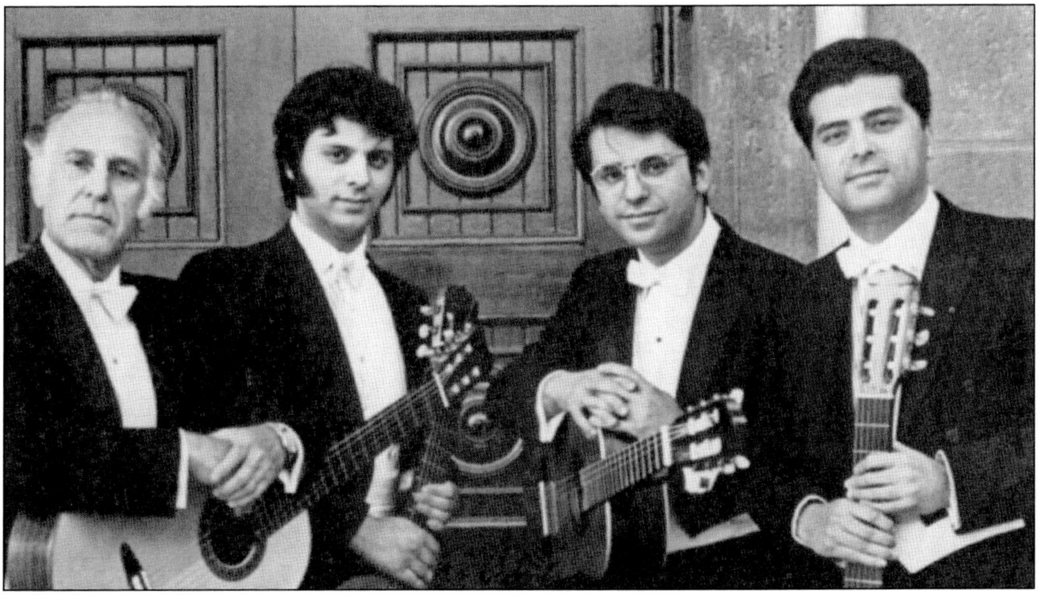

Having first appeared in an Artist Series in 1970, the Romeros returned to Rodeheaver Auditorium in 1978 to please their audience with the finest classical guitar music in the world. Known as "The Royal Family of Guitar," according to their Web site, they are not only the inventors of their musical art form, but they are considered the only classical guitar quartet of real stature in the world. The Romeros originated in Spain under the leadership of Celedonio Romero and encompass three generations of the family.

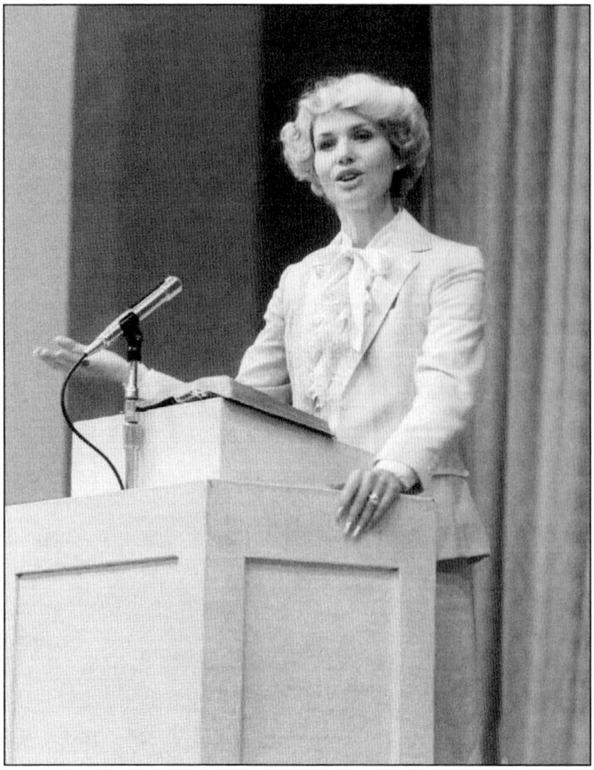

Beneth Jones, wife of Dr. Bob Jones III, speaks to a meeting of the Students' Wives Fellowship in 1988. At this annual meeting, Beneth Jones shared practical information to help students' wives be better helpmeets to their husbands and to experience the blessings of campus life.

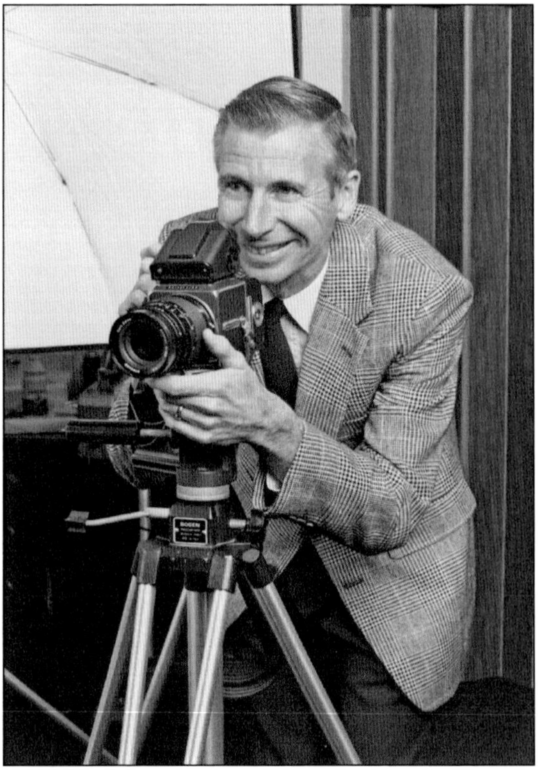

Dan Calnon, who began taking photographs for the *Vintage* as a BJU freshman in 1962, was honored in the 2005 yearbook for his long and faithful service to the university. A familiar face on campus and seldom seen without a camera, Calnon earned both a bachelor's and master's degree in cinema from BJU.

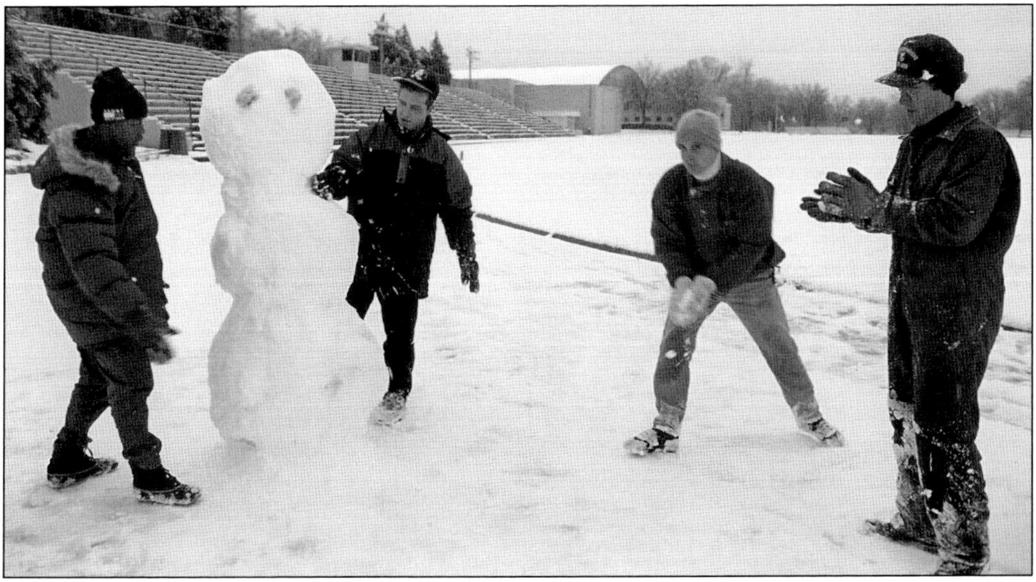

There is something about snow that brings out the "boy" in these students, who could not resist going to the soccer field to build a snowman and throw a few snowballs at each other. This 1997 snowfall was sufficient enough to give both men and women students a bit of winter recreation, which is not too common in the Upstate of South Carolina.

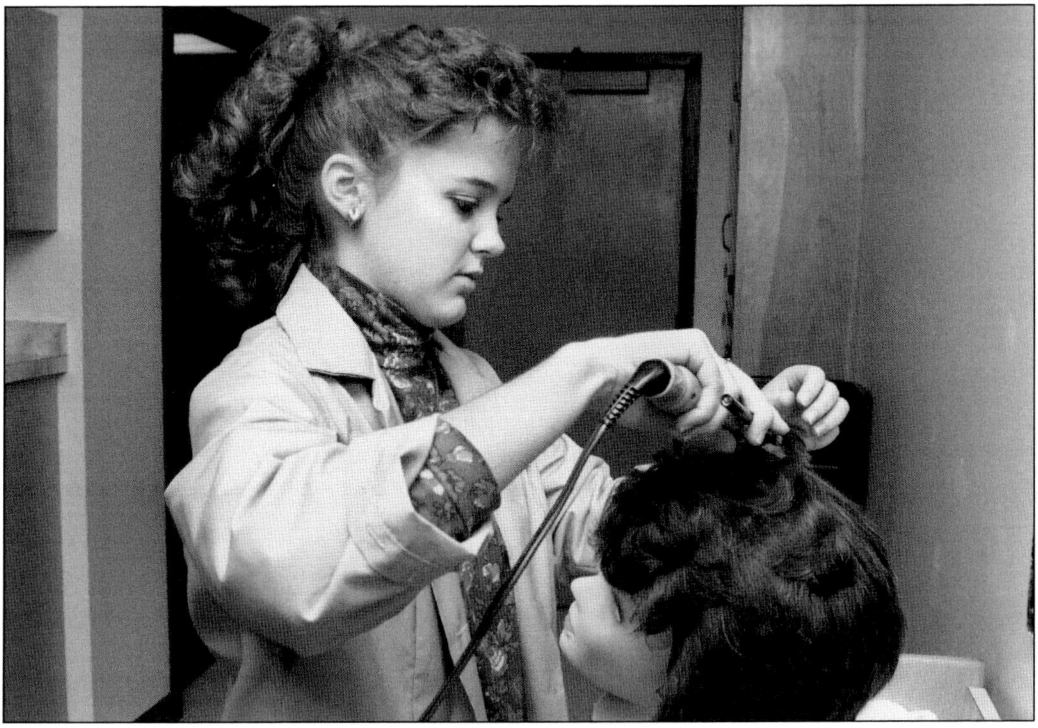

This cosmetology student in a 1984 School of Applied Studies class works on a mannequin's head. She will later practice her art on a live person. Young people enrolled in one- or two-year certificate programs to learn the basics of a trade may apply their work toward receiving an Associate of Science degree and, in some disciplines, a baccalaureate business degree.

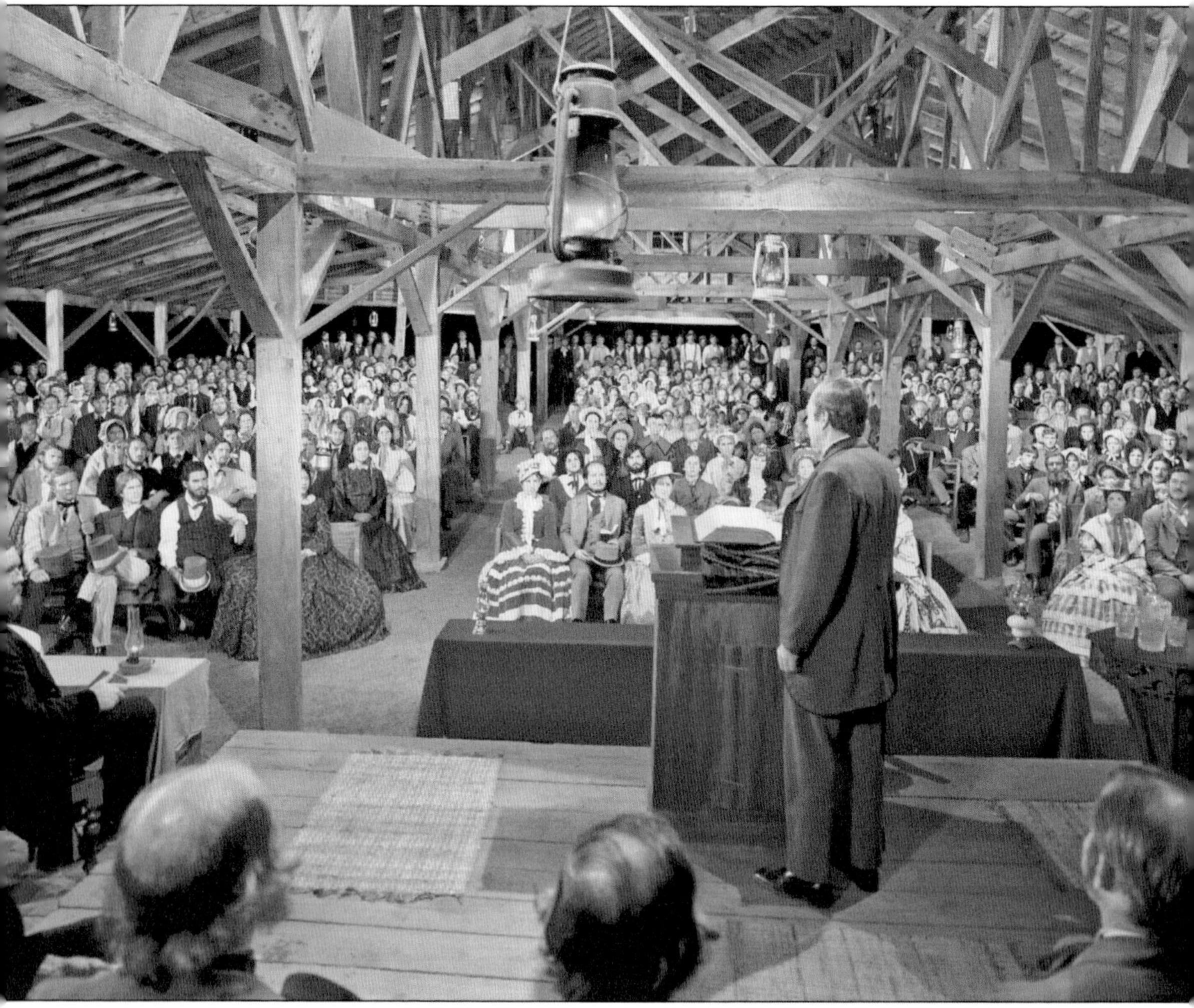

Robert S. Sheffey—a 19th-century circuit-riding preacher—was a rowdy young man who followed some friends to a revival meeting and was converted. He became "a firebrand for God," riding through the Appalachian Mountains to spread the good news that Christ died to save sinners. This 1978 Unusual Films production, *Sheffey*, under the direction of Katherine Stenholm and featuring Harold Kilpatrick as Robert Sheffey, was produced over a period of 32 months and shot in locations in five states: Kentucky, Virginia, North Carolina, South Carolina, and Tennessee. In making the film, BJU cinema students logged more than 63,920 man-hours.

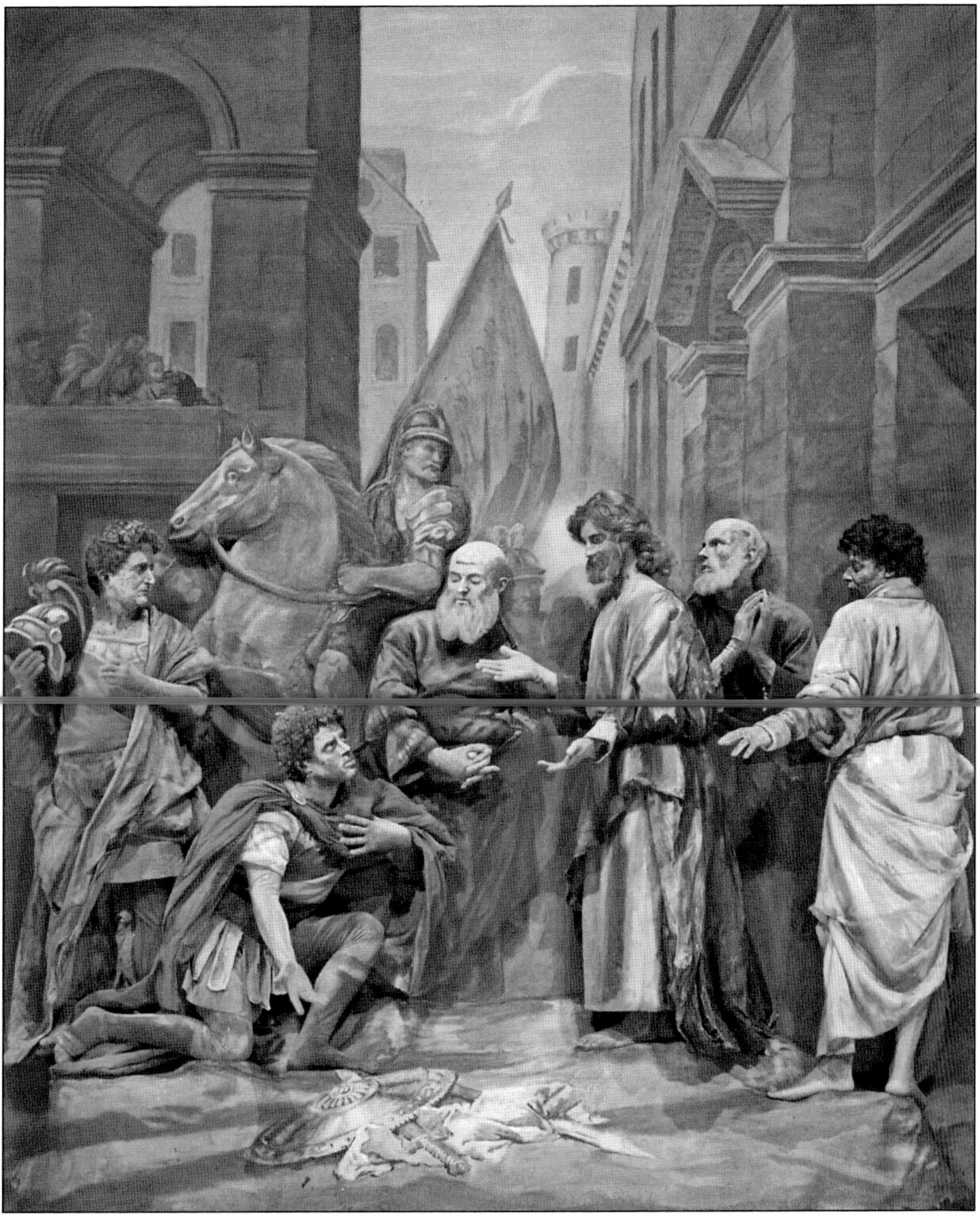

Jean Baptiste Jouvenet's *Christ with Roman Centurion* is one of the many works of art in the Museum and Gallery at Bob Jones University that has been featured in BJU's Living Gallery production. In the production, the set, costumes, makeup, and lighting expand the painting to more than three times its original size. Living Gallery programs in which "art comes to life" consist of an original drama, special music, and breathtaking portrayals of great works of art by live characters—all focused on the life of Christ. Living Gallery is presented each spring.

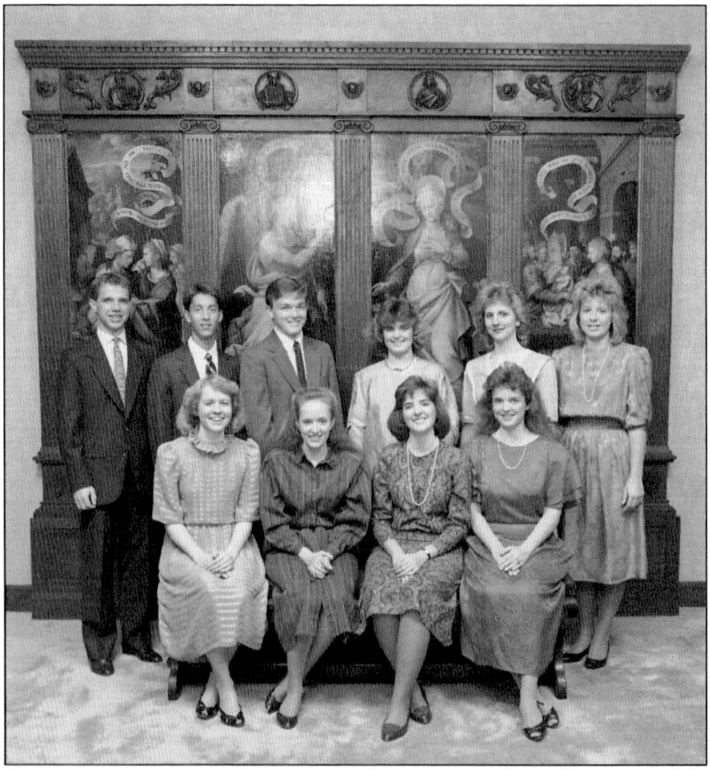

In the 1987–1988 school year, Vol. I, No. 1, of the student newspaper, the *Collegian*, was distributed. This group of journalism students, led by editor Bob Jones IV (standing on the left) was the first year's staff. Others on the staff were John Matthews, business manager (today BJU's vice president for finance); Elizabeth Lyall, reporter; John Boone, sports; Kathleen Ramsey, copy editor; Carol Childress, photographer; Denise Hughes, bulletin board; Kristin Hosaflook, secretary; Vicki Holston, features; and Lena Skistimas, staff writer.

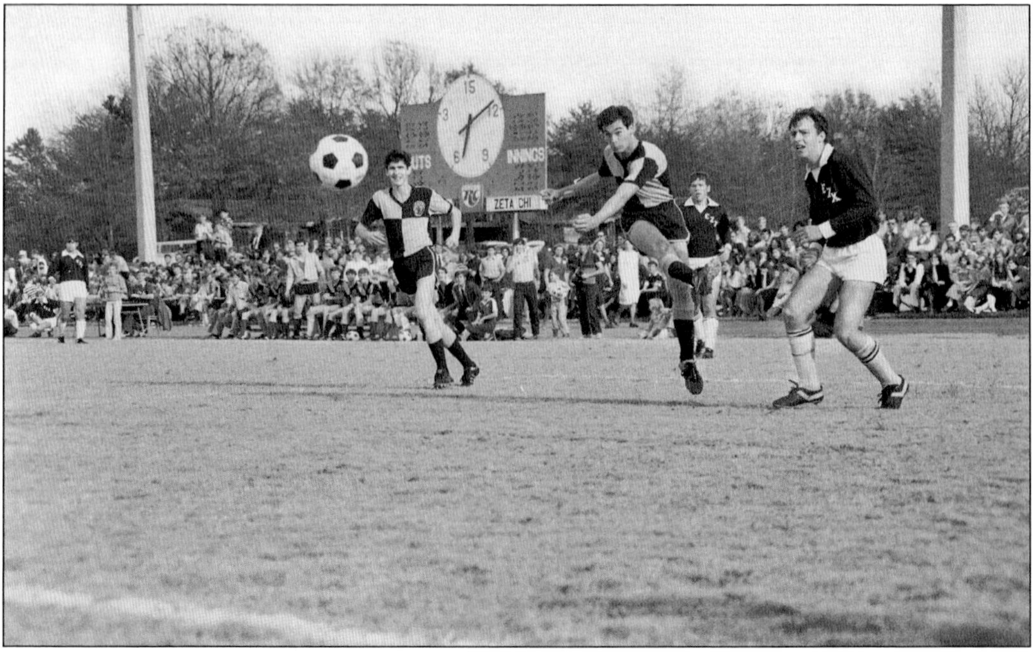

Alpha Omega Delta's Keith Pratt goes high into the air as he gives the ball a vigorous boot toward the cage in Omega's 3-1 victory over Epsilon Zeta Chi in the 1980 Turkey Bowl. Dick Stratton, now the president of Clearwater Christian College in Tampa Bay, Florida, kicked the first Omega goal of the second half and was given the Most Valuable Player award.

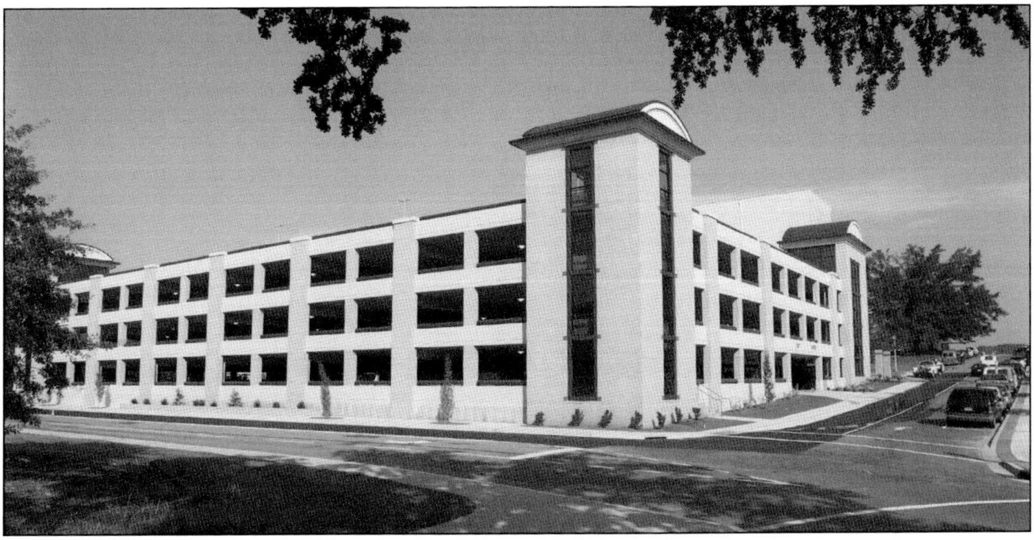

A 400-car parking garage greeted students and faculty when the new school year started in August 2007. Located directly behind Rodeheaver Auditorium, the facility has made parking on campus much easier than before. Its proximity to Rodeheaver and Founder's Memorial Amphitorium is a great help to visitors who come on campus for Artists Series, church services, and other events held in either of the two auditoriums.

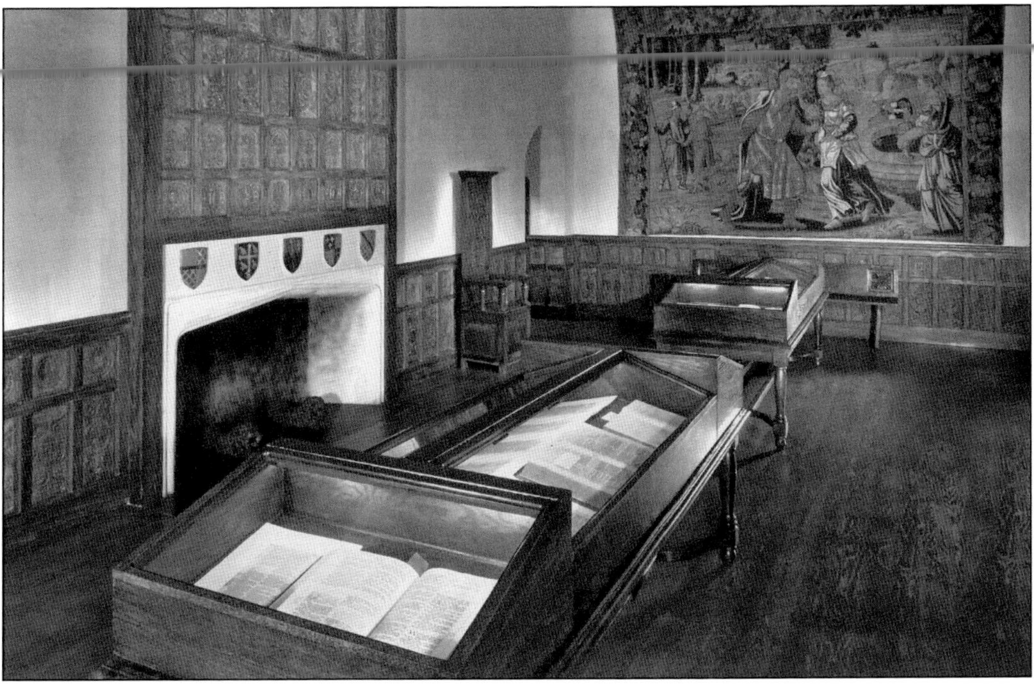

With the permission of the dean and chapter of Westminster Abbey, the university has replicated the Jerusalem Chamber, used in 1611 by the translators of the King James Bible. Since the original Jerusalem Chamber in London serves as the official reception room for the dean of Westminster, it is not open to tourists. The BJU Jerusalem Chamber, open to visitors, serves as the display area for the university's collection of rare Bibles. Dixie Baptist Church in Clarkston, Michigan, pastored by Dr. Paul Vanaman, provided funds for its construction in the J. S. Mack Library.

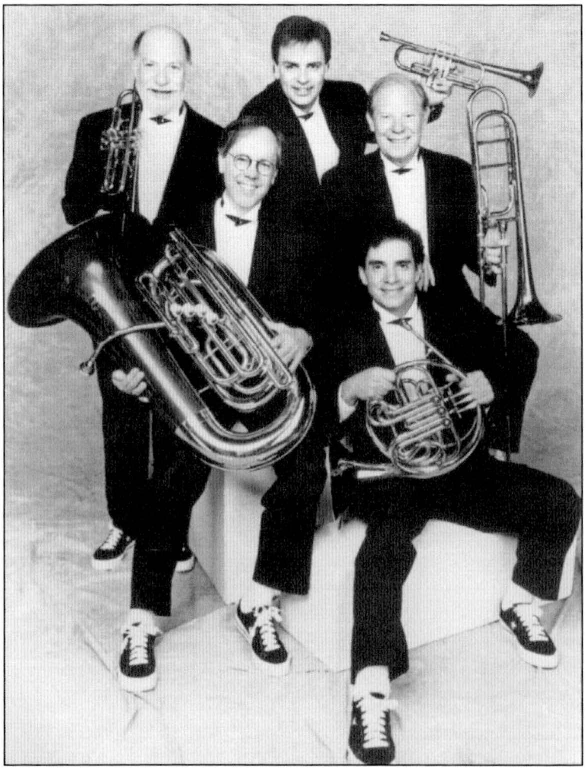

Much to the delight of the audience in a 1998 Artist Series, the performance of the sneaker-clad Canadian Brass left everyone wanting more. The world-renowned brass ensemble at that time was in its 26th year. Writing about the Canadian Brass, the *Washington Post* said, "These are the men who put brass music on the map; with their unbeatable blend of virtuosity, spontaneity, and humor, they brighten the rosters of concert halls, international festivals, and orchestra series throughout the world." The BJU audience agreed.

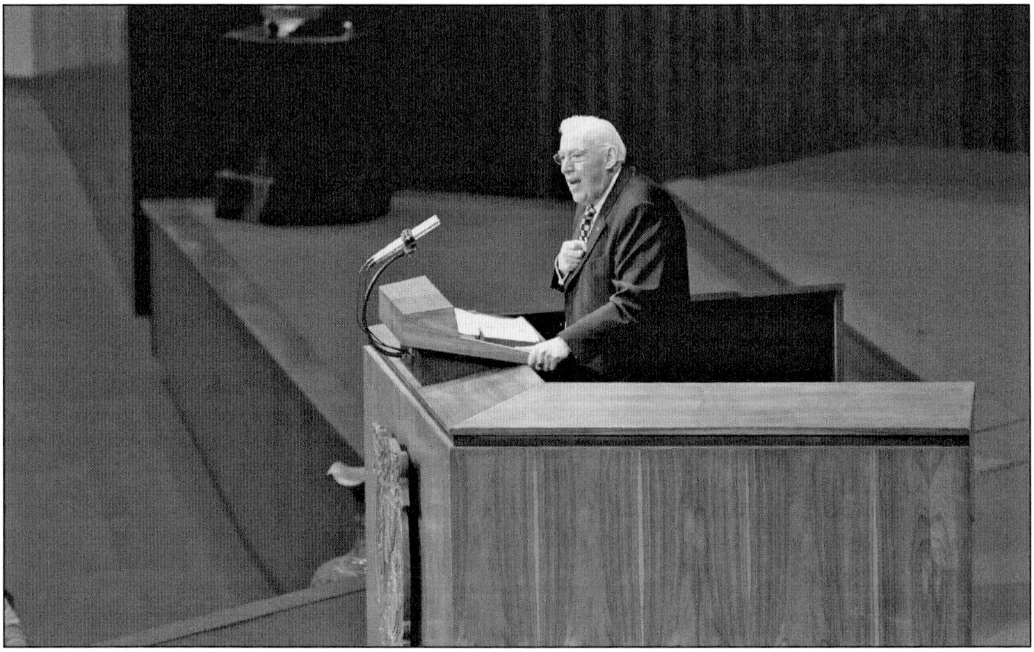

Dr. Ian Paisley of Belfast, Ireland, has been a frequent Bible Conference speaker at BJU over many years. Speaking at the dedication of Founder's Memorial Auditorium in 1973, Dr. Paisley said that Dr. Bob Jones Sr. was as important in American church history as John Calvin and John Knox were in European church history.

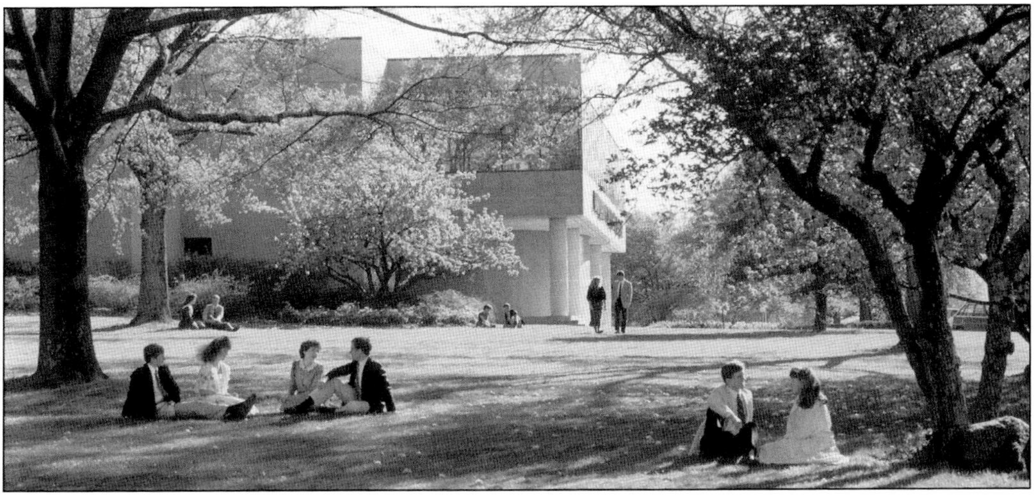

Springtime Bible Conference can be a beautiful time of year in South Carolina, with flowering trees and shrubs in bloom and warm sunshine that invites friends to sit on the grass and visit near the Student Center on the front campus. Classes are set aside for the week, and visitors and alumni come from all over the country to enjoy the special speakers and other campus activities.

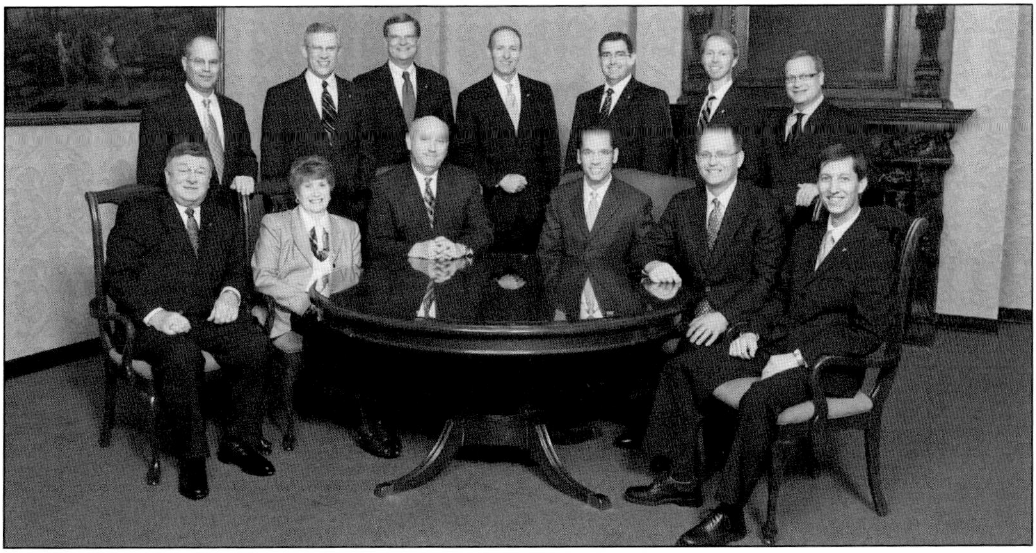

In view of the large growth and expansion of the university, in May 2004, Dr. Bob Jones III formed the president's administrative cabinet, putting in place a clearly delineated corporate structure that facilitates a strong management focus on key operations. The cabinet meets with the president weekly to conduct the university's operational business. Members of the 2007–2008 cabinet include, from left to right, (seated) Dr. Bob Wood, executive vice president emeritus; Carol Keirstead, chief communications officer; Alan Carper, executive vice president and chief operations officer; Dr. Stephen Jones, president and CEO; Dr. Gary Weier, vice president for administration and chief administrative oversight officer; and John Matthews, vice president for finance and chief financial officer; (standing) Dr. David Fisher, provost and chief academic officer; Jim Berg, dean of students and chief student life officer; Jeff Hargraves, chief constituency relations officer; Mark Kopp, chief facilities management officer; Tim Morgan, chief technology and publication officer; Brent Honshell, chief ancillary services officer; and James Cook, chief human resource officer.

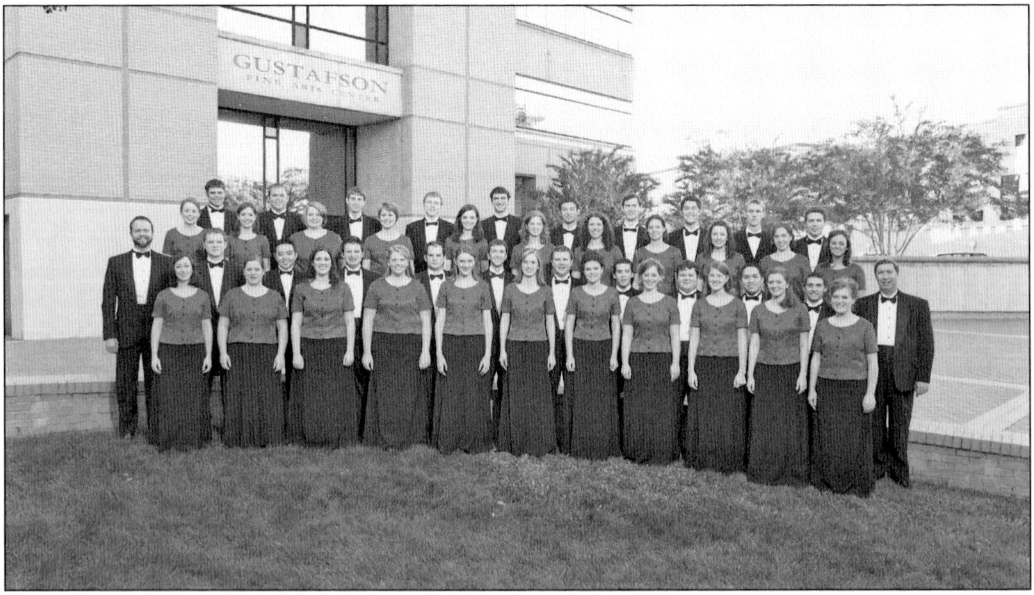

The 50-member 2007 University Concert Choir, standing in front of the Gustafson Fine Arts Center, is one of eight choirs in the BJU choral program. Interested students audition and are placed in choirs according to their classification and ability. The other seven choirs are University Singers, Conductor's Chorus, College Choir, Lyric Choir, Men's Glee Club, University Chorale, and University Chamber Singers. Duane Ream (second row, far right) was the pianist for the Concert Choir, and Dr. Christopher Gilliam (second row, far left) was the conductor.

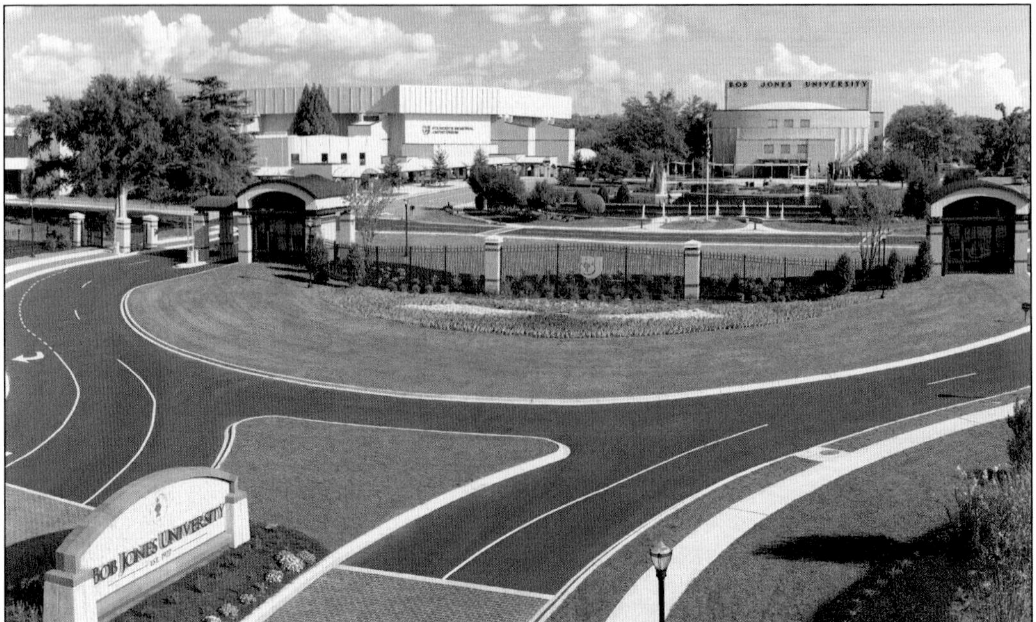

Construction crews worked diligently during the weeks prior to the opening of the 2007–2008 school year to build this new entrance to the front campus on Wade Hampton Boulevard. The new sign, the twin buildings of the Welcome Center, and the carefully planned landscaping form a warm welcome mat for visitors.

Five

Outreaches

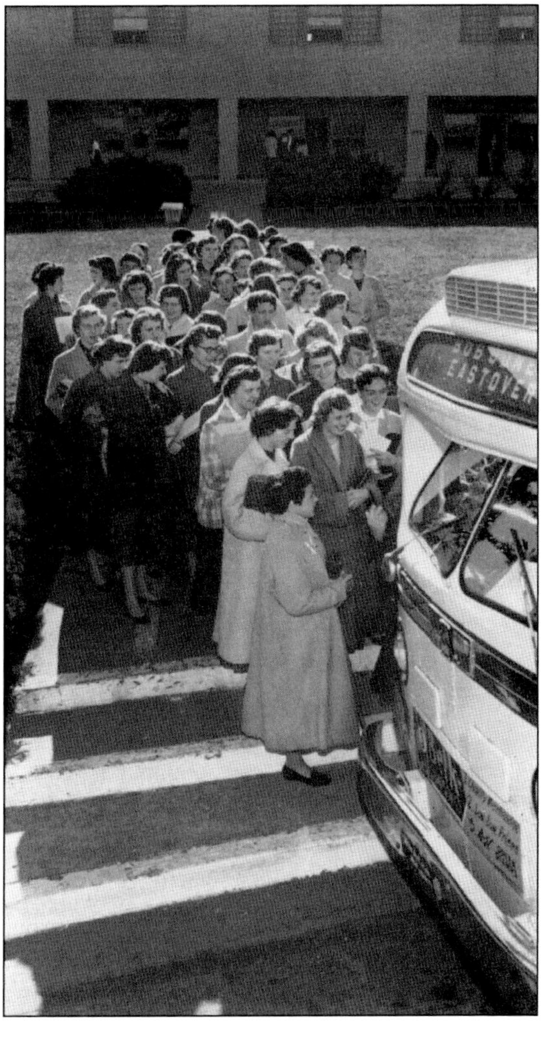

Members of the 1956 Life Service Band board a city bus to conduct child evangelism. Under the motto "Workers Together With Him," the group sought to win souls for Christ by visiting hospital patients, distributing tracts, conducting youth meetings, holding Bible studies groups, and giving personal witness. In the mid-1950s, approximately 500 girls engaged in this outreach throughout Greenville and surrounding counties each week, conducting more than 130 classes and clubs.

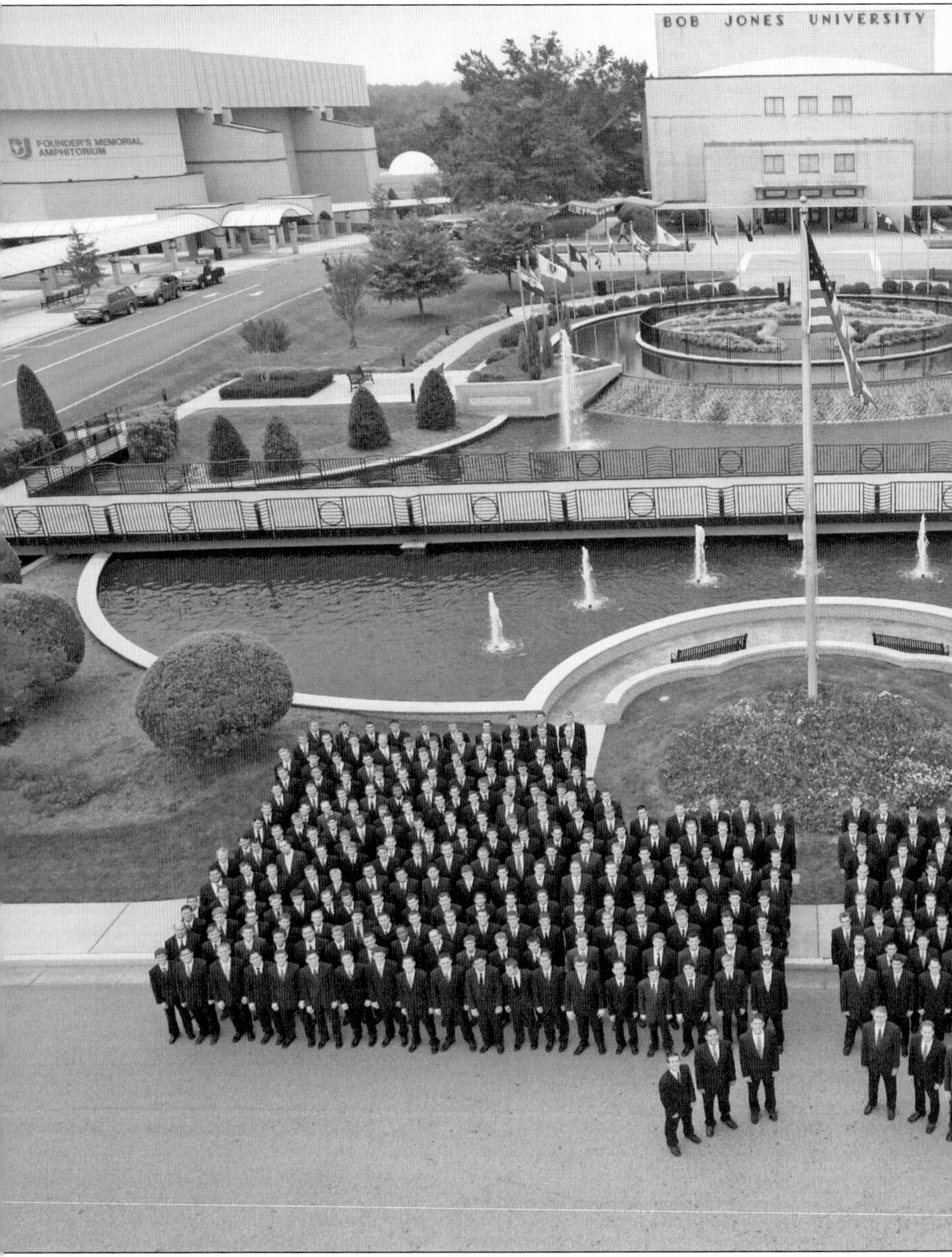
BOB JONES UNIVERSITY
FOUNDER'S MEMORIAL AMPHITORIUM

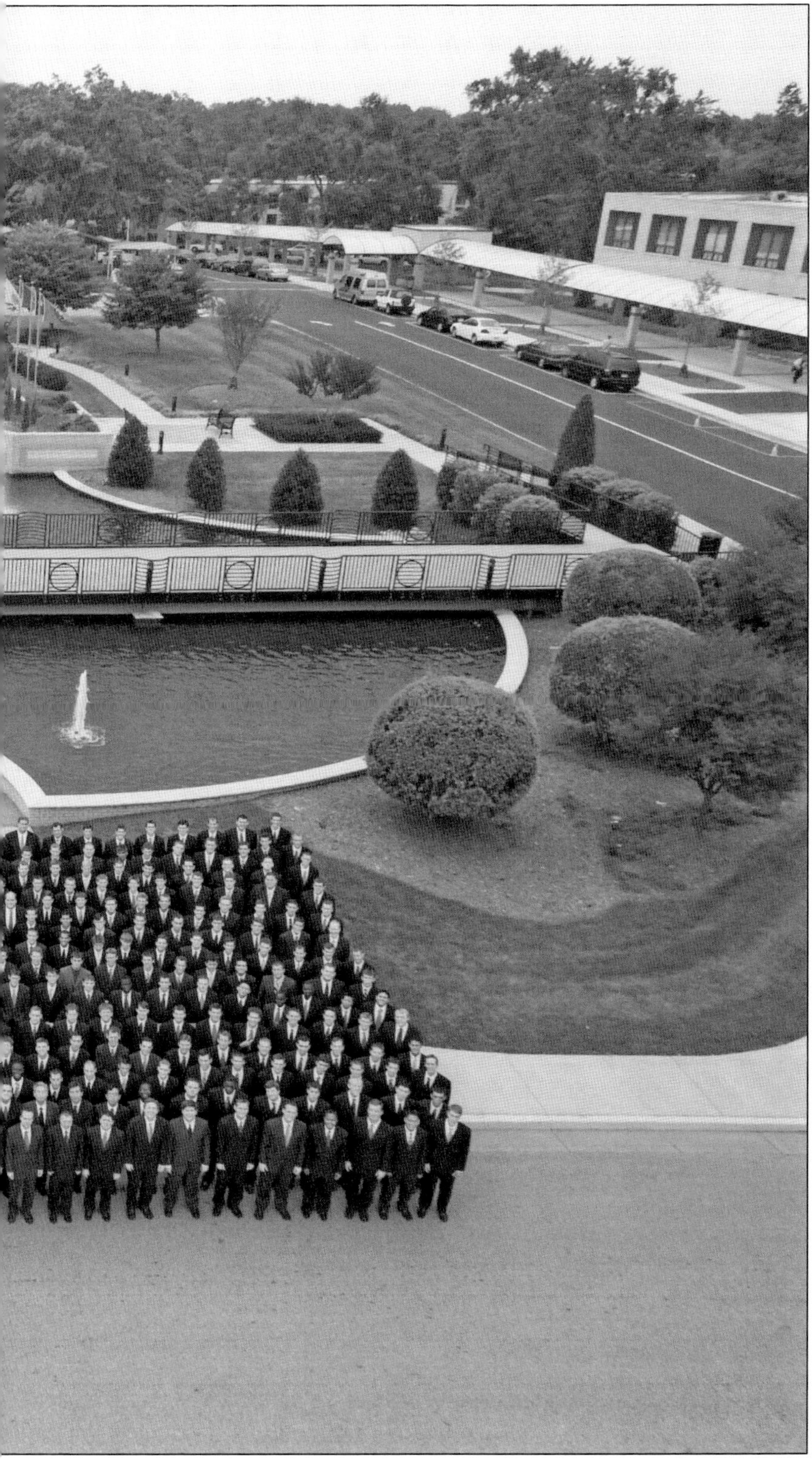

About 500 strong, the 2007 Ministerial Class is under the instruction of experienced teachers and pastors who share the burden of the founder, Dr. Bob Jones Sr., whose evangelistic goals are expressed in the group's theme song: "Souls for Jesus is our battle cry; souls for Jesus we'll fight until we die. We never will give in, while souls are lost in sin. Souls for Jesus is our battle cry." While they study doctrine in other classes, the men receive practical training in church operation in the Ministerial Class. These men, whom the founder always referred to as his "preacher boys," fan out all over the Southeast on weekends on extension ministries that are aimed at winning people to the Lord Jesus Christ. The 2007 officers were Joshua Hurst, president; Thomas McAvoy, vice president; David Cortes-Plata, treasurer; and Jonathan Schnur, secretary.

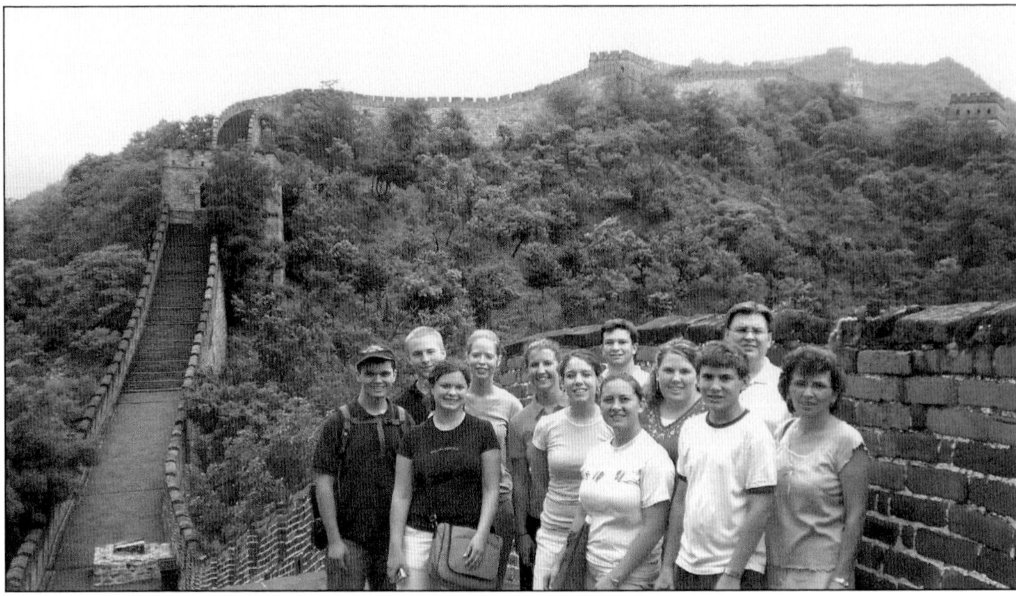

China's Great Wall forms the backdrop for the 2006 China Mission Team. Led by Mark Vowels Sr., BJU's director of missions, the team spent eight weeks in Shanghai and Datong, China, teaching English—with the goal of winning people to Christ. From left to right are Matthew Skaggs, Robert Chernow, Renee Payne, Julia Nevens, Kasey Wilson, Adriana Murias, Emerald Haiger, Patrick Tilson, Carissa Vowels, Mark Vowels Jr., Mark Vowels Sr., and Cary Vowels.

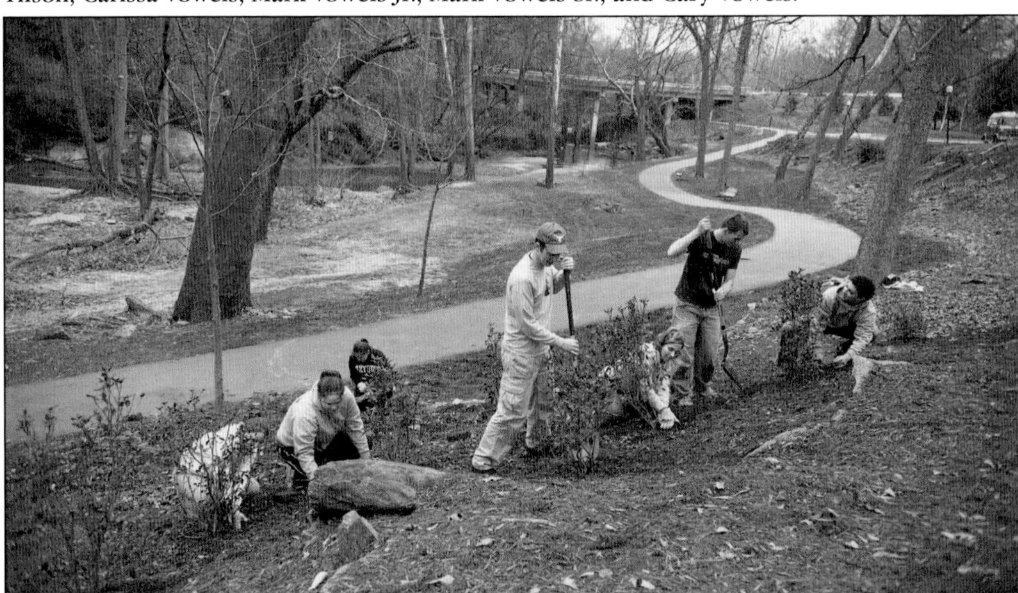

The Community Service Council (CSC), founded in 1986 by Dr. Bob Jones III, each year channels hundreds of volunteering BJU students into the city of Greenville to perform community service projects. From removing litter from the Reedy River, to cleaning up and beautifying local parks, from taking part in projects, to aid disabled children or senior citizens, to serving meals at the downtown rescue mission, the CSC is an active group that believes civic responsibility is important if one is to give a good witness for Christ.

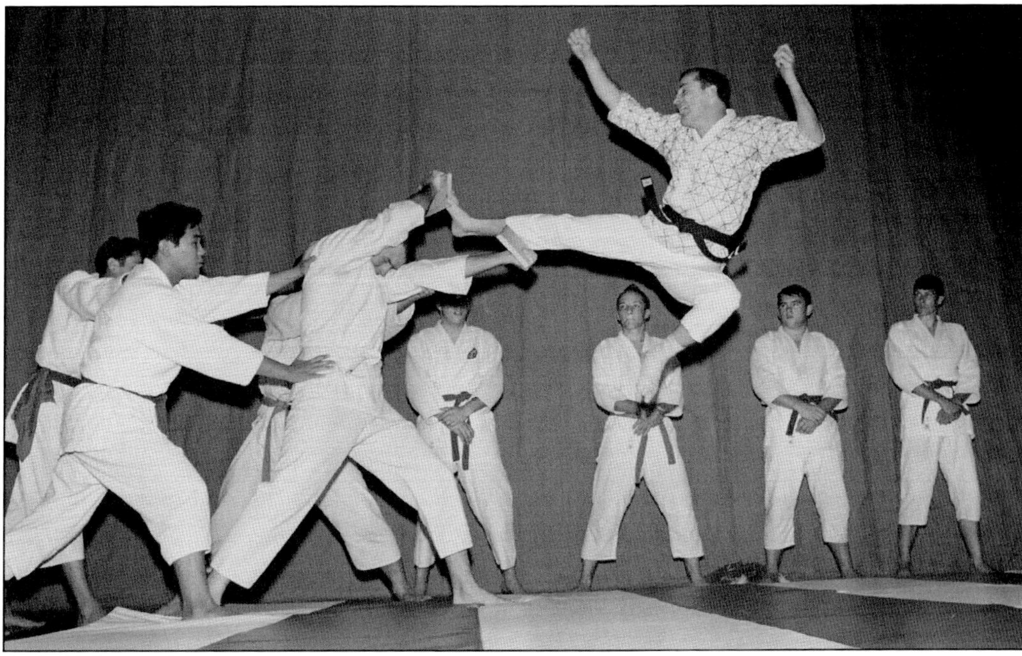

BJU students use various talents to get people into an audience where they can hear the good news that Jesus saves. Using the art of judo, the 1969 university "Judo Gentlemen" entertained young people and oldsters alike so they could have an opportunity to tell the audience what Jesus Christ means to them.

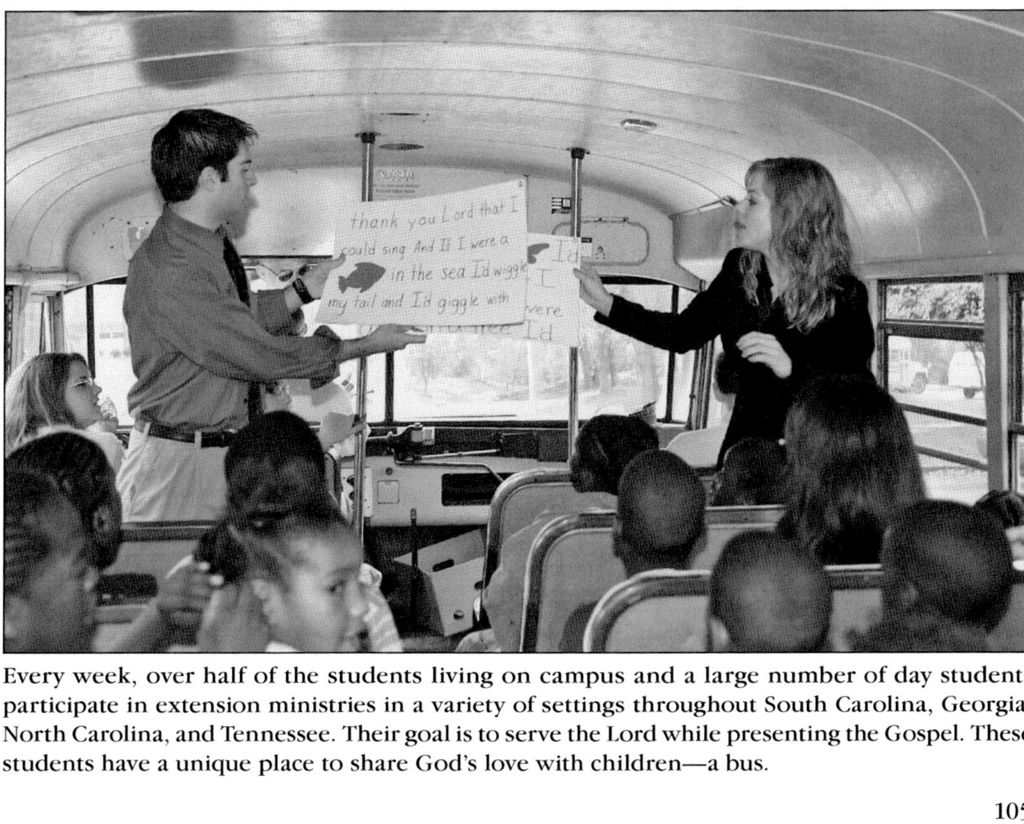

Every week, over half of the students living on campus and a large number of day students participate in extension ministries in a variety of settings throughout South Carolina, Georgia, North Carolina, and Tennessee. Their goal is to serve the Lord while presenting the Gospel. These students have a unique place to share God's love with children—a bus.

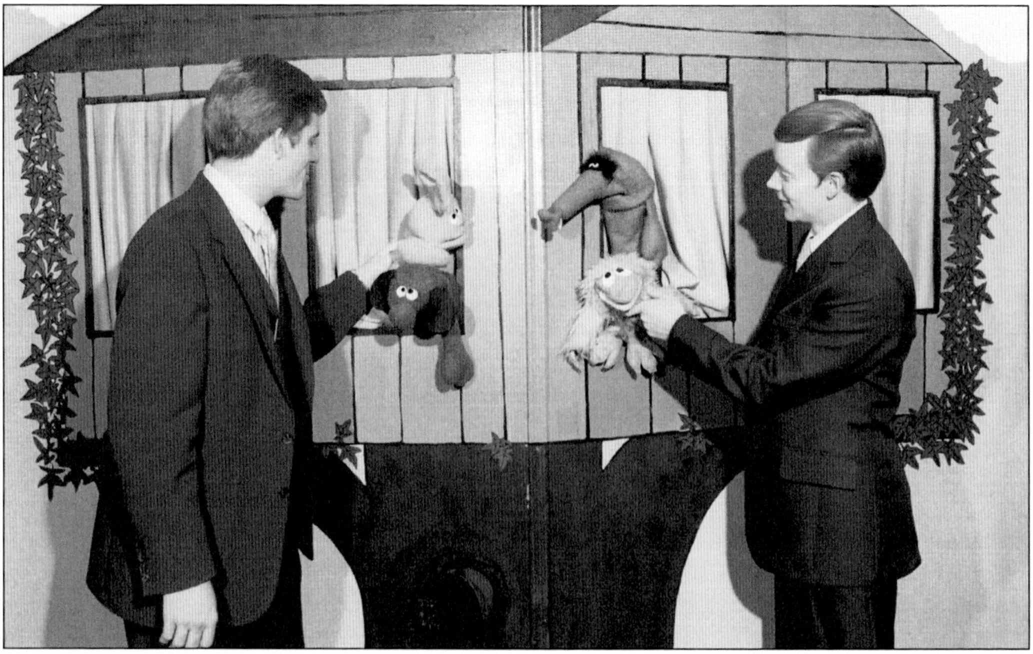

The 1981 Basilean literary society's traveling puppet team members had a sure way of delighting children while at the same time making the Gospel plain to them. They knew that winning children to the Lord is pleasing to Christ, who said, "Suffer little children to come unto me; for of such is the kingdom of Heaven."

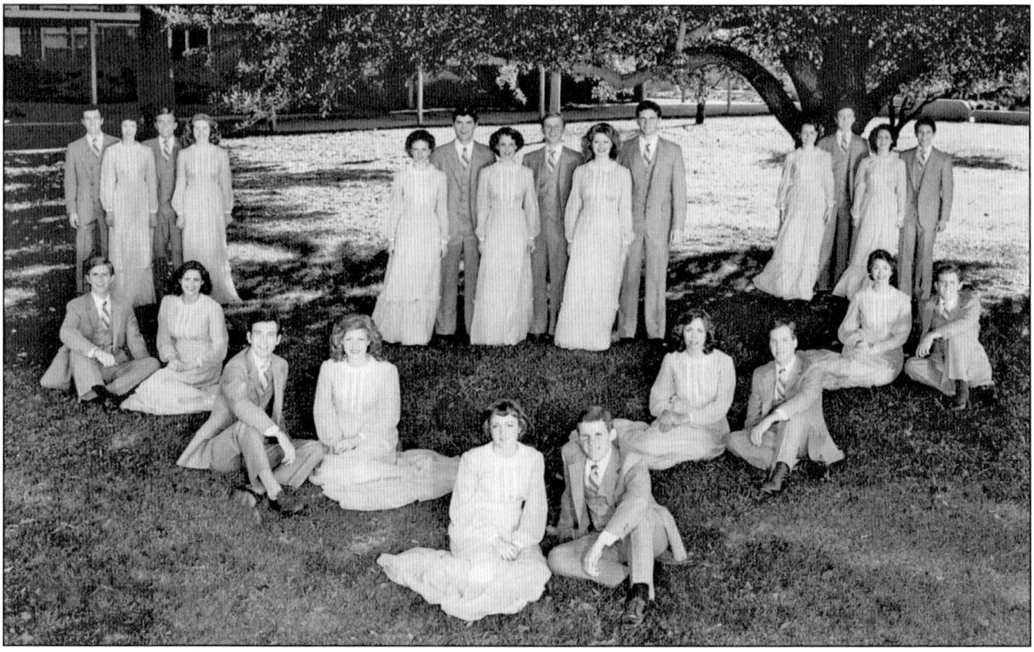

The 1980 *Show My People* television choir blessed many listeners with Christ-centered music. The program first aired nationally in 1976 and continued for 10 years. Many of the taping sessions were held outside on the BJU campus. The programs featured interviews, special musical ensembles, testimonies of students and faculty, and a message from God's Word by Dr. Bob Jones III.

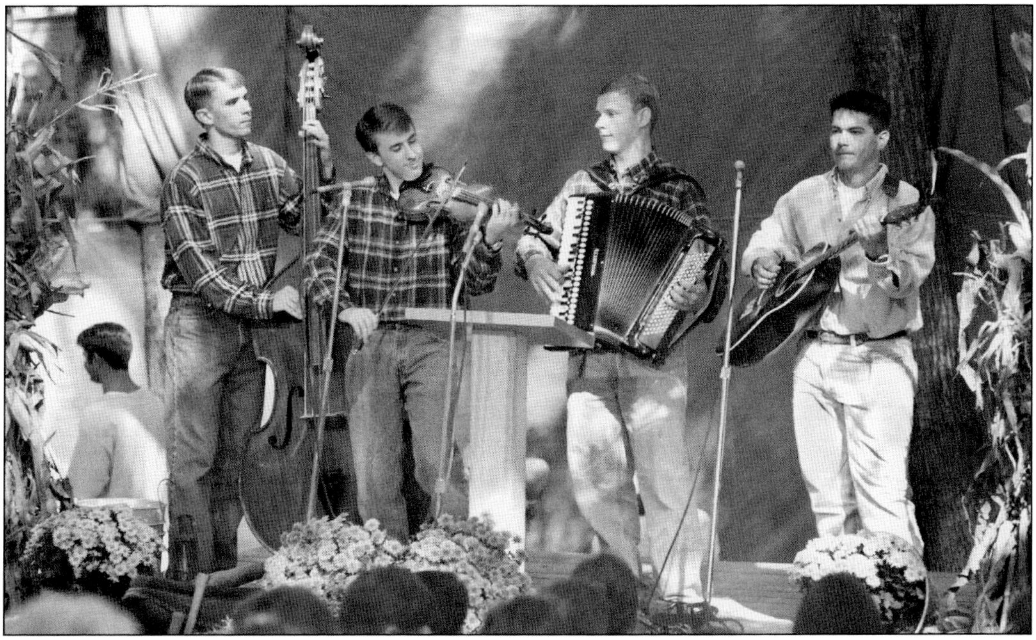

This musical group (above), manning three strings and an accordion, played at the 1998 Farm Fest, an annual occurrence since 1987. In 1986, Dr. Bob Jones III spoke at a Harvest Rally in Connersville, Indiana, where he caught the vision for a BJU Farm Fest ministry. Since 1987, BJU has sponsored a Farm Fest for area teens each fall. Scores of students help plan, prepare the food, and entertain the approximately 2,000 young people from across the Southeast who attend each year. Three Gospel messages are presented throughout the day, and many young people make decisions for the Lord. In the photograph below, young people attending the 2004 Farm Fest enjoy their lunch picnic-style on the grass.

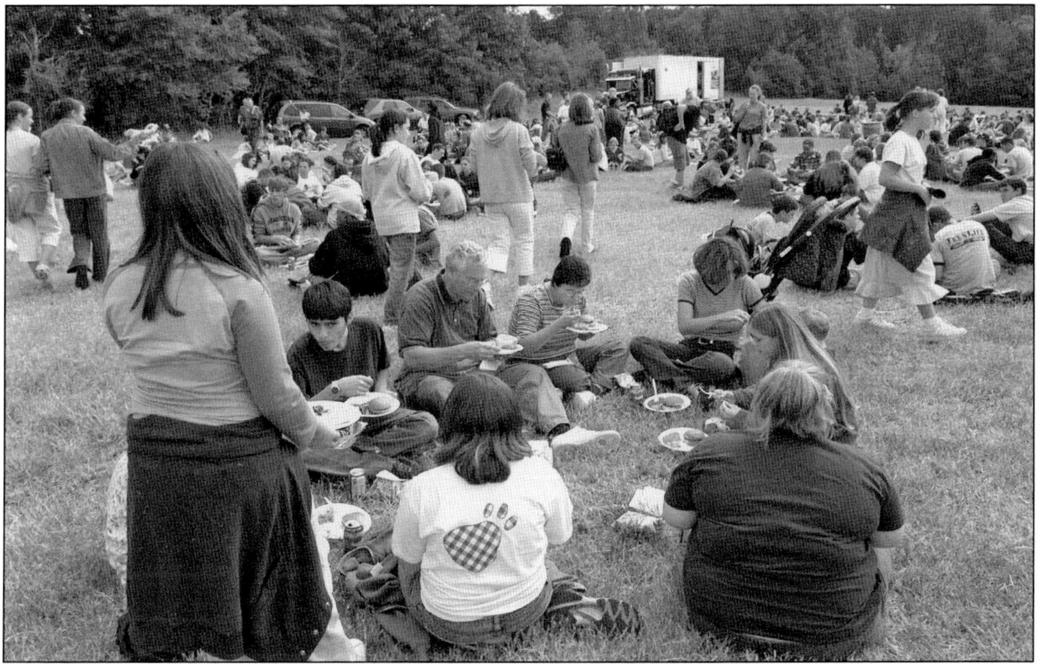

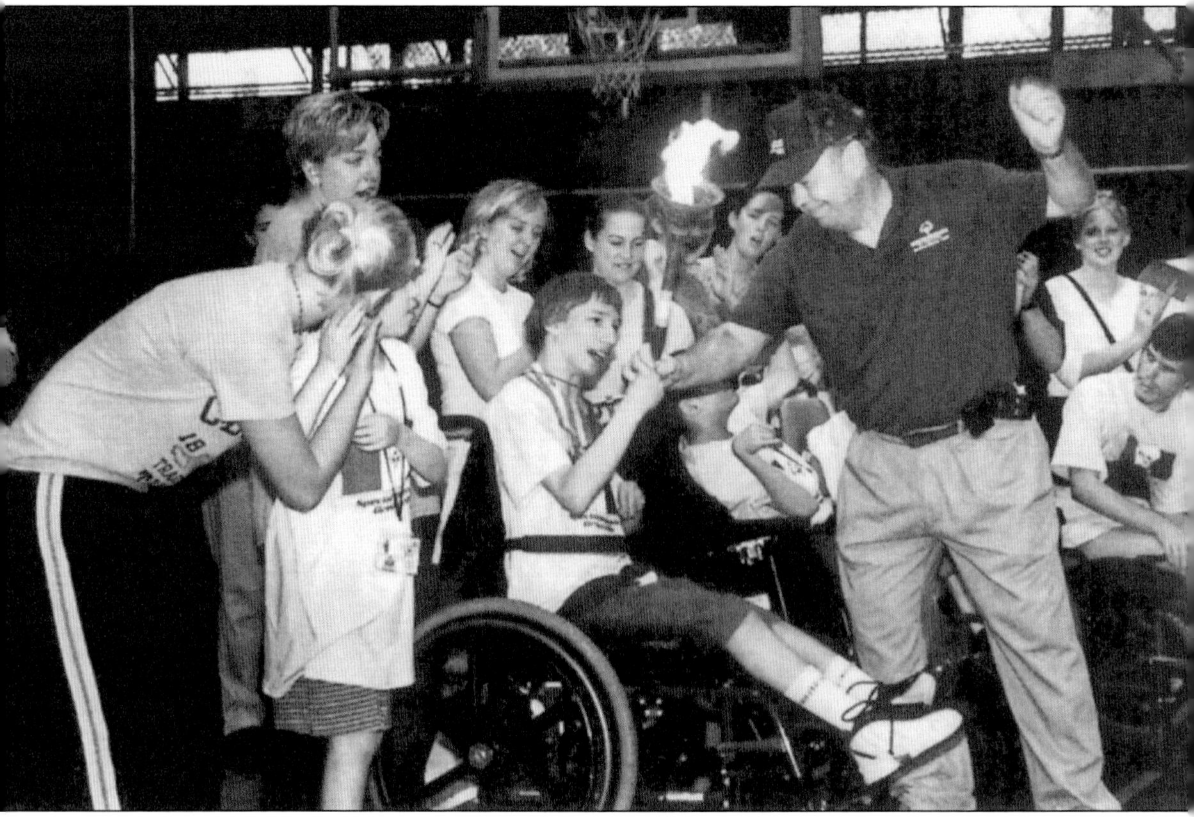

The kind of service Chuck Luttrell has rendered to the community for more than 40 years is the epitome of the community outreach that characterizes BJU students, faculty, and staff. During the 40 years Chuck was on the physical education faculty, he also directed Camp Spearhead, a program ministering to children with special needs. Though he retired from his BJU responsibilities in 2004, he continues to be involved in Special Olympics for handicapped children. He involves as many as 300 student volunteers when events for special-needs children from Washington Center are held at Furman University and as many as 700 students when competition is staged at BJU. Above, Luttrell takes the Olympic torch from a young man in a wheelchair. Looking back to the roles he has been able to play in his work with special-needs children, Luttrell said, "I think I was put there by the Lord. I enjoy the opportunity of being with physically handicapped and special-needs children and listening to what they are saying. They are no different from other children. I am grateful to the Lord for giving me the privilege of working with them."

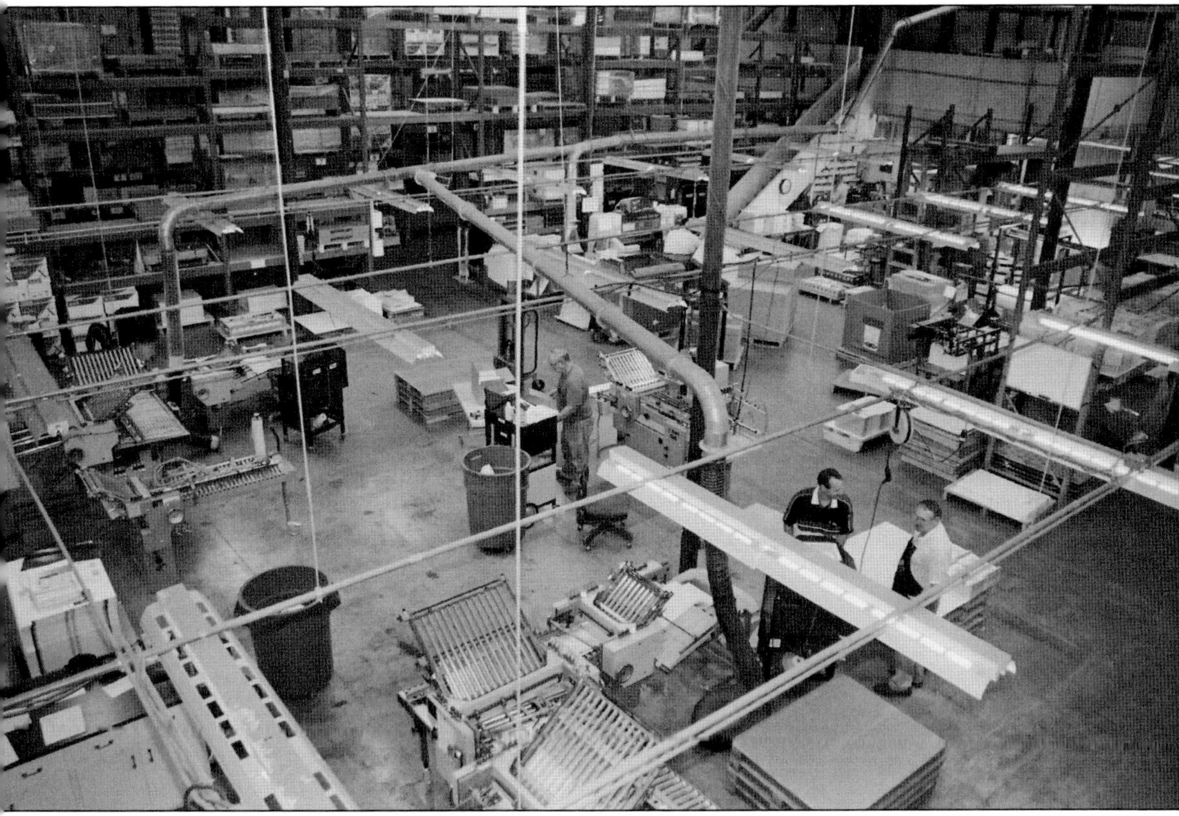

Since 1974, BJU Press has been a source of quality K4-through-grade-12 textbooks and teaching aids for Christian schools and homeschools. It currently offers more than 3,400 products, including music, children's books, Christian living books, and scholarly religious works. Pictured above is one of the work areas in the BJU Press Printing Division.

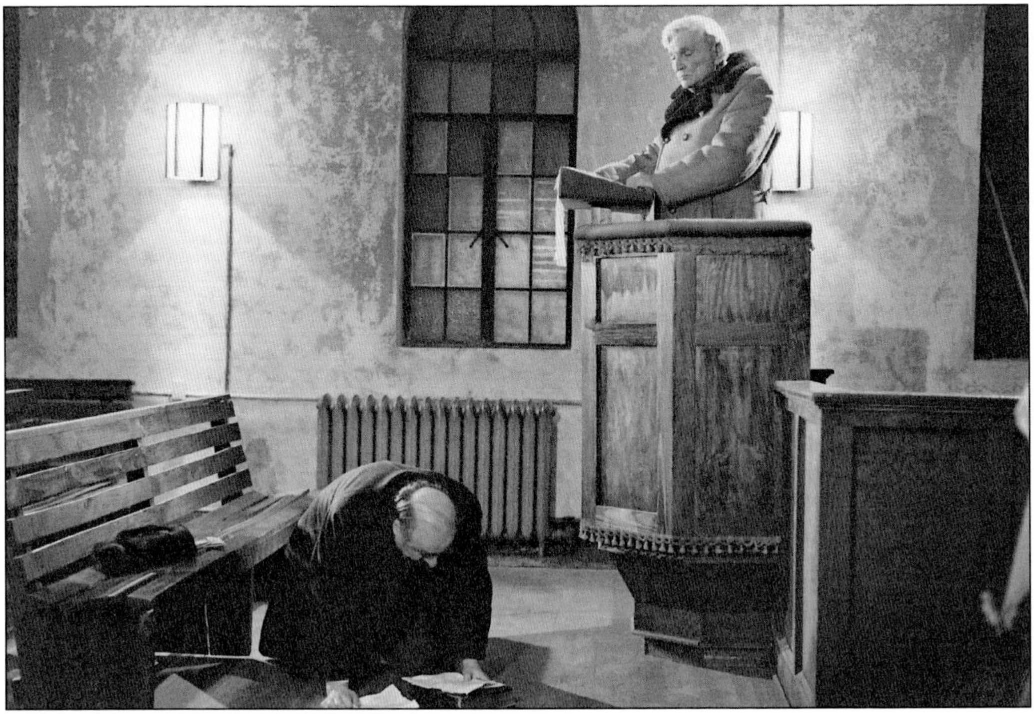

Through Unusual Films, Bob Jones University is able to present the Gospel to multitudes who otherwise would not hear it. *The Printing*, a story set in the Soviet Union during days of great religious suppression, powerfully conveys a challenge for Christians to resist government efforts to stifle their testimony for Christ as well as a salvation message. Dr. Bob Jones Jr., portraying a Soviet official, is standing behind the pulpit, while Dr. Richard Rupp, portraying a pastor who had been compromising his convictions, kneels on the floor.

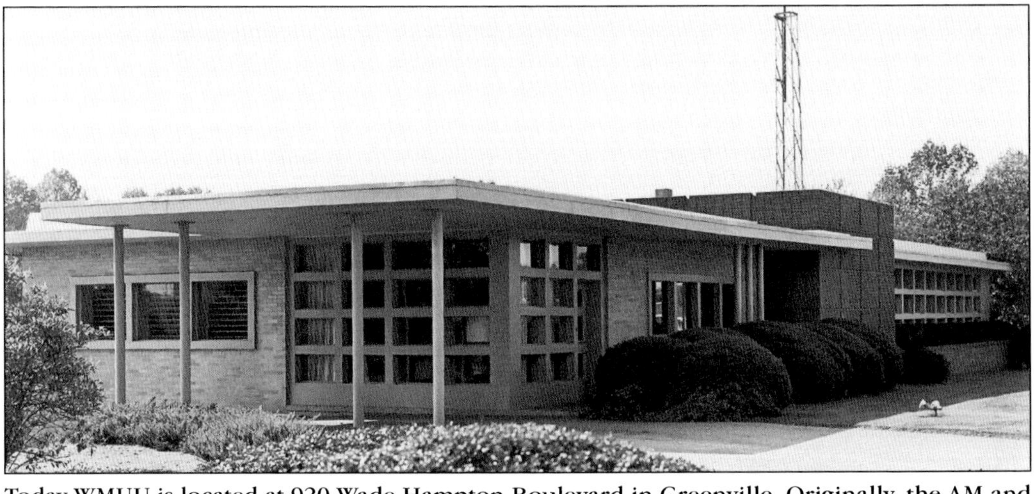

Today WMUU is located at 920 Wade Hampton Boulevard in Greenville. Originally, the AM and FM studio was on campus where the Founder's Memorial Amphitorium now stands. For more than a half century, WMUU has been faithfully broadcasting the never-changing good news of salvation along with beautiful music, news, and other special features that together set it apart from most other stations. Paul Wright has been the general manager since 1994. In 2008, BJU sold the AM station and adopted new digital FM technology for WMUU-FM.

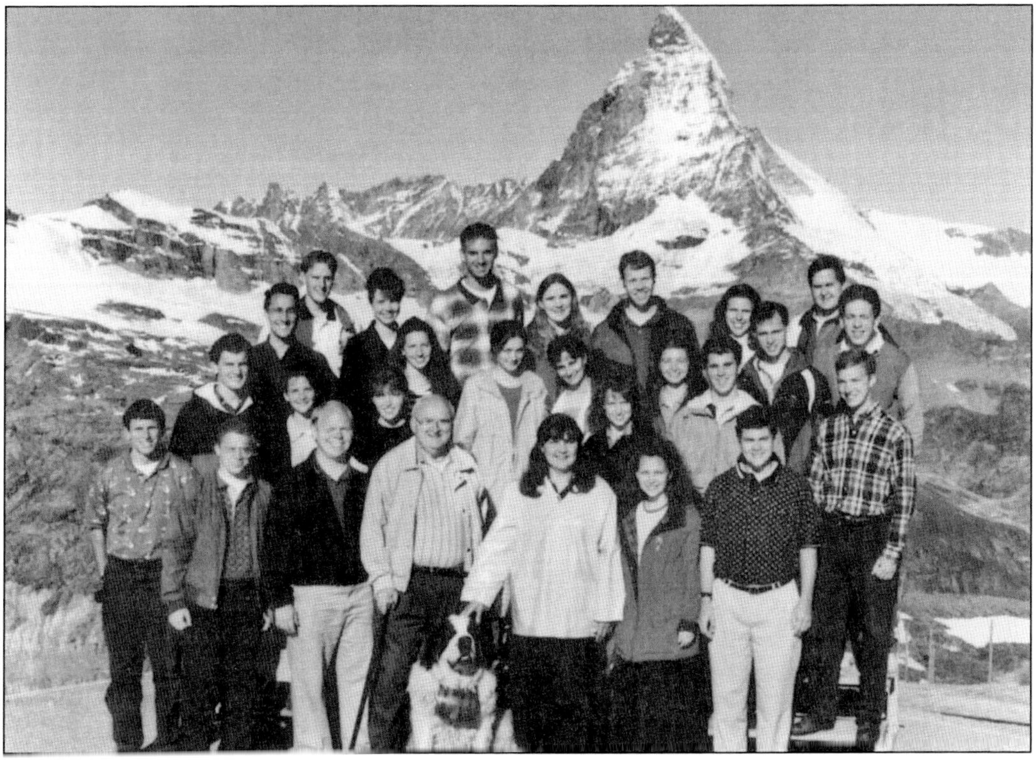

Drs. Bill and Janie McCauley and the Musical Mission Team spent 10 weeks in the summer of 1997 ministering to the people of Northern Asia through music and preaching. As the 1998 *Vintage* recorded, "Sensing God's hand of protection around the Polish border and praying for lost souls in a Russian Church are only a few of the memories that the team will never forget." The team had the joy of seeing many people come to know Christ through their efforts.

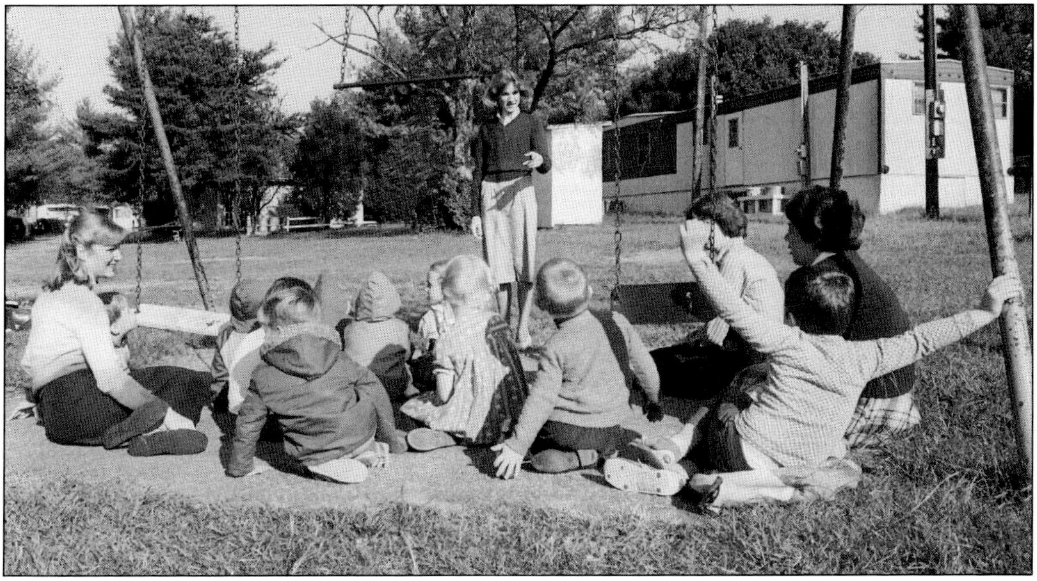

BJU women students minister to children where they are, in this case, in a mobile home park. Telling Bible stories, playing games, and singing songs are all a part of the programs for the children.

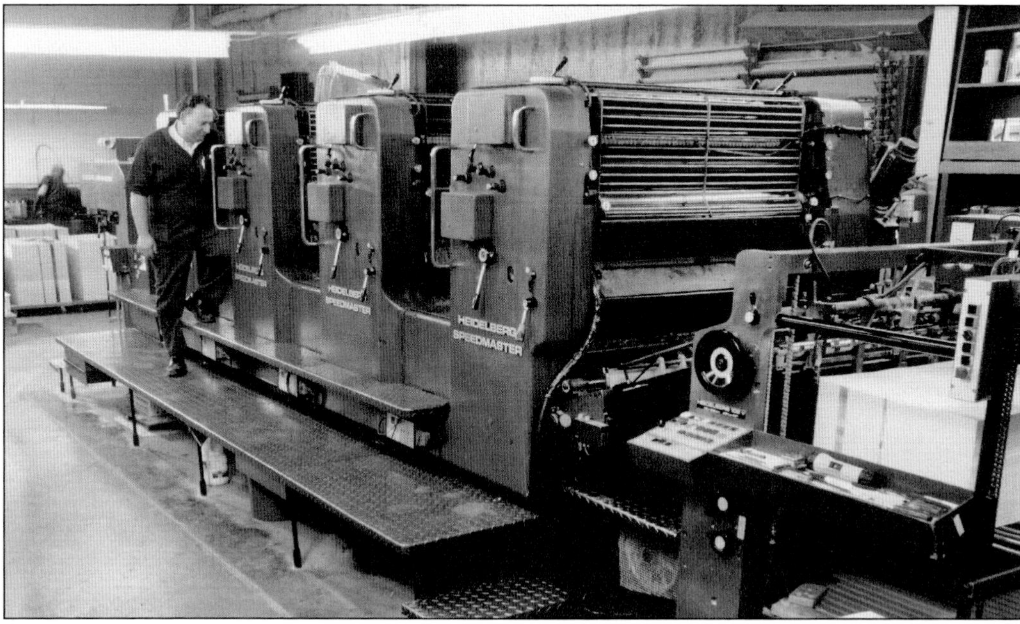

BJU Press uses this giant press to print choral and instrumental music, juvenile fiction, and biography in addition to textbook production. Every BJU employee renders a sacred service to the Lord, whether he is a press operator, librarian, mechanic, or professor. As the founder said, "For a Christian, life is not divided into the secular and the sacred. To him, all ground is holy ground, every bush a burning bush, and every place a temple of worship."

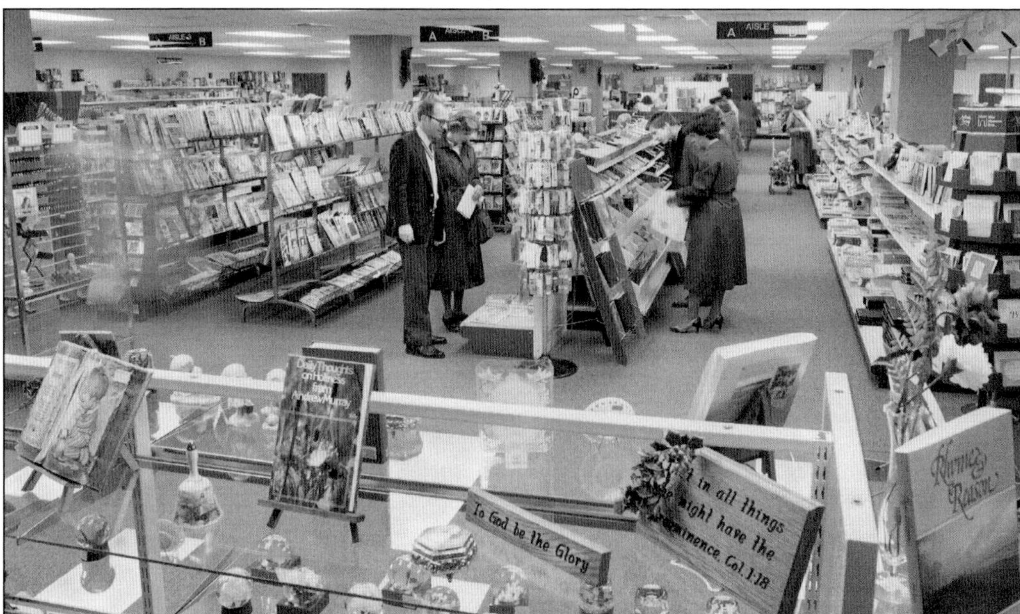

The Campus Store, located in the Student Center mall, is a favorite stopping place for visitors on campus. Care is taken to stock the store with Bibles, biblically sound books, and fine Christian music, as well as a large selection of other merchandise. It, too, is an avenue for reaching out to people to help them grow spiritually or come to know Christ as their Savior.

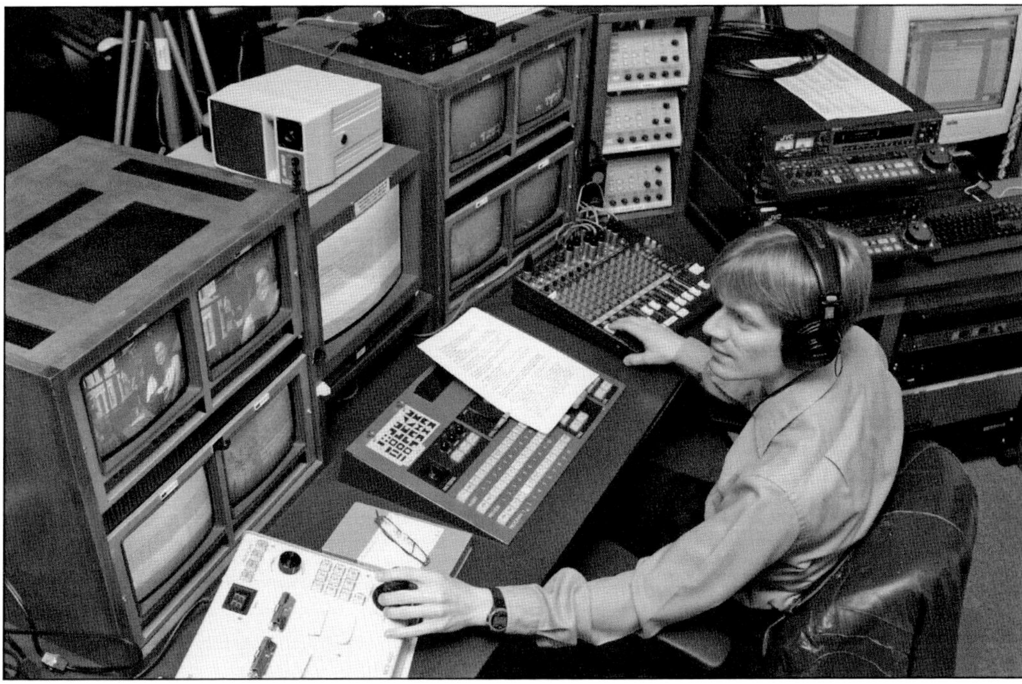

A large amount of technology is involved in the BJ LINC (Bob Jones Live Interactive Network Classroom) and the BJ HomeSat Network, as the above photograph suggests. Satellite courses are offered by the university to help students gain academic credit even though they are off-campus. From the BJ LINC studio or classroom, class instruction is transmitted to participating BJ LINC sites across the United States. Students may interact with the instructor by using an Interactive Response Unit. Christian schools that are short on qualified instructors in some subject areas have found the satellite instruction an answer to their prayers. Parents homeschooling their children are also subscribers to the service, which provides classroom instruction as pictured below via satellite or DVD.

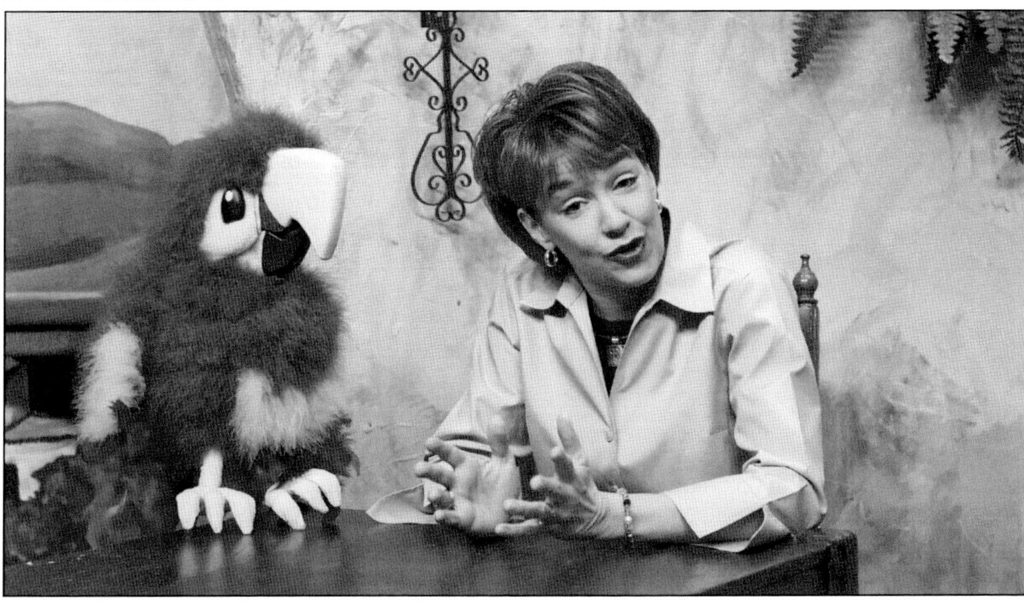

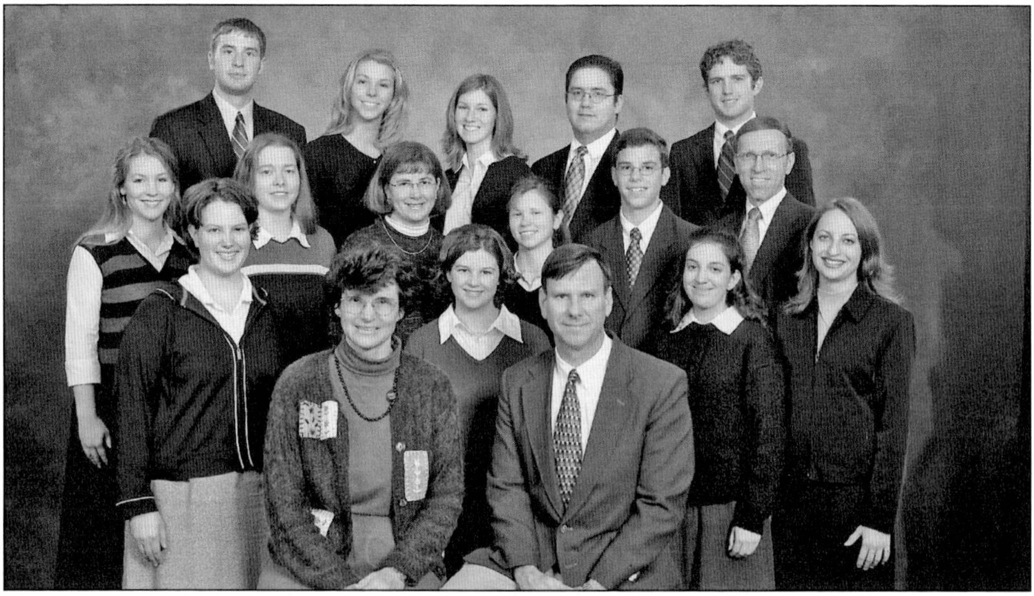

For five weeks, the above team members were in the People's Republic of China with Dr. Tom and Mary Lamb (first row, seated), sharing Christian love as they taught both science and Bible in English to students and staff members at Shanghai's Second Medical University. The students are, from left to right, (first row) Amy Ritter, Hannah White, Anna DeBaggis, and Rachel Browning; (second row) Becky Adams, Sarah Weidenburner, Sue Biddle, Rachel Biddle, Jonathan Biddle, and Dr. Verne Biddle; (third row) Joseph Croates, Jessica Lamb, Anna Christopher, Jamey Pachter, and Bryan McKinnon.

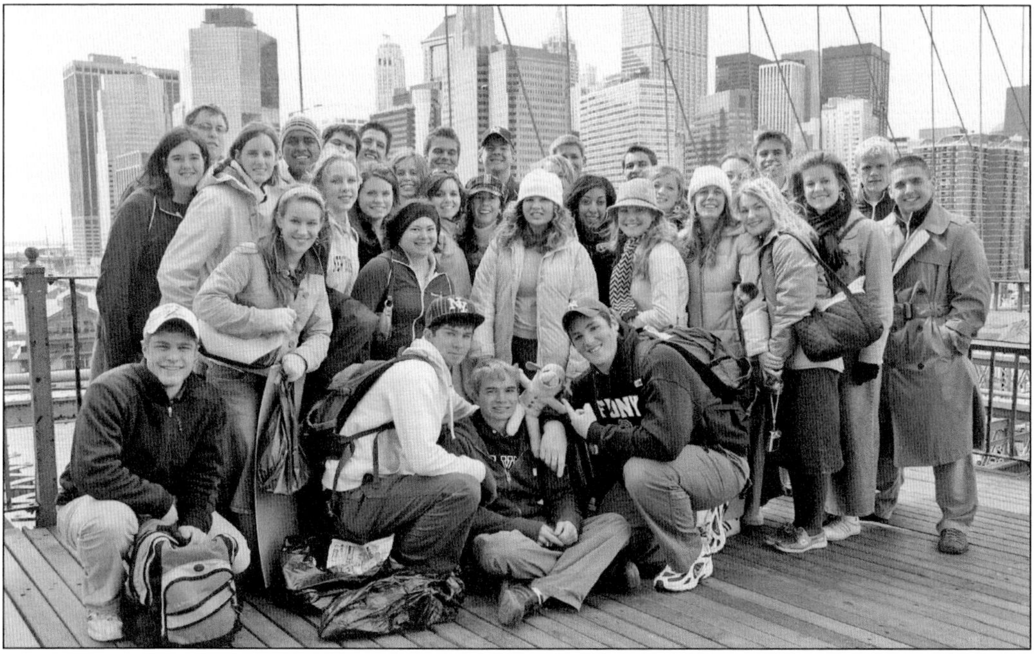

Bob Jones Academy students participate regularly in giving the Gospel through rescue mission, hospital, and music group extensions and camp work. A highlight each year is the trip to New York City, when a number of students and faculty minister with and serve in several inner-city churches.

Six

THE FOUR PRESIDENTS

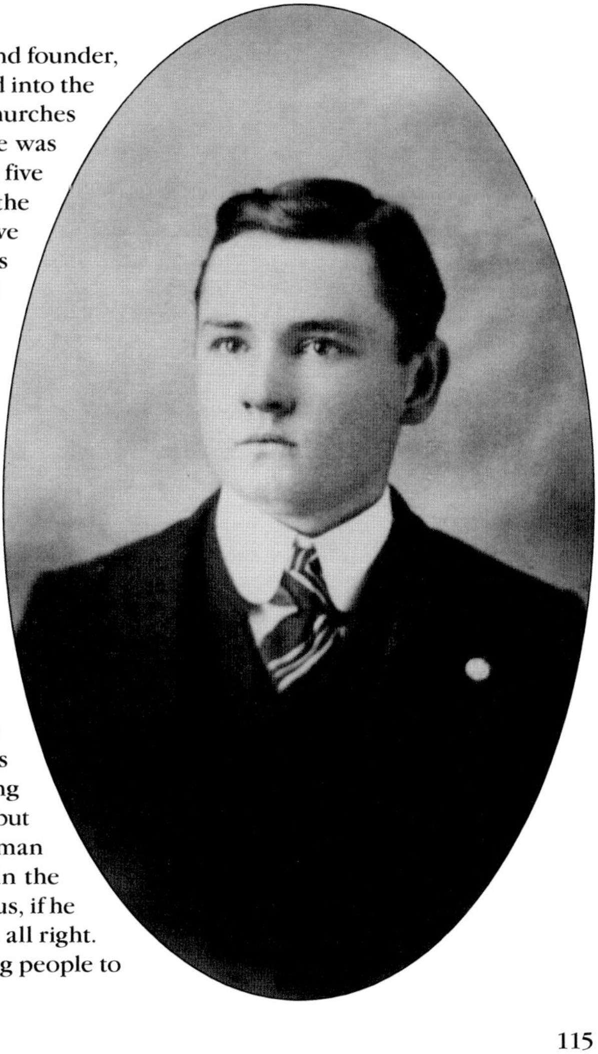

At the age of 15, the first BJU president and founder, Bob Jones Sr., had already been ordained into the Gospel ministry and was preaching in churches and brush-arbor settings. By the time he was 16, he served as a circuit-riding pastor to five churches in the Alabama Conference of the Methodist Church. His salary from the five churches totaled $25 a month. Five years earlier, when he was 11 years old, he had heard an 80-year-old preacher deliver a message about a sick man who was lowered through the roof of a house so that he could be in the presence of Jesus (Mark 2:4). When an altar call was given, he was one of the first persons to go forward in the little Methodist church to publicly confess his sin and accept Christ as his Savior. When he was 12, he was Sunday school superintendent in his home church, where he also held a one-week revival meeting at which 60 people were converted. At the age of 13, he built a brush-arbor shelter and organized his own congregation of 54 members. Dr. Bob said many times after the day when he was converted that he did not know everything there was to know about spiritual things, but he knew that, just as in the case of the man who was lowered through an opening in the roof so he could be in the presence of Jesus, if he could get people to Jesus, they would be all right. And throughout his long ministry, getting people to Jesus was his passion.

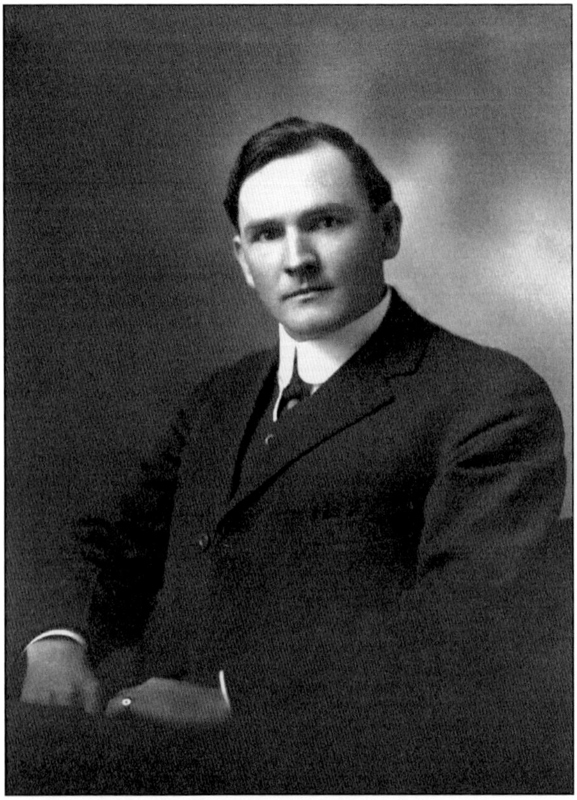

Dr. Bob Jones Sr., prior to his founding of Bob Jones College, was involved in evangelistic campaigns in numerous American cities, both large and small. By the 1920s, he was the best-known evangelist in the United States, with the exception of Billy Sunday, who became his dear friend and colleague. Some of his crowds were as large as 15,000, and amazingly, he preached to them without any amplification. In 1917, when he held a seven-week campaign in Zanesville, Ohio, a town with a population of 22,000, more than 3,284 people were converted to Christ, of whom 2,200 joined local churches on Easter Sunday. Attendance on closing day was 18,000. The left photograph was taken of Dr. Bob in Wheeling, West Virginia. Below is a photograph of the audience in one of Dr. Bob's meetings in Altoona, Pennsylvania.

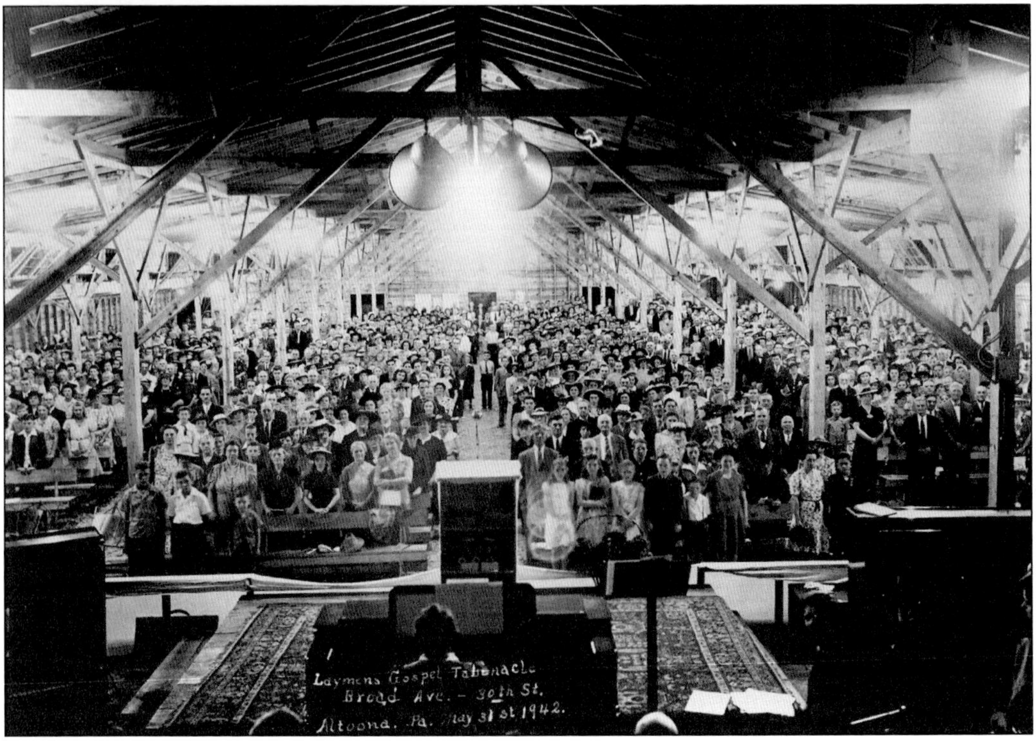

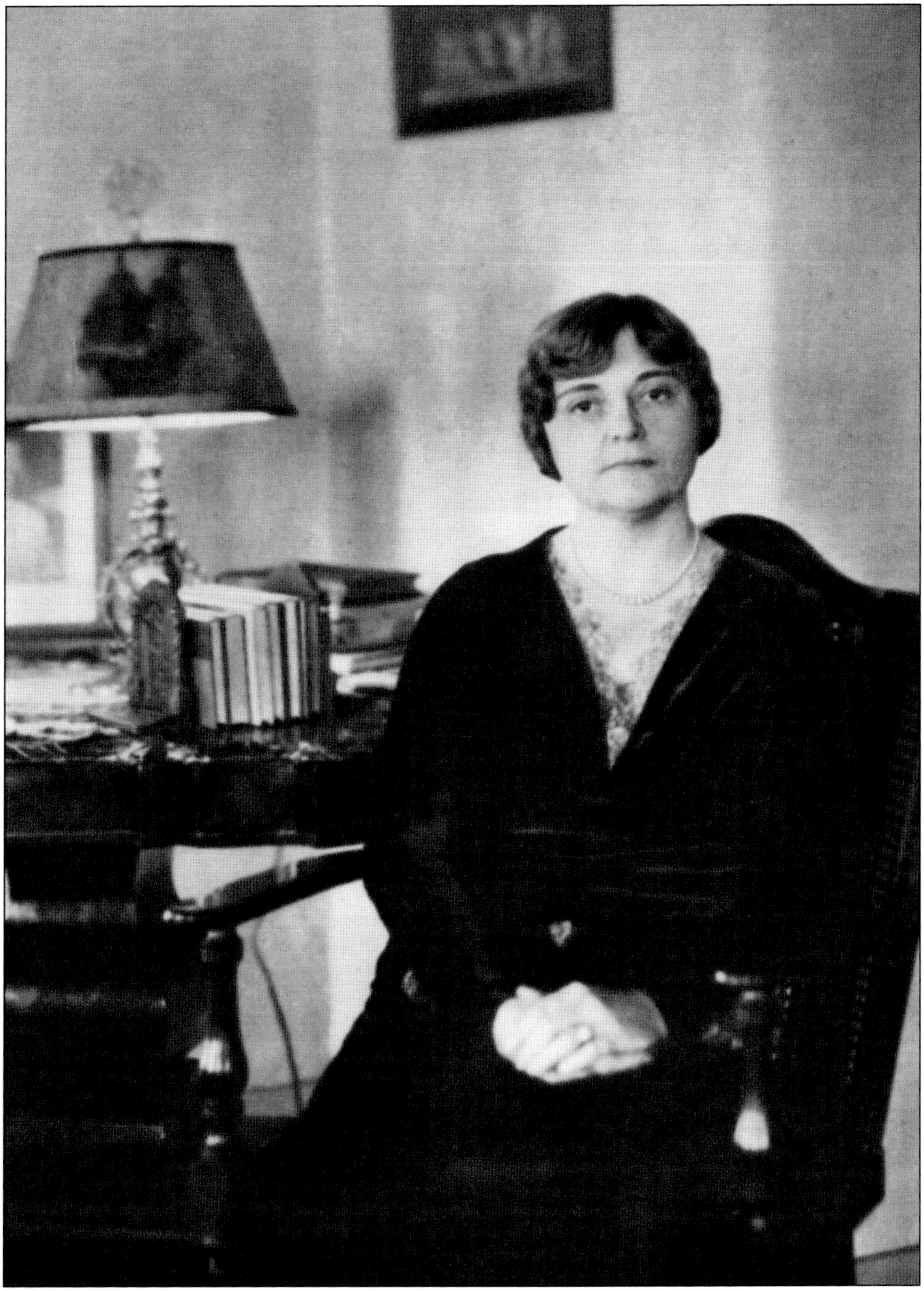

When Dr. Bob Jones Sr. was 25 years of age, he married Mary Gaston Stollenwerck (above) on June 17, 1908. She was a choir member in a church where he was holding a meeting in Uniontown, Alabama. Throughout the next 60 years, this cultured, Southern lady was a wonderful helpmeet to the BJU founder and first president of the school. She died in 1989 at the age of 101. Dr. Bob's first wife, Bernice Sheffield, whom he had married in 1905, died of tuberculosis less than a year after they were married.

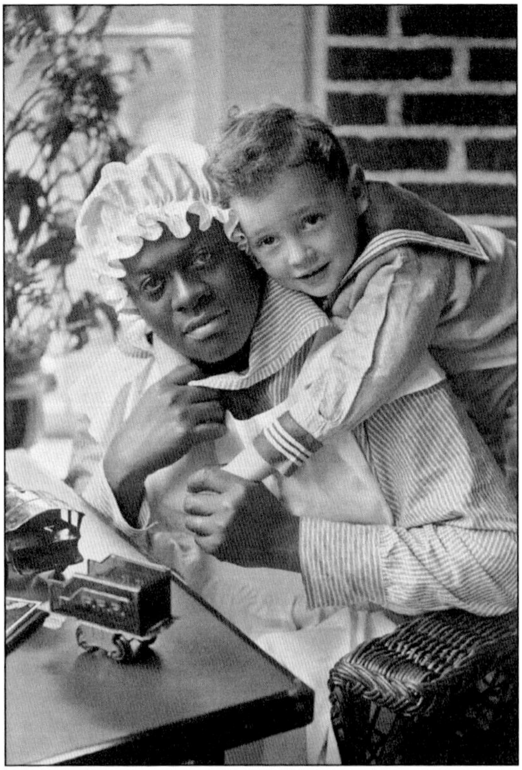

Bob Jones Jr. was born in Montgomery, Alabama, on October 19, 1911. During his early years, he had a nanny named Emma (left), for whom he had great affection. She assisted in caring for him while he was on the road with his parents for evangelistic crusades. Mary Gaston Jones needed such help because she, too, had many responsibilities relating to the evangelistic meetings. As a child of six years, Bob Jr. accepted Jesus as his Savior after hearing one of his father's sermons.

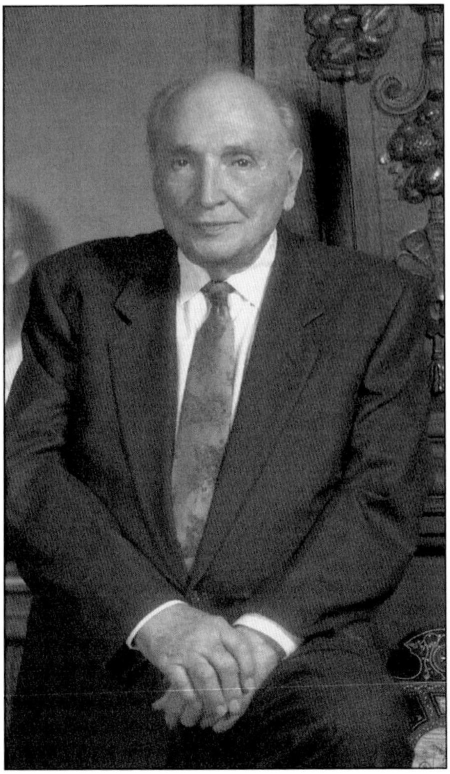

Dr. Bob Jones Jr. entered Bob Jones College in 1928, having been a member of the first Bob Jones Academy graduating class. Graduating in 1931, he studied at the University of Chicago and in 1932 earned a master's degree at the University of Pittsburgh. In 1933, Asbury College honored him with the degree doctor of letters. He served first as BJC history teacher and acting president, and was elected president when the college moved to Greenville and became a university. In his 24-year presidency, he oversaw the strengthening of the academic programs and cultural emphasis, founded the Museum and Gallery, and significantly expanded the Greenville campus. As both president and chancellor, he was poet and author, and was renowned the world over for his preaching, fidelity to the Word of God, and defense of Fundamentalism. In his self-authored obituary in November 1997, he said, "One of the great joys I have had in life, possibly my greatest joy aside from my family, has been to see Bob Jones graduates in various occupations, particularly in pulpits large and small, and on the mission field, standing firm for the Word of God, winning men and women to Christ, and having a positive influence for the authority of the Scriptures."

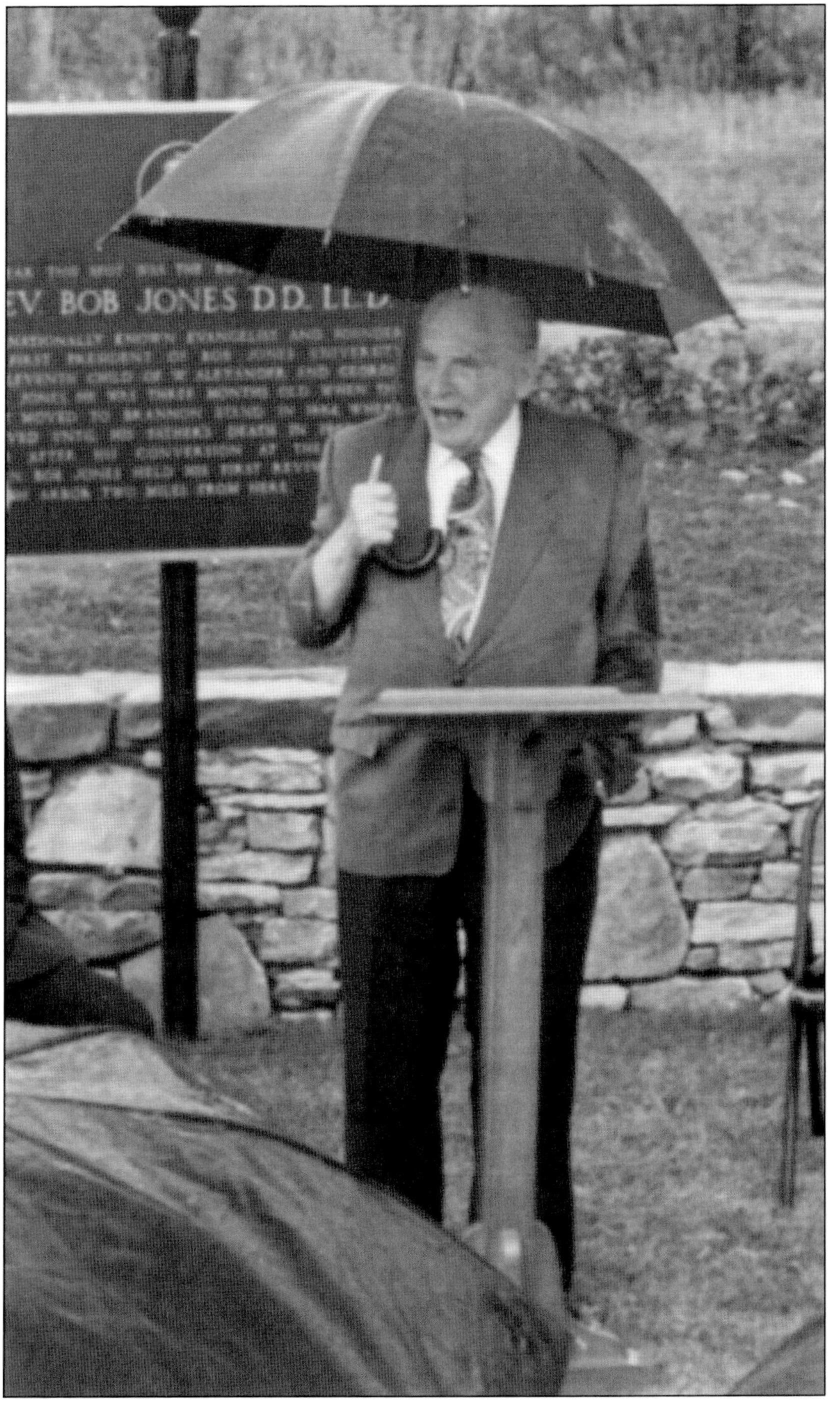

Dr. Bob Jones Jr. speaks at the dedication of a historical plaque marking his father's boyhood home at Brannon Stand, Alabama, on October 18, 1961. A crowd of more than 200 gathered for the occasion as Alabama congressman George Grant said that the kind of education BJU provides could be the solution to America's problems. Dr. Bob Jones Sr.; his wife Mary Gaston Jones; Dr. Bob Jones Jr.'s wife, Fannie Mae, their daughter Joy, and their sons Jon and Bob III also attended.

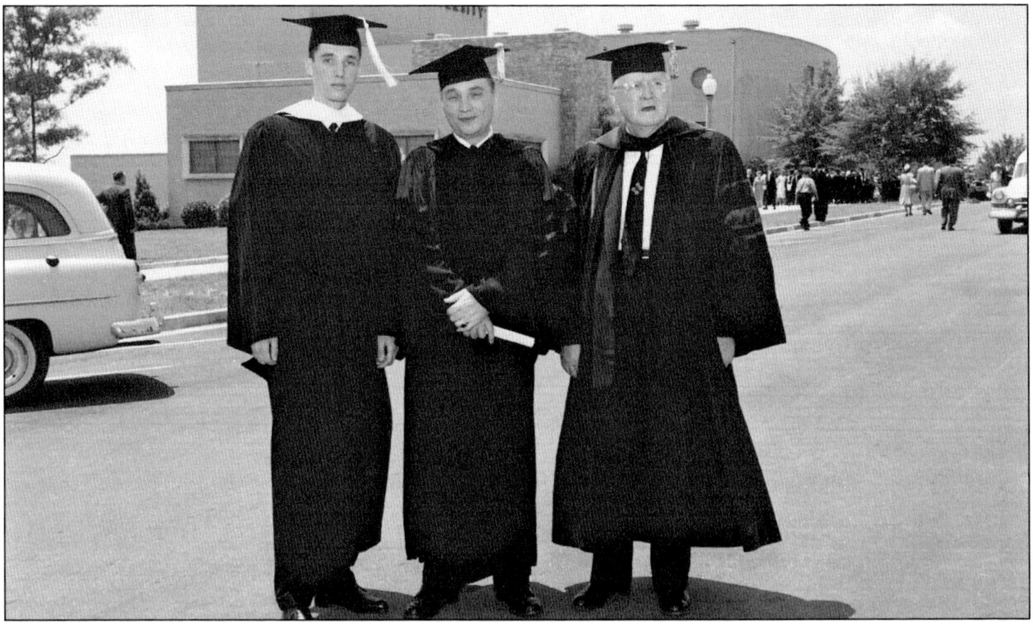

Dr. Bob Jones Jr. (center) and Dr. Bob Jones Sr. (right) were both involved in the 1959 commencement, as Bob Jones III received his bachelor of arts degree from Bob Jones University. Twelve years later in 1971, Bob III succeeded his father as the third president of the university, serving in that capacity until 2005.

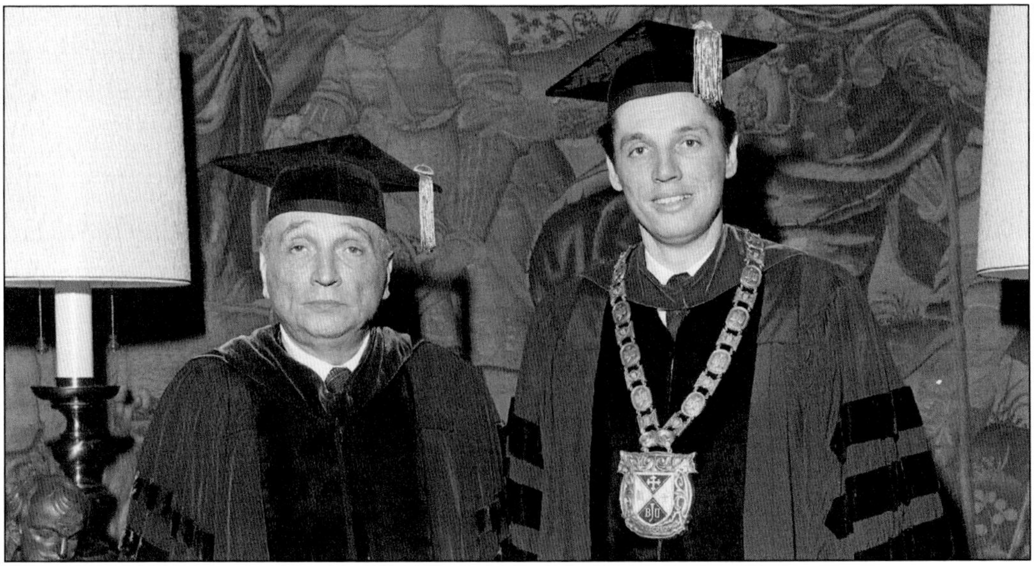

Dr. Bob Jones Jr. (left) and Dr. Bob Jones III pose for photographs after Dr. Bob Jones III is installed as president in 1971. At this installation, the new president said, "Should there be any possible doubt in anyone's mind that this University in the years ahead, as God tarries, will be any less militant in its defense of the Faith, any less earnest in its evangelistic fervor, any less thorough in its academic program, any less resolute in its evangelistic fervor, any less thorough in its academic program, any less resolute in its character-building aspect, let me say with all clarity that I am resolutely and irrevocably committed to the furtherance of what God has ordained from the day of its foundation should be the ministry of Bob Jones University."

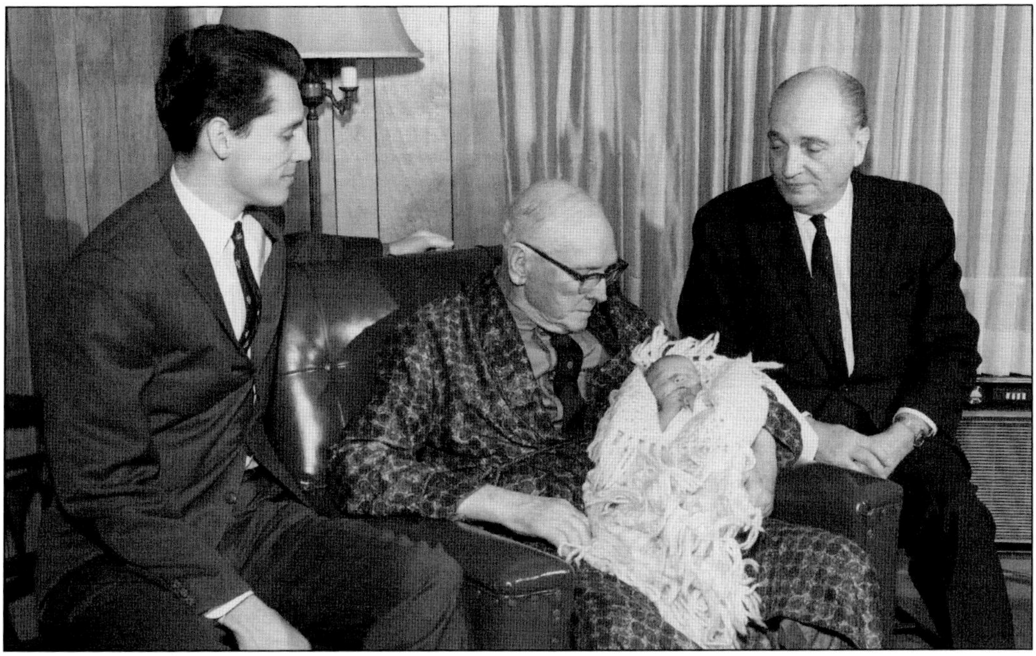

Dr. Bob Jones Sr. holds the infant Bob Jones IV, born on December 11, 1966, at Barge Memorial Hospital. The proud father, Dr. Bob Jones III, and proud grandfather, Dr. Bob Jones Jr., look on. Melton Wright in his book *Fortress of Faith* points out that there were exactly 27 years between each of the births of the second, third, and fourth generations.

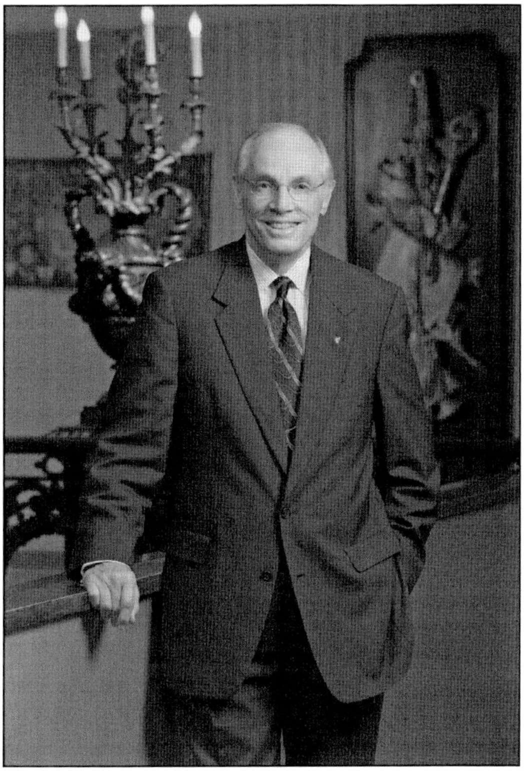

Dr. Bob Jones III became BJU's president in 1971. From that time through 2005, when he turned over the presidency to Dr. Stephen Jones, the university experienced unprecedented growth. Both undergraduate and graduate offerings were greatly expanded. Bob Jones Elementary School and Junior High were added. BJU Press was established; a full K4–12 curriculum was developed for Christian and home schools, and a distance learning program was developed that serves over 45,000 students around the world. A number of new buildings were added and several others renovated or enlarged. Under Dr. Bob's tenure, the university further opened its programs and campus to the community and gained national attention for its stand on issues. Chancellor since 2005, Dr. Bob continues a heavy national and international preaching schedule.

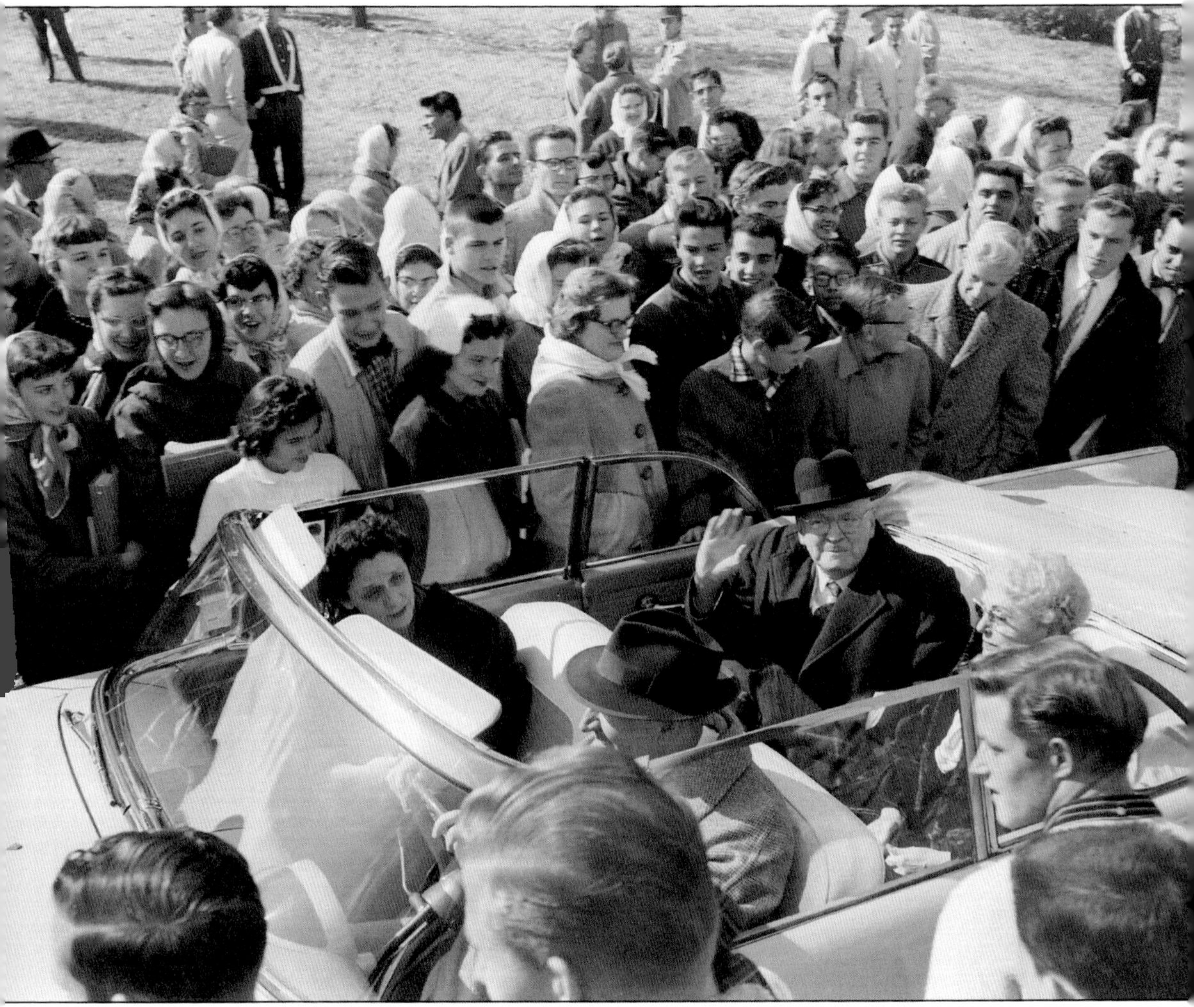

Dr. Bob Jones Sr. waves to well-wishers following the observance of his 75th birthday on October 30, 1958, as he and his wife, Mary Gaston Jones, drive away from Rodeheaver Auditorium. On that "Founder's Day," the chapel service was devoted to honoring the man to whom God gave the vision of starting Bob Jones University. His comments on that day illustrate the staunch stand for the truth of God's Word that has prevailed at BJU since it began in 1927: "I am 75 years old today. Someone recently criticized me by saying I am getting old and unpredictable. I suppose he meant that he did not know what I might do. Well, I am not unpredictable. I know what I am going to do. I am doing exactly what I have done for 62 years since I began to preach at the age of 13. I am standing uncompromisingly for the Bible as the Word of God and for all the fundamental essentials of the faith, such as the virgin birth, the incarnation, the vicarious atonement, and the bodily resurrection of our Lord." The founder's influence is still very much felt on the university campus. Founder's Day is now called Heritage Day, a day on which the university celebrates various aspects of its history.

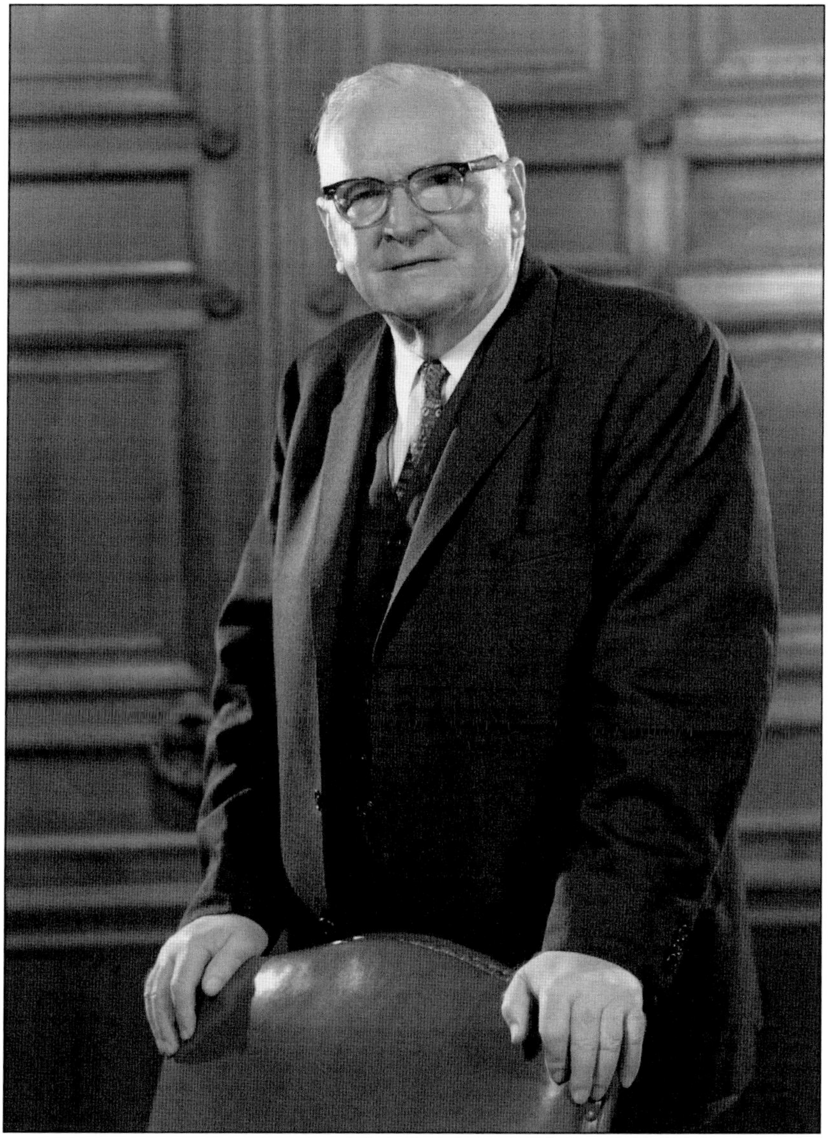

During his many chapel talks, Dr. Bob Jones Sr. made statements that became indelible in the minds of the students and faculty, and keep his influence alive in the lives of the thousands who heard them. In every BJU classroom, his sayings, such as the following, are posted and recommended as guidelines for living successful Christian lives:

You can borrow brains, but you cannot borrow character.
You and God make a majority in any community.
The greatest ability is dependability.
Finish the job.
Don't sacrifice the permanent on the altar of the immediate.
The test of your character is what it takes to stop you.
It is never right to do wrong in order to get a chance to do right.
Beware of the man who kowtows to his superiors or who is rude to his inferiors.
The door to the room of success swings on the hinges of opposition.
The religions of the world say "Do and live." The religion of the Bible says, "Live and do."

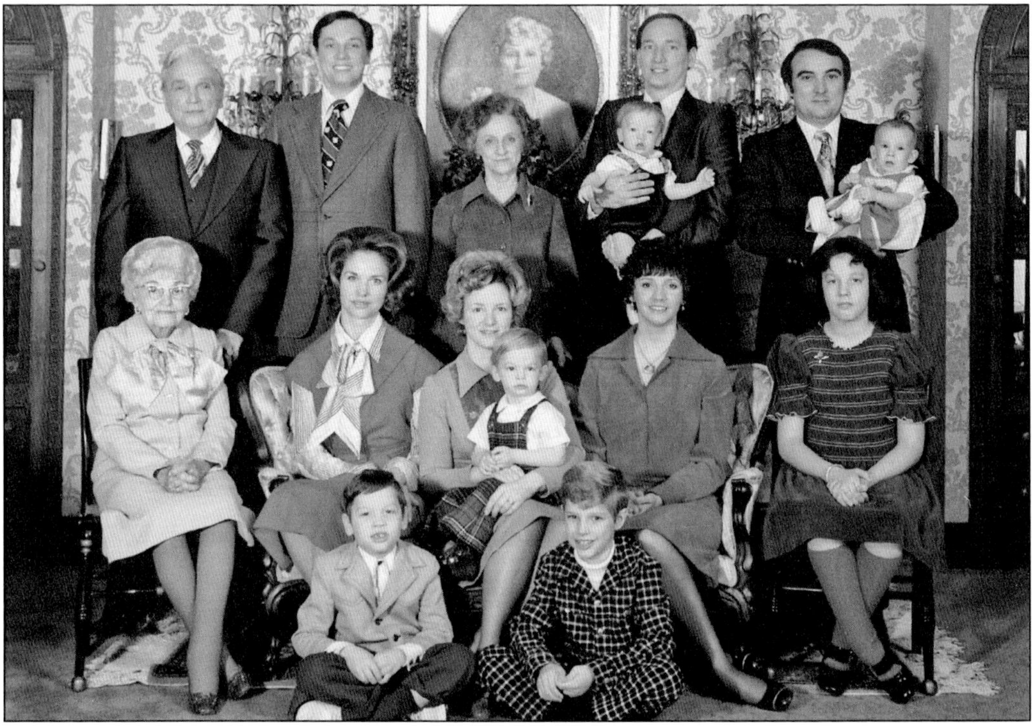

This family portrait was taken during the 1977 golden anniversary year of Bob Jones University. Seated on the floor are Stephen Jones, who assumed the school's presidency in 2005, and Bob Jones IV. Seated from left to right are Mary Gaston Jones, Beneth Jones, Betty Jones holding son Matthew, Joy Jones Jordan, and Roxanne Jones; (standing) Dr. Bob Jones Jr., Dr. Bob Jones III, Fannie Mae Jones, Jon Jones holding son Michael, and Gerald Jordan holding daughter Jessica.

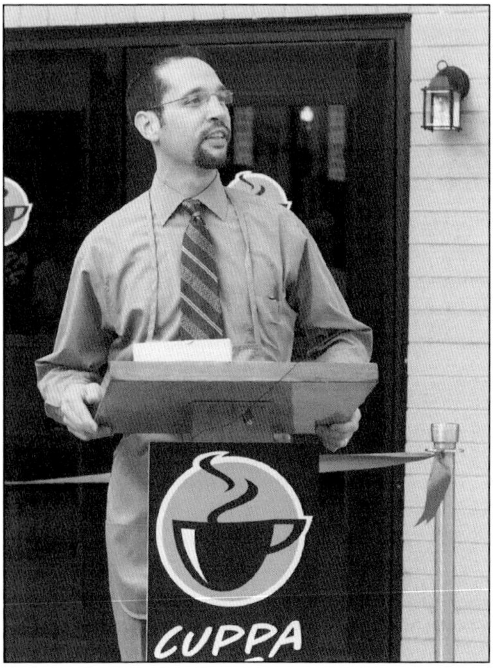

Who wants Starbucks when Cuppa Jones is available? Dr. Stephen Jones cut the ribbon at the grand opening of the new coffee shop in 2007 and acted as guest barista for the first hour on opening day. Constructed in 42 days from start to finish, Cuppa Jones is located at the west end of the Alumni Building and between the seminary and the library. It makes coffee more accessible to students on the west end of the campus. The building has inside seating and wireless Internet access. Dr. Jones told the large group at the opening ceremony, "Necessity is the mother of invention, and this is for those of us who need our coffee. The coffee shop is here for us to feed our addiction; the Seminary is next door to address our addiction."

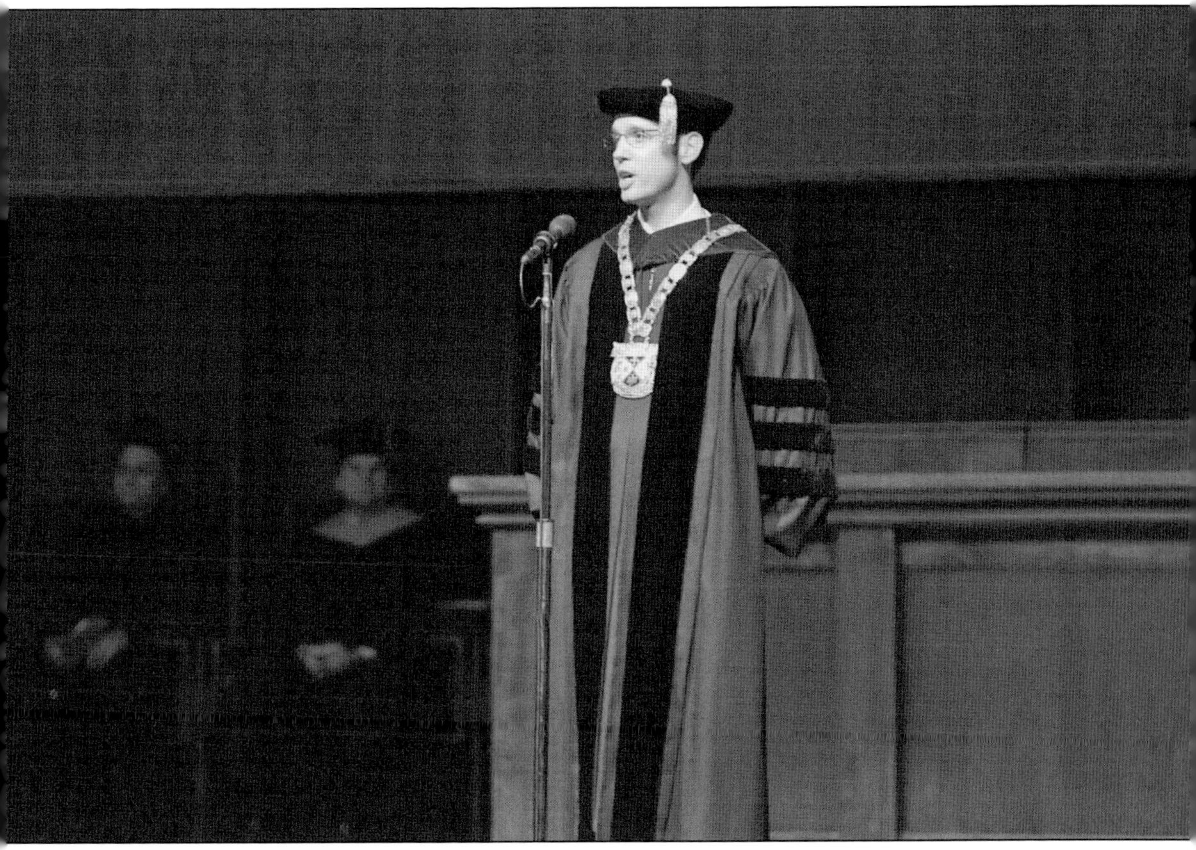

The fourth president of BJU, Dr. Stephen Jones, addressed the 2005 commencement audience following his investiture as president. A great-grandson of the founder, Stephen has earned a bachelor's degree in public speaking, a master of divinity, and a Ph.D. in liberal arts studies with concentrations on business, education, and organizational communications. He previously served in a number of capacities at the university, including vice president for administration, instructor of Speech Communication and Pulpit Speech, residence hall supervisor, and assistant to the president.

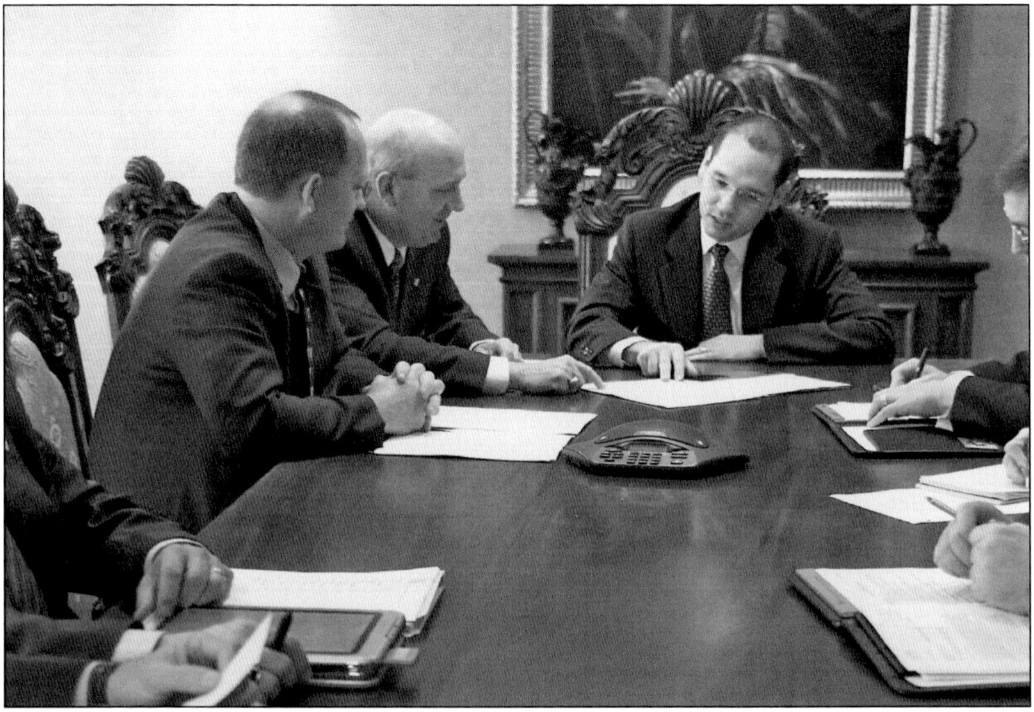

Dr. Stephen Jones takes his place at the head of the conference table with two of his administrators, Dr. Gary Weier (left), vice president for administration, and Alan Carper (right), executive vice president. Dr. Weier is filling the position formerly occupied by Dr. Jones, and Carper succeeds Dr. Bob Wood.

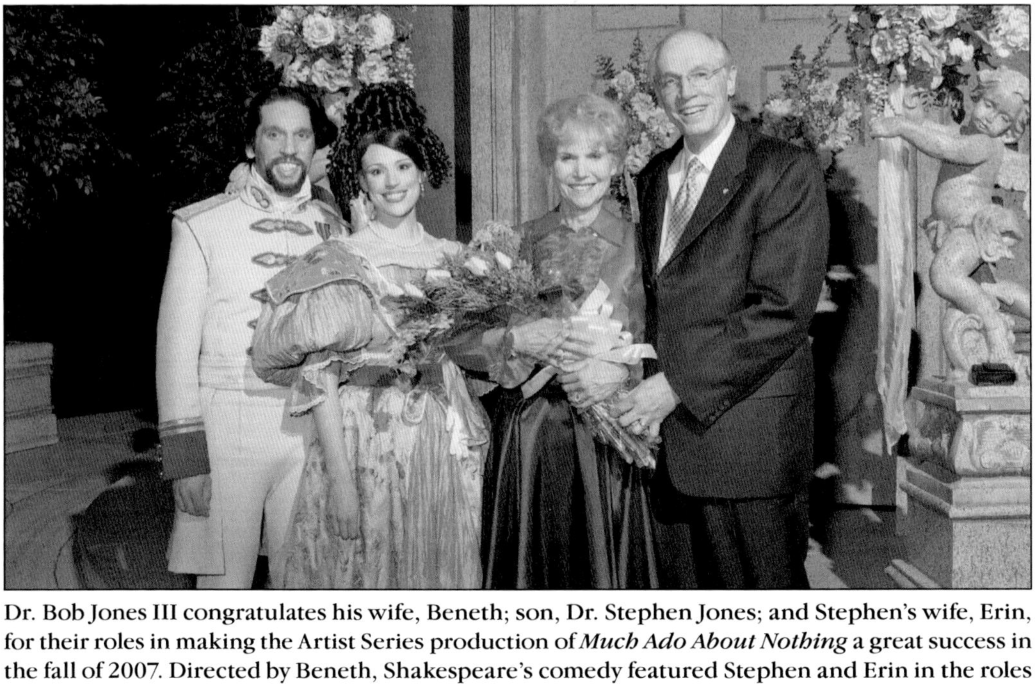

Dr. Bob Jones III congratulates his wife, Beneth; son, Dr. Stephen Jones; and Stephen's wife, Erin, for their roles in making the Artist Series production of *Much Ado About Nothing* a great success in the fall of 2007. Directed by Beneth, Shakespeare's comedy featured Stephen and Erin in the roles of Benedict and Beatrice, a couple whose witty verbal sparring seemingly disdains marriage.

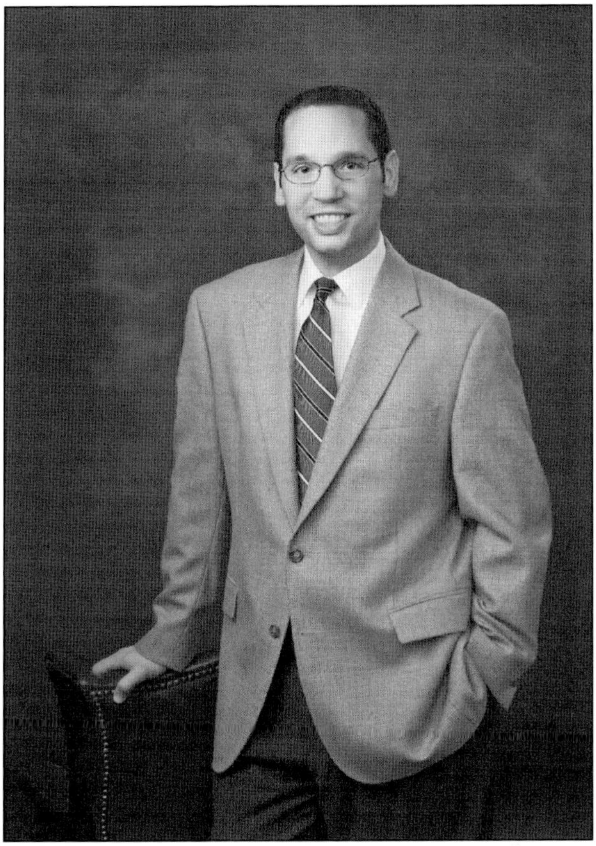

As Dr. Stephen Jones assumed the presidency in 2005, he declared his intention to keep Bob Jones University committed to its Bible-based heritage, to its mission of Christlike character development, and to its emphasis on academic and cultural excellence. The new president continually emphasizes to faculty and staff the importance of mentoring and discipling individual students to help them grow in their walk with the Lord. A short time into his administration, he and an administrative committee documented the following nine institutional goals, which reveal both the president's heart for the mission of the university and what Bob Jones University is all about:

Bob Jones University's goals are

1. To inspire regenerated students to know, love, and serve Jesus Christ
2. To strengthen each student's belief in the truths of God's Word
3. To develop in students Christlike character through disciplined, Spirit-filled living
4. To direct students toward a biblical life view that integrates God's Truth into practical Christian living
5. To prepare students to excel intellectually and vocationally by offering diverse academic programs rooted in biblical truth and centered on a liberal arts core
6. To develop in students the cultural breadth and social skills that enhance their lives and also equip them to communicate biblical truth effectively
7. To instill in students a compelling concern for reaching the unconverted with the saving truth of the gospel of Christ
8. To implant in students an eagerness for vital involvement in the life and ministry of a biblically faithful local congregation
9. To develop educational materials and services that extend these objectives beyond the university campus